WI
UT:

RENEWALS 458-4574

GAYLORD			PRINTED IN U.S.A.

The Second Information Revolution

The Second Information Revolution

Gerald W. Brock

HARVARD UNIVERSITY PRESS

Cambridge, Massachusetts

London, England

2003

Library of Congress Cataloging-in-Publication Data

Brock, Gerald W.
    The second information revolution / Gerald W. Brock.
        p. cm.
    Includes bibliographical references and index.
    ISBN 0-674-01178-3 (alk. paper)
    1. Telecommunication. 2. Information science. 3. Electronic
information resources. 1. Title.

TK5101.B6883 2003
384'.0973—dc21   2003044973

To Ruth

CONTENTS

ACKNOWLEDGMENTS

I appreciate the wide range of students, faculty, government officials, and industry executives with whom I have had the privilege of discussing telecommunication and computer policy questions over many years. The opportunity to participate directly in policymaking under FCC chairmen Mark Fowler and Dennis Patrick during the 1980s was particularly useful. The students and faculty of the Graduate Telecommunication Program at The George Washington University have provided numerous insights in many seminars and discussions since 1990. While a Ph.D. candidate, Yuntsai Chou helped me understand the importance of institutional economics for analyzing telecommunication policy. I particularly appreciate the support of program director Christopher Sterling.

I am grateful to Michael Aronson at Harvard University Press for his enthusiasm for this project from the time it was only a concept and for his patience when I took longer than expected to complete the manuscript. Richard Audet's careful editing of the manuscript provided numerous improvements. Two anonymous referees for Harvard University Press provided detailed expert comments on the draft manuscript that helped guide the revisions.

Portions of this book are adapted from my earlier published work. Chapters 10–12 include a condensation of material developed in detail in my 1994 Harvard University Press book, *Telecommunication Policy for the Information Age: From Monopoly to Competition,* used with permission. Chapter 2 includes material first printed in my "Historical Overview" in Martin Cave, Sumit Majumdar, and Ingo Vogelsang, eds., *Handbook of Telecommunications Economics,* volume 1 (Amsterdam: Elsevier, 2002), used with permission. Other chapters include occasional excerpts from my previous work.

I am especially thankful for the love, encouragement, and support of my wife, Ruth, and our children and their spouses, Jane, George, Sara, David, Charlotte, and Jimmy, throughout the research and writing process.

ABBREVIATIONS

1927 Act	Radio Act of 1927
1934 Act	Communications Act of 1934
1996 Act	Telecommunications Act of 1996
AEC	Atomic Energy Commission
AMPS	Advanced Mobile Phone Service
ARPA	Advanced Research Projects Agency
AT&T	American Telephone and Telegraph
BBN	Bolt Beranek and Newman
BIOS	Basic input-output system
BOC	Bell Operating Company (after divestiture)
CAP	Competitive access provider
CDC	Control Data Corporation
CDMA	Code division multiple access
CLEC	Competitive local exchange carrier
CPE	Customer premises equipment
CPU	Central processing unit
DCA	Defense Communications Agency
DDD	Direct distance dialing
DEC	Digital Equipment Corporation
DOD	Department of Defense
DOJ	Department of Justice
DOS	Disk operating system
ENFIA	Exchange Network Facilities for Interstate Access
ERA	Engineering Research Associates
ESP	Enhanced service provider
FCC	Federal Communications Commission
FIR	First Information Revolution
FRC	Federal Radio Commission
FTP	File Transfer Protocol
GE	General Electric
GHz	Gigahertz (billions of cycles per second)
HTML	Hypertext Markup Language
HTTP	Hypertext Transfer Protocol

IAS	Institute for Advanced Study
ICC	Interstate Commerce Commission
ILEC	Incumbent local exchange carrier
IPO	Initial public offering
ISP	Internet service provider
ITU	International Telecommunication Union
IXC	Interexchange (long distance) carrier
LAN	Local area network
MCI	Microwave Communications Incorporated
MFJ	Modified Final Judgment (AT&T divestiture)
MFS	Metropolitan Fiber Systems
MHz	Megahertz (millions of cycles per second)
MITI	Ministry of International Trade and Industry
MSA	Metropolitan Statistical Area
NCSA	National Center for Supercomputing Applications
NIE	New Institutional Economics
NPL	National Physical Laboratory
NSA	National Security Agency
NSF	National Science Foundation
NTT	Nippon Telegraph and Telephone Corporation
OPP	Office of Plans and Policy (FCC)
OSRD	Office of Scientific Research and Development
PBX	Private branch exchange
PCA	Protective Connecting Arrangement
PCM	Plug-compatible manufacturer
PCS	Personal Communications Service
POP	Point of presence
PUC	Public Utility Commission
RCA	Radio Corporation of America
RCC	Radio common carrier
RFC	Request for Comments
RSA	Rural Service Area
SAGE	Semiautomated Ground Environment
SIR	Second Information Revolution
SLC	Subscriber line charge
SNA	Systems Network Architecture
TCP/IP	Transmission Control Protocol/Internet Protocol
TDMA	Time division multiple access
TI	Texas Instruments
WDM	Wave division multiplexing

1

Introduction

Before 1845 long distance communication in the United States was slow and expensive. While the postal system was widely used for business, the basic charge of twenty-five cents per sheet of paper for letters sent more than 400 miles put routine communication out of the financial reach of ordinary workers who earned wages of $1 per day. The Post Office Acts of 1845 and 1851 simplified the rate structure and drastically reduced the prices to a flat rate of three cents for letters sent anywhere in the country. The three-cent basic rate remained generally in effect for over one hundred years until it was raised to four cents in 1958 (U.S. Census, 1975, p. 19; John, 1995, pp. 159–161). The three-cent flat rate stimulated a massive increase in the volume of mail, from an average of three letters per person per year in 1840 to an average of sixty-nine letters per person per year in 1900 (John, 1995, p. 4; U.S. Census, 1975, pp. 8, 805). The flat rate also accentuated the previous practice of subsidizing the sparsely populated areas of the country through charges on the densely populated areas.

The Post Office Act of 1845 coincided with the initial private development of the electric telegraph. While the Post Office did not place any legal restrictions on the development of the telegraph, the telegraph companies were required to respond to Post Office prices and policies for financial viability. Telegrams were expensive fast letters that consumers would choose when the value of fast transmission was greater than the price differential between mail and telegrams. By 1870 the number of Western Union telegram messages was 2 percent of the number of letters while Western Union's revenue was 35 percent of the Post Office's revenue (computed from U.S. Census, 1975, pp. 788, 805). The invention of the telephone in 1876 added a third product to the nation's rapidly expanding information infrastructure. By 1900 many people had a choice of three communication technologies: inexpensive universally available mail service, expensive fast telegrams for time-sensitive written communication, and widely available local voice telephone service together with limited high-cost long distance telephone service.

This book refers to the combination of reliable inexpensive mail service and widely available telegraph and telephone service as the First Information Revolution (FIR). The FIR began with the early telegraph network combined with the mid-nineteenth-century innovations in postal technology and prices and matured with numerous innovations that increased the efficiency and reliability of these services. As discussed in Chapter 2, the FIR was a critical component of the transformation of the U.S. economy in the late nineteenth century. The development of giant industrial enterprises to take advantage of the economies of scale and scope in many different sectors of the economy could not have occurred without the improvements in information technology that allowed managers to control their widely distributed operations.

The technological base for the FIR was steam-powered railroads for the transportation of mail and electrical innovations for the development of the telegraph and telephone industries. At a later stage it included early vacuum-tube electronics for telephone amplifiers, wireless point-to-point communication, and radio broadcasting. The electrical telegraph was introduced soon after the invention of a reliable battery, and its maturation followed the trajectory of increasing sophistication of electrical products. The telephone began as an attempt to crowd more telegraph messages onto a telegraph wire and advanced with the development of sophisticated electrical relay technology for control and switching.

While many countries combined their postal service, telephone, and telegraph into a single government agency, the United States retained a government Post Office and privately owned telegraph and telephone companies. Nevertheless, the privately owned telephone company sought regulation as a defense of its monopoly position. By emphasizing politically controlled monopoly rather than market-oriented competition, the U.S. private telephone company developed many characteristics similar to the European publicly owned telephone companies and to the U.S. Post Office. The domestic telegraph service declined to secondary importance as long distance voice service eroded demand for telegraph, but the telephone monopoly, shielded from competition by state laws and regulatory policies, achieved a thoroughly protected position. Prices were designed to produce enough revenue to cover total cost (including depreciation and return on capital), but the prices of individual services were determined by political considerations rather than the cost of service. The extensive implicit cross-subsidies built into the price system provided a political rationale for excluding competition in any particular service because limited competition could take away profits used to subsidize favored users. The telephone company accepted end-to-end responsibility for the service and strictly limited the ability of any other company to connect to its network.

While great progress was made on improving the efficiency of FIR production, the actual products remained highly stable. From a consumer perspective, mailing a letter or sending a telegram was essentially the same in 1950 as in 1875. The institutions created to control the FIR output (government-operated monopoly for mail, regulated privately owned monopoly for telephone) channeled technological progress into reducing the cost of providing a standardized basic service rather than into finding innovative new services. The FIR was very successful in establishing communication among all parts of the United States and creating the necessary conditions to establish a national market rather than numerous local markets. The stable uniform prices facilitated by government ownership of the mail service and government regulation of the telephone industry allowed businesses to confidently plan to utilize the communication infrastructure without having to establish their own private communications to guarantee service.

Technological innovations during the 1940s and early 1950s created the foundation for a Second Information Revolution, but it took many years of development before the new information structure was widely utilized. World War II created an extensive demand for computing, especially in the code-breaking and atomic bomb projects, and that demand led to the creation of electronic digital computers. The war also created urgent requirements for improved radar and induced extensive research on electronic components, crystals, and methods of utilizing electromagnetic waves of much higher frequencies than prewar technology utilized. Building in part on improved understanding of crystals developed through its wartime radar efforts, AT&T's Bell Laboratories established an extensive postwar semiconductor research effort that led to the invention of the transistor and the beginning of rapid sustained price declines in electronic components.

The Soviet Union's detonation of an atomic bomb in 1949 and the beginning of the Korean War in 1950 revived intensive U.S. military efforts with a particular emphasis on developing new technologies for air defense. The early Cold War military effort created extensive price-insensitive demand for improved transistors. The military demanded multiple suppliers for critical transistors and helped develop improvements in semiconductor technology outside of the control of AT&T. Transistor radios created an early consumer market and induced semiconductor companies to develop mass-manufacturing techniques and cost-saving innovations in order to compete in the price-sensitive consumer market. The military also pressed forward on radar and computer developments with generous funding to both industrial firms and academic researchers in order to accelerate the process of moving from basic innovation to deployed product.

The SAGE air defense system of the 1950s provided a prototype for the Second Information Revolution. SAGE (for "Semiautomated Ground Environment") was an ambitious effort to develop and deploy a sophisticated computer communications system in order to link distant radar sites, air defense control centers, and large-scale computers that could process and interpret data as it was received. IBM's contract to produce the SAGE computers established IBM's preeminent position in the early computer industry and provided more revenue than all commercial computer sales for several years. The System Development Corporation was created to develop the computer programs for SAGE, and its 800 programmers pioneered the techniques of creating large complex programs. AT&T's contract to supply the communications for SAGE led to the development of the first modem and practical experience with transmitting digital data over communication lines designed for analog voice signals.

While the SAGE air defense system provided an early large-scale computer communications system, it was far too expensive and specialized to be copied in the commercial world. The then-existing combination of mail, telegraph, and telephone communication satisfied most corporate communication requirements as they were perceived at the time. However, extensive corporate demand for improved data processing created rapid growth in the emerging commercial computer industry. Continuous improvements in manufacturing processes for transistors changed them from a specialty item to a general replacement for vacuum tubes by 1960 when most computer producers shifted from vacuum tubes to solid-state components. With the invention of the integrated circuit and continuing rapid improvement in the price and performance of electronic components, computer prices fell drastically. It became economically feasible to substitute computers for an increasingly wide range of functions previously provided by human control or earlier kinds of electronic and mechanical controls.

As computer prices continued to fall, it became economically desirable during the 1980s to supply individual workers with computers in order to enhance their productivity, first with expensive workstations for engineers and then with inexpensive personal computers for a wide range of workers. Many of the workstations were linked together by fast local area networks (LANs) in order to share information and collaborate on projects. The LANs were often linked to wider networks, first to internal corporate networks to provide communication among distant workers in the same company and later to the public Internet. The "client-server" model of computing (small computers able to communicate with any of a wide variety of information servers) began to replace the earlier mainframe model of computing. The data communications systems (LANs, corporate wide-area systems, Internet) that developed in the data processing industry provided an alternative to the voice telephone and postal systems.

Sustained progress in electronics and computing created continuous opportunities for new products. Consequently, efforts to craft a stable replacement for the initial regulated monopoly continually failed as the underlying technological conditions changed. The corporate and government structures of the FIR were best suited to a capital-intensive stable technology. So long as the primary policy goal was providing guaranteed access to communications at reasonable prices for consumers and guaranteed recovery of sunk cost investments for suppliers, the regulated monopoly structure worked reasonably well and enjoyed widespread political acceptance, but the regulated monopoly was less successful in adapting to rapid technological change. The Bell System incorporated electronics into its previous electromechanical operations but did not develop radically new products based on the drastically reduced price of electronic components.

The new opportunities created by the high rate of technological progress in electronic components generated increasing pressure on the regulated monopoly telephone industry. The values protected by the regulated monopoly (stable uniform prices, cross-subsidies among services for a politically determined sharing of the cost burden, reliable stable technology with slow depreciation) came into conflict with the values of an open-market system (freedom to develop innovative products, freedom to enter any market and set the price without political interference). The conflict began in fringe areas of the market (the right to build a private microwave communication system for the internal communications of a company, the right to connect specialized customer-provided equipment to the network) and then spread to all parts of the market. Initially, the questions were narrowly circumscribed, accepting the general concept of the regulated monopoly but attempting to give individual customers more freedom than AT&T's policies allowed. At an intermediate stage the questions broadened to consider what portions of the network should remain a monopoly and what portions should be competitive. By the mid-1990s the policy perspective had changed to an acceptance of competition for all parts of the market while attempting to preserve certain characteristics of the previous structure such as subsidies to high-cost areas of the country. The new technologies increased the complexity of regulation and created a requirement to determine the boundaries of the regulated monopoly while technology continued to change and create new opportunities and new forms of interaction between regulated and nonregulated services. The solution of abandoning regulation and relying on market outcomes did not appear to be feasible during most of the period of regulatory evolution because it appeared that certain portions of the industry were potentially subject to competition while other portions were most efficiently served by a single supplier.

As the price of electronic components and computer processing continued to decline and the regulated monopoly structure was modified into a more flexible and competitive communications sector, powerful inexpensive combinations of computer processing and communications capability created a Second Information Revolution (SIR). The SIR is characterized by computer-enhanced communication with usage costs and prices that are distance-insensitive and very close to zero. Much greater capabilities than possessed by the multibillion-dollar SAGE computer and communications system of the 1950s are now available to ordinary consumers and office workers at nominal cost. While late nineteenth-century innovations allowed telegrams to be sent among major cities around the world when their importance was high enough to justify the substantial cost, the current structures allow e-mails to be exchanged and information from web sites to be accessed at a zero marginal cost regardless of the location. Just as the nineteenth-century information innovations facilitated major business and political changes, the current information revolution is providing the conditions for major business and political changes. Some of those are already evident (provision of software support for U.S. corporations from India, for example) while other implications are only beginning to be developed or have not yet been discovered.

This book tells the story of the development of the Second Information Revolution. It is a complex story because of the interaction of technological opportunities, business decisions, and political decisions. The driving force in the story is the sustained rapid technological progress in electronic components that created continuous new opportunities in computers and communications. The computer industry was generally quicker to take advantage of the new opportunities than the communications industry because the regulated monopoly communications industry was more constrained by compatibility and other regulatory requirements than the unregulated computer industry. The interaction of the computer and communications industries created political pressure for a more flexible communications structure.

A simple (but not really accurate) version of the story is that political authorities observed the more rapid technological progress in computers compared to communications and decided to eliminate many regulatory requirements in order to make communications more like the computer industry. The actual process of adjusting the institutional structure designed for the electromechanical technology of the First Information Revolution into a structure more compatible with the technology of the Second Information Revolution was messy and controversial. It involved significant changes in implicit property rights of various groups with corresponding effort to influence the new structures in a way favorable to them or to preserve benefits of the old structure against the efforts of other groups to change it. Two major themes of this book include:

1. A comparison of the relative responses of the unregulated data processing industry and the regulated communications industry to new technological opportunities.
2. An analysis of the process of changing the institutions designed for one technology into those suitable for a different technology.

The Promise of Regulation

The development of the Second Information Revolution was greatly influenced by the practice of public utility regulation at both the state and federal level. Public utility regulation is focused on the operation of infrastructure industries (first railroads, then electricity and communications) and should be distinguished from health, safety, and environmental regulation that has very different characteristics and is not discussed in this book. Public utility regulation was developed in the late nineteenth century for railroads and reached its most optimistic period in the New Deal legislation of the 1930s. From the late 1970s through the present there has been an increasingly strong regulatory reform and deregulation movement that has modified or eliminated portions of public utility regulation. In the late twentieth century "regulation" generally had a negative connotation, and few politicians or business leaders would openly advocate increased regulation. That attitude was in sharp contrast with an earlier era when the expert regulatory agency was viewed as the best way to combine the efficiency of private enterprise with public objectives for infrastructure industries. Despite a quarter-century of rhetoric attacking regulatory agencies and the practice of regulation, regulation continues to play a major role in the opportunities and incentives of the telecommunication industry.

Early regulation was a uniquely American institution that was a substitute for the state control of critical industries developed in Europe. Robert Horwitz characterizes the early regulatory agencies as an outgrowth of common law requirements imposed on industries of special importance to the economy:

> English common law courts gave certain kinds of occupations, hence certain kinds of property, a special status which incurred privileges and obligations . . . [Those occupations] were awarded local monopolies in exchange for an obligation to serve all at reasonable charges . . . The

modern regulatory agency in many ways constituted a new institutional form of the common law . . . In the most general and abstract sense, early regulatory agencies arose to create a predictable environment for *national* economic activity. A primary means of creating such a predictable environment for economic activity was through the regulation of infrastructure industries (first transportation, later communication, banking, and energy), and the oversight of their commerce-bearing function. (1989, p. 47)

Even in its early years the United States did not leave infrastructure industries entirely to private enterprise. The stagecoach industry in the first half of the nineteenth century was privately owned but so dependent on Post Office contracts that "stagecoach proprietors . . . competed for the mail contract and, if they failed to secure it, immediately retired from the field" (John, 1995, p. 94). State and local governments were active participants in the construction of transportation improvements: building public roads, providing a majority of the financing for canals, and paying for a minority share of the early railroads. The government also facilitated the early transportation networks by providing land for rights-of-way and using its powers of eminent domain to establish government or privately owned transportation routes.

While the government continued to provide land, eminent domain privileges, and some financial subsidies, the massive railroad investment of the mid- and late nineteenth century was largely privately financed. However, both shippers and railroad managers were dissatisfied with the results of market-oriented railroad pricing. Railroads had a high fixed cost and a low marginal cost for additional traffic. Building the road required a heavy investment, but adding traffic only required adding a car to an existing train, or at most adding a train, up to the capacity of the tracks. That cost structure created incentives for the railroad to practice price discrimination (also known as value of service pricing) among types of traffic and shipper locations, charging low prices to those who had alternatives (such as water transportation and no time sensitivity) and high prices to those who were entirely dependent on the railroad. Price discrimination seemed unfair to many shippers.

Railroads could charge high prices so long as they had a monopoly, but the high profits encouraged a competitor to build a new railroad. Once two or more railroads competed for the same shipments, it was profitable for either railroad to offer any price above its marginal cost in order to avoid losing the shipment to its competitor. The resulting price wars created "ruinous competition" with prices below the level needed to pay the fixed cost of the railroad, including the interest on bonds issued to finance the track. Railroad managers and their financiers considered the low prices unfair and sought ways to prevent price wars that threatened the financial stability of all railroads involved. The critical role of the railroads in facilitating other forms of commerce meant that the economic fortunes of individual shippers as well as entire regions were dependent on the level of railroad rates. Rational economic decisions regarding where to site a factory or whether to devote a farm to subsistence or export crops depended on the level of railroad rates. Politicians considered it unfair that the economic welfare of their constituents could be severely curtailed by changes in railroad pricing policies.

The earliest theory of public regulation was developed by Boston lawyer and economic analyst Charles Francis Adams (son of Lincoln's ambassador to Great Britain, grandson of President John Quincy Adams, and great-grandson of President John Adams). After leading a Massachusetts regiment in the Civil War, he turned his attention to influencing government interaction with the railroads. Railroad networks were already well developed in Massachusetts at that time, and railroad routes and rates were crucial factors in the decisions of the state's many factory managers. Beginning in 1867, Adams published a number of influential articles analyzing the economic characteristics of railroads. He developed an early theory of what is now known as "natural monopoly." Adams observed that the high fixed cost of constructing a railroad and the low marginal cost of carrying additional traffic made a single firm more efficient than multiple competing firms and concluded that "competition and the cheapest possible transportation are wholly incompatible" (quoted in McCraw, 1984, p. 9).

Adams evaluated the European solution of public ownership of railroads and concluded that public ownership should not be chosen for the United States. He noted that the structure of the U.S. government (separation of executive, legislative, and judicial powers, division between state and federal government authority) was designed to reduce the power of the government and to guard against abuses of that power. However, that intentional diffusion of power built into the foundation of the U.S. government would prevent effective management of a government railroad. Some public limitations on railroad freedom already existed in the form of state charters for the railroad companies and early railroad laws that imposed profit ceilings and other restrictions. Adams considered those provisions too rigid and unable to adjust to changing conditions. His preferred solution was a commission of experts that would devote full attention to railroad problems. Adams advocated what has become known as a "sunshine commission" or "weak regulatory commission." Rather than having the power to issue binding orders, the commission would gather information and study problems, providing advice to the industry, the public, and the state legislature.

Adams showed a clear grasp of railroad industry economics and of the structure of the U.S. government but not of practical politics and government incentives. He wrote: "Work hitherto badly done, spasmodically done, superficially done, ignorantly done, and too often corruptly done by temporary and irresponsible legislative committees, is in future to be reduced to order and science by the labors of permanent bureaus, and placed by them before legislatures for intelligent action" (quoted in McCraw, 1984, p. 15). He did not explain why "irresponsible" and "corrupt" legislative committees would accept the recommendations of the commission or how the regulatory commission would achieve impartial expert views of the best public arrangements for the railroads.

After drafting a proposed law and lobbying extensively for it, Adams succeeded in getting Massachusetts to set up the Board of Railroad Commissioners in 1869 and to appoint him as one of the three commissioners. Adams dominated the board and continued to write extensively, including the board's influential *Annual Report,* which was widely distributed and publicized. According to Thomas McCraw, "These sophisticated general commentaries by Adams included some of the best writing on industrialization produced in nineteenth-century America" (1984, p. 23). Adams and the board sought to promote a harmonious "public interest" by advice and publicity without coercion. They successfully requested safety improvements and rate reductions but had no power to issue binding orders to the railroads. Foreshadowing future problems of regulatory "capture" by the regulated industry, Adams invested in railroad stock while on the board and joined the industry after leaving the board in 1879. He first served as an arbitrator for Albert Fink's cartel, the Eastern Trunk Line Association, and then became the president of the Union Pacific Railroad in 1884.

The first coercive railroad regulation, with power to issue legally binding orders on rates, came from the Granger laws of the 1870s. The farmers of the upper Mississippi Valley who were dependent on the railroads for exchanging their crops for manufactured goods sought to eliminate price discrimination through state laws. The railroads opposed the state regulation but sought federal regulation in order to bolster their ineffective private efforts to maintain price-fixing cartels. Litigation over state railroad regulation led to two influential Supreme Court decisions. In *Munn v. Illinois,* the Court upheld the state regulations as consistent with common law precedent and ruled that the railroads were subject to common carrier obligations because their property was "affected with a public interest" (94 U.S. 113 (1877)). However, the states' power to regulate railroads was largely eliminated nine years later when the Court ruled in *Wabash, St. Louis, and Pacific Railway Co. v. Illinois* that most railroads were engaged in interstate commerce and therefore beyond the regulatory authority of the individual states (118 U.S. 557 (1886)).

The early state regulatory agencies had little obvious effect on the prices or operation of the railroads. Railroad development and prices were determined by market opportunities and efforts to achieve dominance. Railroad entrepreneurs discovered what would later be called "network effects" (the value of a network rises with the number of nodes connected). They utilized interconnection rights with other railroads as a competitive weapon and sought to build complete systems in order to reduce their vulnerability to refusal of interconnection by other lines. The railroads discovered the potential instability of a competitive capital-intensive network industry with large economies of scale. Thomas McCraw's summary of late-nineteenth-century railroad history could also be applied to the 1996–2002 period of telecommunication history:

> Each of the major lines began to build, purchase or acquire through merger . . . tracks leading in and out of all important centers of commerce from the Northeast to the Midwest, plus extensive webs of feeder lines serving the hinterlands. During the 1880s, a wildly competitive construction program, in pursuit of this strategy, compounded the earlier overbuilding . . . Overbuilding in turn led to numerous bankruptcies, capital writedowns, mergers, and abandonments of unprofitable lines. As the number of corporations involved in railroading shrank, a remaining few companies, now of very large size, came to dominate the industry . . . What law and custom had not allowed Albert Fink to do [set up a cartel with pooling and cooperation among

the railroads], subsequent financial distress tendered to the ministrations of J. P. Morgan. And Morgan, unlike Fink, levied colossal fees for his services. (McCraw, 1984, pp. 51, 52)

Despite the ineffectiveness of early regulation, the regulatory movement continued to expand. There was widespread sentiment that some public control over critical infrastructure industries was necessary but equally widespread opinion that government ownership and operation of the industries was undesirable. There was no clear alternative to the regulatory agency in the nation's effort to combine public control with the market-oriented benefits of managerial freedom and access to capital. The politically popular Progressive Movement of the early twentieth century sought ways to orient private companies toward public goals and helped create new regulatory agencies and strengthen the powers of old ones. Massachusetts created the Board of Gas and Electric Light Commissioners in 1887, added telephones to the jurisdiction of the railroad board in 1913, and later merged the two regulatory commissions into the Massachusetts Department of Public Utilities (McCraw, 1984, p. 58). While the details vary by state, many other states followed a roughly similar pattern, and by the early twentieth century many states had Public Utility Commissions that regulated telephone, gas, and electric companies.

Following an 1898 Supreme Court decision that railroads were entitled to a reasonable return on the fair value of the property being used for the convenience of the public, most regulatory agencies adopted some form of rate-of-return regulation. The essential idea was to limit the regulated company's total revenue to the level necessary to cover operating expenses, depreciation, and a normal level of profit on invested capital. Turning that simple idea into legally defensible procedures for approving or disapproving specific rates required specifying accounting systems and determining innumerable other details that have kept the staff and commissioners of regulatory agencies occupied for the past century. The detailed "rate case" to consider the approval of specific price changes, often accompanied by thousands of pages of supporting documentation and formal hearing procedures, became the centerpiece of regulatory activity.

After the Supreme Court largely eliminated state jurisdiction over railroads, the federal government inaugurated federal railroad regulation with the Interstate Commerce Commission (ICC) in 1887. The enabling legislation was vague and adopted common law precedents for common carriers (just and reasonable rates, nondiscrimination) as statutory language. The difference was that the common law principles would now be interpreted on an ongoing basis by an administrative agency rather than by courts. However, the decisions of the ICC could still be appealed through the courts and thus court interpretation of common law principles remained the definitive guide to the legal obligations of common carriers. Congress gradually expanded the powers and scope of the ICC, putting interstate telephone service (in 1910) and interstate trucking service (in 1935) under its jurisdiction along with a number of enhancements to its rate-setting powers.

Federal regulatory commissions were expanded and strengthened by New Deal legislation in response to the depression of the 1930s. At that time, many industries were in severe financial difficulty, and many people believed that laissez-faire capitalism had failed. New Deal regulatory agencies continued the earlier tradition of an independent agency separate from the three major branches of government and combining aspects of all three, but generally contained stronger powers than the earlier agencies. The New Deal emphasis on government planning and direction gained business support by also supporting the creation of monopolies and cartels to eliminate competitive price cutting for critical industries. Robert Horwitz describes the results of New Deal regulatory agencies as a bargain that produced specific benefits for the regulated industries, consumers, and employees of the regulated industries:

> New Deal regulatory interventions accepted pre-existing institutional structures and applied controls that would stabilize the structures of those industries under their jurisdictions . . . [R]egulatory agencies formulated complex rate structures to cross-subsidize certain types of routes and services. The common carrier obligations which guaranteed (often cheap) service thus had the effect of bringing consumers into the regulatory system of mutual benefits and compromises. And the protections provided to regulated businesses also had the effect of bringing labor into the system of mutual benefits and compromises. The stabilization of those industries . . . facilitated the broad unionization of regulated industries. Thus, New Deal regulation defined the public interest as the government oversight of rationally functioning,

privately owned businesses that provided services universally, relatively cheaply, and in nondiscriminatory fashion. The economic consequence of this was to stabilize and universalize the infrastructure for commerce. (1989, pp. 74, 75)

Telecommunication regulation under the Federal Communications Commission (formed in 1934) followed the pattern described by Horwitz. Regulation supported the existing industry structure and protected it against new entrants. The resulting monopoly could then be required to provide subsidized service to politically favored classes of consumers. It could charge high enough prices to provide job security to its unionized labor force without concerns that a company with lower labor costs would undercut its prices. The regulatory structure created an alliance of regulated company managers, unionized employees, and favored consumers that supported continuation of the regulated monopoly.

Throughout the half-century of regulatory development from early state railroad agencies through the New Deal, policies to promote technological progress played no role. It was an era of rapid technological progress (sometimes called the Second Industrial Revolution) as innovations in industrial chemistry, electrical equipment, and internal combustion motors transformed the economy. Yet regulatory theorists and practitioners devoted no attention to the effects that their policies could have on the development of new technology. As industries based on new technologies became important parts of the country's infrastructure, they were often forced into the model developed for railroads. Thus electricity flowing over wires, telephone calls flowing over wires, trucks driving along a road, and airplanes flying through the air could all be regulated as common carriers, utilizing railroad precedents as if each activity was a train moving along the railroad tracks. The implicit assumption was that technological progress was either irrelevant or unaffected by the regulatory process. Regulatory concerns focused on the level and structure of rates and the financial health of the regulated companies. The stable prices and stable companies that were promoted by the regulatory process were achieved by reducing the threat of either price competition or technological competition. Thus the stability that seemed attractive during a time of depression and bankruptcies appeared less attractive when it was viewed as locking in old structures and limiting innovation.

Conceptual Framework

The conceptual framework utilized in this book is based on the New Institutional Economics (NIE), especially as developed by Douglass North (1981, 1990) and Oliver Williamson (1975, 1996, 2000). The essential idea of the NIE is that the success of a market system is dependent on the institutions that facilitate efficient private transactions. While textbook economics assumes that all mutually beneficial transactions will occur, the NIE observes that conducting a transaction requires numerous elements other than the possibility of mutual gain: information about the potential traders, ability to conduct the bargaining, and confidence that the agreement will be carried out once reached. John McMillan summarizes the requirements for effective markets as follows: "A workable platform for markets has five elements: information flows smoothly; people can be trusted to live up to their promises; competition is fostered; property rights are protected but not overprotected; and side effects on third parties are curtailed" (2002, p. 135). Those conditions are dependent on information exchange, commercial law, and enforcement mechanisms. With well-functioning institutions (clearly defined property rights, enforcement of contracts, norms of behavior that promote trust, absence of corruption), the economy will approximate the textbook predictions. In societies with poorly functioning institutions (low respect for property rights, corruption, theft, uncertain judicial behavior), economic performance will fall far below that predicted from standard economic reasoning because people will not be able to make bargains with confidence that they will be carried out.

Economic historian Douglass North defines institutions as "the rules of the game in a society" or alternatively as "the humanly devised constraints that shape human interaction" (1990, p. 3). North finds that the institutions developed by a society (including regulatory rules) are a crucial factor in determining economic success. Poor institutions create incentives for the parties to engage in redistributive activities, expending substantial resources in privately beneficial activity that transfers income from one party to another with no net increase in society's resources. Good institutions promote a long-term path of productive activity rather than redistributive activity.

North illustrates the importance of institutions with the contrasting economic paths of Spain and England during the seventeenth century.

At the beginning of that century Spain was economically dominant over England and appeared to have far brighter prospects with its extensive fleet, its vast colonies, and the great influx of wealth from the New World. Throughout the century both Spain and England sought ways to increase government revenue in order to finance extensive military operations. England increased government revenue by ceding more power to Parliament, strengthening private property rights, and establishing the Bank of England, creating institutions that provided security for private investment and facilitated private enterprise and economic growth. Spain increased government revenue by arbitrary taxation and confiscation of wealth, creating insecurity over private property and disincentives for private investment. Spain's economic position declined precipitously while England rose to the world's leading economic power (North, 1990, pp. 113–115).

Any particular set of institutions creates a corresponding set of property rights and incentives. Property rights may be formally defined as in the U.S. system of real property with its elaborate legal structure of deeds, mortgages, zoning regulations, and procedures for transferring and proving title to a piece of property. Alternatively, property rights may be implicit in the institutional structure without being characterized in the law as property. For example, the regulated monopoly telecommunication structure of the 1960s provided substantial subsidies to rural telephone companies. Those subsidies did not meet the legal definition of property and could have been removed without creating an unconstitutional "taking" of property. Yet those subsidies were a "property right" as the term is used in institutional economics and in this book. They transferred income to a particular group of companies and created incentives for those companies to support the continuation of the institutional structure that provided the benefits. The property rights and the opportunities for changing those property rights that are created by a particular institutional structure determine the incentive structure and help determine the pattern of economic activity. If property rights are vague and can be easily changed, individuals have an incentive to focus on changing property rights to their advantage or protecting themselves against changes in property rights (redistributive activities). If property rights are clearly defined and enforced, individuals have an incentive to focus on increased production because there is limited opportunity for redistribution. Property rights are determined by legal definitions, custom, and enforcement mechanisms. In the economic sense, rights to physical property in a high-crime area are vaguely defined and easily changed. One person may have a clear legal title to an automobile, for example, but have a limited economic property right in the automobile if there is a high probability that it will be stolen and not recovered.

Institutions are created to solve particular problems and incorporate the assumptions of the time they were created, including the relevant production technology, economic conditions, and price ratios. While institutions evolve, there is no automatic mechanism that makes institutions optimally adjust to changes in technology or other conditions. At best, they will lag behind current conditions and at worst they will be counterproductive by creating perverse incentives. A particular set of institutions creates benefits for particular parties, and they are likely to resist any changes that detract from their benefits even if changes would produce an increase in overall efficiency. If those who benefit from a particular set of institutions are able to block any changes to the institutions, then the economy may fail to benefit from technological progress.

Changes in relative prices play a critical role in the process of institutional adjustment. If technological progress causes a substantial decline in the cost of one input while other inputs retain constant prices, for example, managers and entrepreneurs will perceive new opportunities in the changed relative prices, but institutional constraints may limit their ability to exploit the new opportunities. If an opportunity is blocked by an institutional constraint, it creates an incentive to invest resources in attempting to modify the institutions. Success for entrepreneurs is in part determined by their ability to influence institutional change in a way favorable to themselves. In the telecommunication industry, for example, substantial decline in the cost of electronic components created many opportunities for innovative wireless communications systems, but exploitation of those opportunities was limited by Federal Communications Commission spectrum licensing policies developed for earlier conditions. Substantial profits were made by entrepreneurs who were able to obtain policy changes that favored their particular approach to the market. More generally, the political pressure created by blocked technological opportunities created significant change in the process of spectrum allocation and licensing in order to allow more of the new technological opportunities to be utilized.

North describes the process of institutional adjustment to changes in relative prices as follows:

Institutions change, and fundamental changes in relative prices are the most important source of that change. To the noneconomist (and perhaps for some economists as well), putting such weight on changing relative prices may be hard to understand. But relative price changes alter the incentives of individuals in human interaction, and the only other source of such change is a change in tastes.

All of the following sources of institutional changes are changes in relative prices: changes in the ratio of factor prices . . . changes in the cost of information, and changes in technology (including significantly and importantly, military technology). (1990, p. 84)

The initiator of the institutional change in telecommunication examined in this book is the sustained rapid technological progress in electronic components. That progress can be considered largely exogenous to the communications industry. It was begun with innovations in Bell Labs but the continuous improvements were primarily developed by companies outside of the communications industry. Electronic components were widely available on a reasonably competitive market throughout the relevant time period and there was no need to have an integrated manufacturing operation or an internal electronic research organization in order to take advantage of the fall in price and improvement in capability of electronic components.

The fall in the price of electronic components introduced a major change in the relative price ratios for the relevant factors of producing communication service. Expensive and rigid control and switching functions performed by electromechanical technology became inexpensive and more flexible, allowing improvements in the supply of voice telephone service (digital transmission, electronic switching) and entirely new products. As prices of electronic components continued to fall, services based on extensive computer processing (packet-switching, cellular radio, compression algorithms to save transmission bandwidth) became economically feasible. The development during the late 1960s of time-sharing computers that could be accessed remotely and the development of distributed processing with client-server architecture during the late 1980s and the 1990s brought the unregulated data processing industry into close association with the regulated communications industry. Computer manufacturers and users sought freedom to integrate their services with communication services in a more flexible way than was allowed by the then-existing regulations. That pressure began an evolution of the institutional structure toward partial competition and caused the reconsideration of many implicit assumptions of the regulated monopoly era.

As the institutional structure evolved, it also changed the property rights within the communication industry. Much of the controversy over changing institutions related to the changing property rights, with the various parties seeking to improve their own position through the political process. Yet it was not simply a matter of voting or lobbying. The specific policymakers who were able to craft a widely accepted justification for particular institutional changes were able to gain political support for those changes. Parties supporting changes in the institutional structure generally argued for freedom and competition, widely accepted political values. Parties opposing changes in the institutional structure generally argued for subsidizing the price of basic telephone service to promote universal service, also a widely accepted value. Throughout the evolution of the institutional structures, many complex compromises between the competing values were fashioned in order to gain political support for implementing particular changes.

As the institutions and property rights evolved, the new structure created additional opportunities for new products. The provision of those new products generally increased political support for maintaining the changed structure. It also brought new participants into the policy process who could provide alternative information and perspectives to support the institutions that allowed their entry. As new products came into the industry from new suppliers, new technological trajectories were created. Those suppliers stimulated technological progress in their particular products as they took advantage of improving input products, engaged in research and development, and gained experience in producing their particular product. Because progress in electronic components was continuous, the process of institutional change required adjusting to a continuously changing set of input prices with a consistent direction: rapidly falling price of electronic components, creating incentives to utilize more and more electronics as substitutes for other inputs.

2

The First Information Revolution

The U.S. Post Office Act of 1792 established the structure for early expansion from the limited mail service provided by the colonial postal system. It instituted favorable rates for newspapers, privacy for the mail, and a procedure for expanding the number of post offices. Many communities petitioned for the establishment of mail service and the petitions were freely granted, increasing the number of post offices from 75 in 1790 to 8,450 in 1830. By 1831 the Post Office was a dominant part of the federal government, with three times as many postmasters as all other federal civilian employees combined and more postmasters than soldiers and officers in the army (John, 1995, p. 3). While tremendous efforts were made to increase the speed of the mail, the poor roads and dependence on horse-drawn vehicles limited the opportunities. Major routes were served by stagecoaches that averaged four miles per hour, while special horse expresses could reach twelve miles per hour. Nevertheless, administrative improvements and attention to coordinating schedules gradually increased the speed of letters. On the East Coast route that had been established in colonial times, the round-trip time for a letter from Portland, Maine to Savannah, Georgia dropped from forty days in 1780 (colonial post) to twenty-seven days in 1810 (early U.S. post) to twelve days in 1831, without any fundamental change in technology (John, 1995, pp. 17, 18).

The most time-sensitive information was information related to market prices, and a time advantage in obtaining price information could be very profitable. Postal regulations designed to guarantee that the mail would travel faster than other sources of information were a direct result of arbitrage in commodity prices. As recounted by postal historian Richard John:

[Postmaster General John] McLean's interest in the high-speed transmission of market information was the direct result of a celebrated bit of commodity trading that occurred in the spring of 1825. An enterprising group of merchants based along the Atlantic seaboard . . . netted several hundred thousand dollars by taking advantage of their advance knowledge of a sharp rise in cotton prices in the European markets. The key to their gambit was their ability to commandeer the horses and riders that the government used to transmit the mail and, in so doing, to greatly reduce the delay that ordinarily separated the arrival of European market information along the Atlantic seaboard from its arrival in the cotton ports of Mobile and New Orleans . . . The merchants were able to place their purchase orders long before news of the price rise became generally known, thus undermining the implicit trust that the planters in the cotton ports had come to place in the postal system as the authoritative source of information on changing market trends. (1995, pp. 83, 84)

The early information transmission capability was almost entirely a function of Post Office policies and the laws controlling those policies. The efforts to increase speed, to expand to rural areas, to move toward railway transmission of the mail, and to provide subsidies to stagecoach lines all determined the initial information infrastructure.

While the early nineteenth-century improvements in the Post Office provided a regular means of communication, the mail was too expensive for routine use. Prior to 1845, postage was computed based on the mileage traveled and the number of sheets of paper in the letter. Postage was an important cost of doing business for merchants, and required care in deciding what communications were worthwhile. Two laws (in 1845 and 1851) simplified the rate structure and greatly reduced the price, introducing a largely distance-insensitive rate (now known as postalized rates). Beginning in 1851, a letter to most regions of the country was charged three cents instead of the twenty-five cents charged before 1845 for letters traveling over 300 miles (U.S. Census, 1975, p. 19). The U.S. rate reductions followed similar British postal reforms of 1840 that reduced prices for a letter carried 100 miles from nine pennies to a distance-insensitive rate of a single penny, the "penny post" (Noam, 1992, p. 17). The rate reductions inspired a dramatic increase in correspondence among ordinary citizens, as well as the initiation of junk mail as businesses found it profitable to mail advertisements and solicitations.

The Development of Telegraph Services

Telegraph development in the United States began in 1844, under the sponsorship of the Post Office. After operating an experimental telegraph line, the Post Office declined to purchase the patents from inventor Samuel Morse and allowed the telegraph to be developed as a private enterprise. Morse then licensed several different entrepreneurs to build individual lines along the East Coast and west to St. Louis. A dispute over royalties with the license holder for the western line led to a breakup of the patent organization and to efforts by many parties to build telegraph lines outside of the control of the Morse patent. Court efforts to shut down the lines that were not licensed by Morse were unsuccessful and telegraph building became an industry with quite free entry. Capital costs were relatively low. Early telegraph-building techniques were improvisational because of lack of experience and lack of fundamental understanding of electricity. However, the Morse Code and the apparatus designed to utilize that code could be used even in very poor conditions, and lines were built rapidly through the sparsely populated but large U.S. territory. With the initial telegraph development, the Post Office lost its status as the source of the most up-to-date information on prices and other time-sensitive material, but retained a legal monopoly on letters and remained the primary source of information transmission.

Early railroad development increased both the supply and the demand for communications. Railroads provided a faster and cheaper method of transporting mail than stagecoaches and also provided a conveniently accessible route for building telegraph lines. The railroads also needed communication to prevent accidents and to manage the much more complex operations of a large railroad compared to the other businesses of the time. The first railroad-related communication problem was preventing accidents on single-line tracks. Initial short-line railroads could complete the trip one-way before a train began the return trip in order to avoid collisions, and they had few enough employees and short enough track that a single manager could personally oversee all operations. With longer lines, it was necessary to precisely schedule train "meets" where one train would go onto a siding while the other passed, and to account for contingencies such as failure to follow schedules or mechanical breakdowns. After a notable fatal head-on collision on the Western Railroad's Worcester to Albany line in 1841, the railroad began developing precise methods of control that were greatly facilitated by the telegraph.

As railroads expanded in size and geographical scope, the problem became efficient management rather than merely preventing collisions. By 1851 the Erie Railroad had expanded to over 1,000 freight cars on 445 miles of track with 1,325 employees utilized in moving 250,000 tons of freight and almost 700,000 passengers, and it continued to grow rapidly in subsequent years (Beniger, 1986, pp. 226, 227). The size of the Erie Railroad and the complexity of managing its operations produced a crisis. Twenty-six people were killed on the railroad in 1851, and, according to a railroad writer of the time, "utmost confusion prevailed, so much so, that in the greatest press of business, cars in perfect order have stood for months upon switches without being put to the least service, and without its being known where they were" (quoted in Beniger, 1986, p. 227).

Daniel McCallum, the superintendent of the Erie Railroad, found that the company was experiencing diseconomies of scale because of management obstacles. He observed that operating costs per mile increased with the size of the system. He wrote:

> A Superintendent of a road fifty miles in length can give its business his personal attention and may be constantly on the line engaged in the direction of its details; each person is personally known to him, and all questions in relation to its business are at once presented and acted upon; and any system however imperfect may under such circumstances prove comparatively successful. In the government of a road five hundred miles in length a very different state exists. Any system which might be applicable to the business and extent of a short road would be found entirely inadequate to the wants of a long one; and I am fully convinced that in the want of system perfect in its details, properly adapted and vigilantly enforced, lies the true secret of their [the large roads'] failure. (Quoted in Beniger, 1986, pp. 227, 228)

McCallum established a highly structured management system for the Erie Railroad, with emphasis on information flows to the appropriate decisionmaker. He required hourly reports by telegraph on the location of all trains, accompanied by a staff at headquarters that analyzed the reports and charted the position and progress of each train. Daily and monthly reports on financial transactions and freight movements provided for financial control and provided information for improving the efficiency of operations. After McCallum left the Erie Railroad, he served as superintendent of the Union railroads during the Civil War and supervised the construction or repair of over 2,700 miles of track for the war effort (Beniger, 1986, p. 232).

Western Union utilized the complementary nature of railroads and telegraph to develop into a major telegraph company during the 1850s and then dominated the telegraph industry during and after the Civil War. Western Union developed contracts with the railroads in which the railroad would be a partial owner of the telegraph and would give Western Union exclusive use of rail right-of-way for telegraph messages. Western Union agreed to give priority to railroad operational messages and provide them without charge. Initially, Western Union was one of many telegraph companies serving the United States but increased its position throughout the 1850s as railroads expanded their networks. Just before the beginning of the Civil War, Western Union secured a government contract to build a telegraph line to the West Coast. When war began, that line became extraordinarily profitable and could command rates of up to $1 per word because of the great time savings in communicating over telegraph versus any other method through the long distance not yet served by railroad. Western Union lines were almost entirely in the states that remained with the Union. Many other telegraph lines extended across the boundary between the Union states and the Confederate states and were cut at the outbreak of hostilities. Furthermore, Anson Stager, the general manager of Western Union, was appointed Director of Military Telegraphs for the Union army without resigning his Western Union position. He directed the construction of 15,000 miles of military telegraph lines during the war and those were absorbed into Western Union's system after the war.

In the year following the war's end, Western Union purchased two other telegraph companies that survived the war and established a nationwide telegraph system (Thompson, 1947, pp. 399–442; Brock, 1981, pp. 73–83). Western Union expanded rapidly in the decade following the Civil War, increasing its offices from 2,250 in 1866 to 7,072 in 1876, while increasing its miles of wire from 76,000 to 184,000 over that same time period, and increasing its revenue from $4.6 million to $9.1 million (U.S. Census, 1975, p. 788). The Post Office made no at-

tempt to control or regulate the telegraph industry, but postal rate policies partially determined the telegraph rate structure. Mail and telegrams were imperfect substitutes for each other. Mail was the cheapest
means of communicating over long distances and it remained the dominant form of long distance communication, with telegrams providing
time-sensitive communications at much higher prices. On routes with
no competing telegraph line, Western Union's monopoly power was limited by the opportunity to substitute a slower three-cent letter for the
telegram.

Western Union dominated the post–Civil War telegraph industry but
never attained a sustained monopoly. Several small telegraph companies
continued in business, providing a potential source of competition if
Western Union's prices made it profitable for the competitors to expand.
The close connection between telegraph and railroads made it possible
for the railroad entrepreneurs to establish a competing telegraph if Western Union prices were too high. The combination of competition from
mail and potential competition from railway-based telegraph companies
limited Western Union's market power even in the absence of regulation or substantial direct competition. Western Union imitated the Post
Office practice of rarely changing prices and, for example, offered a price
between fifty and sixty cents for a telegram from New York to Chicago
for most years between 1876 and 1946 (U.S. Census, 1975, p. 790).

As the railroads continued to expand their operations after the Civil
War, they faced new management challenges. By 1891 the Pennsylvania
Railroad employed 110,000 workers, more than the Post Office and almost three times the number of men in the armed services. That railroad's revenue was 35 percent of the federal government's receipts, and
its capitalization was almost equal to the national debt. Alfred Chandler
states:

> The railroad was . . . in every way the pioneer in modern business ad-
> ministration. The great railway systems were by the 1890s the largest
> business enterprises not only in the United States but also in the world
> . . . In Europe, on the other hand, the much larger military and govern-
> mental establishments were a source for the kind of administrative
> training that became so essential to the operation of modern industrial,
> urban, and technologically advanced economies. (1977, pp. 204, 205)

The transportation and communication advances during the post–
Civil War period paved the way for the rise of the United States to global

economic power. The new information availability and managerial systems allowed the creation of far larger enterprises than in the first half of the century, and therefore allowed companies to take full advantage of the economies of scale and scope that were technologically possible. Chandler notes:

> It was not until the 1870s, with the completion of the modern transportation and communication networks—the railroad, telegraph, steamship, and cable—and of the organizational and technological innovations essential to operate them as integrated systems that materials could flow into a factory or processing plant and finished goods move out at a rate of speed and volume and with the precise timing required to achieve substantial economies of throughput . . . Thus the revolution in transportation and communication created opportunities that led to a revolution in both production and distribution. (1990, p. 26)

The large scale of operations and increasing complexity of sales and service required for the new products led to extensive vertical integration as well as increased size of factories. The massive new companies had to ensure their sources of supply and provide distribution channels, displacing earlier market structures that were less suited to the new conditions.

The incentive to create large integrated firms came from the efficiencies that could be gained by taking full advantage of the economies of scale and scope in the production technologies of the time if the diseconomies of size that came from coordination problems could be overcome. The communication revolution provided the necessary tools to coordinate geographically dispersed time-sensitive operations. Those methods were pioneered on the railroads and then adapted to many other industries. While the railroads could have built private communication systems along their rights of way to solve their own coordination problems, the public nature of telegraph and mail service (and later telephone service) facilitated the use of the new communication technologies to control large vertically integrated companies with more diffuse communication requirements than railroads. Companies could utilize the public communications networks without investing capital and managerial attention in the development of a private communication system. The nineteenth-century version of the "National Information Infrastructure" was largely complete by 1876 with the extension of telegraph lines and post offices beyond the major urban centers to most small towns.

The Telephone and State Regulation

With rapidly increasing telegraph demand, an incentive was created to transmit multiple messages over the same wire simultaneously. In 1872, a duplex patent (ability to transmit two messages simultaneously on one wire) was purchased by Western Union. In 1874, Thomas Edison developed a quadruplex apparatus. Other inventors continued the effort to improve the capacity of telegraph lines. Elisha Gray, an electrician for Western Electric, partially owned by Western Union, developed in 1876 a method of carrying up to fifteen conversations by using different tones on the telegraph. That same year, Alexander Graham Bell filed a patent application titled "Improvement in Telegraphy" that contained a vague speech claim. Both Western Union and Bell considered themselves the inventor of the voice telephone. After unsuccessful initial negotiations, both began establishing telephone services in 1877, with the first telephone switching exchanges in 1878.

In 1878 the Bell Company was reorganized with professional management, and Theodore Vail was hired to develop the company. The next year, he reached an agreement with Western Union in which Western Union and Bell agreed to pool their patents in telephone under the control of Bell while Bell would stay out of the telegraph business and send all telegraph messages it received by phone to Western Union. Western Union agreed to finance 20 percent of the Bell research, and Bell agreed to pay Western Union 20 percent of Bell's telephone rental receipts during the seventeen-year agreement.

The 1879 agreement between the Bell Company and Western Union led to a strict patent monopoly on voice telephone service by Bell while Western Union continued to develop the telegraph business. The Bell patents were upheld as controlling all voice communication over wire, not merely the specific apparatus originally patented to transform voice into electrical signals. Had the courts ruled for a narrow interpretation of the patents, they would have become largely irrelevant because the specific apparatus was quickly superseded by greatly improved telephone instruments. With the broad interpretation, Bell gained a full monopoly until the expiration of the basic patent in 1893 (Brock, 1981, pp. 89–104; Mueller, 1996). It enforced the monopoly vigorously and succeeded in shutting down any companies that attempted to provide telephone service outside of Bell control.

During the Bell patent monopoly, telephone service was largely confined to local areas, and therefore was complementary to the long distance service provided by Western Union telegraph, rather than directly competitive. In that time period Western Union continued to grow rapidly as telegraph communications became a critical component of the rapidly expanding U.S. economy of the late nineteenth century. Between 1876 and 1893 (the telephone patent period), Western Union increased its annual messages from 19 million to 67 million, at the same time increasing its net revenue from $9.1 million to $23 million (U.S. Census, 1975, p. 788). Western Union messages expanded at a compound annual rate of 7.5 percent per year during that time period, while the average revenue per message dropped from forty-nine cents per message to thirty-five cents per message.

The Bell System initially focused on building telephone exchanges in the center of the cities, and on developing short toll lines. The technology of the time was not yet developed to build true long distance lines, but it was gradually improved to increase the range of voice conversations. By the expiration of the patent monopoly in 1893, the Bell System had installed 266,000 telephones or four telephones per 1,000 of population, and was approaching the size of Western Union.

In the years following the expiration of the Bell patent monopoly, telegraph messages carried by Western Union remained the dominant form of long distance communication in the United States. However, Bell put great efforts into developing long distance voice technology and expanding its system. Western Union had a dominating price advantage for very long routes but a lesser advantage for shorter routes. For example, by the turn of the century, the price of a basic long distance telephone call (three minutes) was twice the rate for a basic telegram (ten words) between New York and Philadelphia (109 miles), but ten times the price of a basic telegram between New York and Chicago (821 miles). At that time voice telephone service was unavailable across the country. When transcontinental telephone service first became available in 1915, a New York to San Francisco call (2,946 miles) was priced at twenty times the telegraph rate between those points (U.S. Census, 1975, pp. 784, 790).

After the expiration of the basic Bell patents, many new companies entered the telephone business in the United States. Initially, entry occurred in places that had not been served by the Bell System. Having concentrated its efforts on the major cities, Bell had left large portions of the country without telephone service, creating an extensive demand in small towns and rural areas. Commercial companies and cooperative arrangements were formed to serve these areas. In many cases the equipment was primitive and of low quality. During the patent monopoly, the Bell Company had purchased a controlling interest in the Western Electric Equipment Manufacturing Company and had signed an exclusive dealing arrangement in which Bell agreed to purchase only from Western Electric, and Western Electric to sell only to Bell-licensed companies. Consequently, the independents were required to develop their own equipment or find an alternative source other than the Western Electric Company that had previously dominated telephone equipment manufacturing.

Many independent telephone companies were formed in different parts of the country and they expanded rapidly. As they developed, they also began supplying competition directly to the Bell companies in areas already served by Bell. With the advent of competition, prices were reduced and growth accelerated. The early competition was noninterconnected competition in which network effects were a dominating factor in the choice of a telephone. Individuals could not make calls from an independently owned telephone to a Bell-licensed telephone. Consequently, the choice of company depended on which company had the most subscribers with whom one was likely to wish to communicate. In many cases that simply meant the most total subscribers, but in some cases a smaller network that contained people with whom communication was important could be more desirable than a large network containing a random mix of the population.

With the entry of new telephone companies and a reduction in prices, the growth rate of telephone service accelerated from an average of 7 percent per year during the monopoly period to an average of 25 percent per year. The growth rate of Bell-owned telephones rose even while the company was facing competition from non-Bell-owned telephones. The period of intense competition between 1893 and 1907 caused the total number of telephones to increase from 266,000 at the end of the monopoly period to over six million by 1907. At that time the United States had an average of seven telephones per 100 population (U.S. Census, 1975, pp. 783, 784), a telephone density not achieved by the government systems of France or Great Britain until after World War II (Noam, 1992, p. 140).

The development of the telephone in the United States during the monopoly period was comparable to the early development in the government-owned companies of Europe during the same time period. In both cases the companies focused on telephone development in the major cities with relatively high prices and slow growth and little effort to explore the limits of demand in the smaller areas. However, the rapid development under competition in the United States was not matched by the government-owned telephone operations of Europe. During the competitive period, U.S. telephone development increased faster than telephone development in Europe, with particularly notable differences in small towns and rural areas. For example, at the beginning of the twentieth century, Berlin and New York City had almost equal telephone coverage with approximately 2.5 telephones per 100 population. However, at that date, the rural state of Iowa had twice the telephone development of New York City with 5 phones per 100 population (provided by a total of 170 different systems within that state), while rural districts in Germany had less than one-tenth the development of Berlin with two-tenths of a phone per 100 population (Brock, 1981, p. 144; Holcombe, 1911, pp. 418–438).

During the monopoly period the Bell System had financed its growth largely through retained profits. With rapid growth during the competitive period and reduced profitability because of price competition, the company needed outside capital in order to finance its growth. Early in the twentieth century, the Bell System began regular interaction with the New York financial markets. In one particularly important transaction the company placed a very large set of convertible bonds with J. P. Morgan and Associates. The bonds failed to sell and Morgan and Associates took an active role in reorganizing the company. In 1907, Theodore Vail (who had left the company after initial leadership to pursue other business interests) was appointed as president with the support of J. P. Morgan. Vail began a vigorous strategy to restore the market power of AT&T, the parent company of the Bell System.

Vail developed a three-part strategy to restore market power: (1) merger with the independent telephone companies; (2) increased emphasis on fundamental research and the purchase of outside patents; (3)

advocating regulation with legal and political support for monopoly telephone service. At that time the United States was in the late stages of its first great merger wave in which large numbers of companies were consolidated in order to eliminate competition and gain potential advantages of economies of scale and scope. J. P. Morgan and other New York financiers were deeply involved in the merger wave, and Vail's merger strategy was comparable to that being used in other industries. In 1909, AT&T purchased a controlling block of Western Union stock, and Vail was chosen president of Western Union as well as of AT&T, creating an effective merger between the telegraph and telephone companies. Vail also began purchasing individual independent telephone companies. In 1911, an effort was made to consolidate the industry through a complete purchase of all independents, but the negotiations broke down because of disagreements among the many independent telephone companies. Vail continued to purchase individual companies, reducing the market share of independent telephone companies from 49 percent to 42 percent between 1907 and 1912.

As Vail purchased independent telephone companies, the remaining ones became more isolated and vulnerable. Bell had the only long distance network of the time, but some independents were planning a separate long distance network to connect with other independents across the country. However, that plan was threatened as potential participants in the network became Bell companies and connected with the AT&T long distance network while refusing interconnection to remaining independent companies. The remaining independents sought Department of Justice (DOJ) antitrust enforcement against the Bell System to prevent further mergers. The Attorney General expressed an opinion that a planned merger of independent companies already purchased by J. P. Morgan into the Bell System would be a violation of the Sherman Act, leading to settlement negotiations.

In 1913, the Bell System reached a settlement known as the Kingsbury Commitment in which AT&T agreed to sever its ties with Western Union, allow interconnection with the remaining independent telephone companies, and refrain from acquiring any more directly competing companies. At that time the Bell System provided most of the telephone service in cities while the independent telephone companies supplied most of the service in small towns and rural areas. After the agreement the independent companies that were directly competing with Bell companies exchanged territories so that each had a geographic monopoly. The Bell and independent companies connected to a single long distance network and to each other to create a system in which any telephone could be reached from any other telephone. The telephone industry structure established after the Kingsbury Commitment remained quite stable until the AT&T divestiture in 1984.

The second component of Vail's effort to reestablish Bell dominance in telephone service was an increased emphasis on research. Bell had been performing research and had generated many patents beyond the original telephone patents. However, those patents were not nearly so dominating as the original telephone patent, and competitors were able to find ways to operate outside of the Bell patents. The early twentieth century was a time of rapid technological advance, and two innovations in particular created possibilities for competition with the telephone system. Marconi's early radio-telegraph service could not at that time carry voice but it provided an alternative to wires for communication and could potentially compete with voice communication after further technical refinement. The triode vacuum tube invented by Lee DeForest and first patented in 1907 was in an early stage of development but showed promise for telephone amplifiers and other new products.

AT&T purchased the patent rights to the DeForest triode vacuum tube for use in telephone repeaters and wireless applications in 1913 and 1914 and continued developing it to create a telephone repeater. There was no practical way to amplify voice circuits before the development of triode vacuum-tube amplifiers. Long distance communication was limited and expensive because increasing distance required using thick wires to reduce attenuation and allow the conversation to be heard. The Bell System also greatly expanded its internal research capability, multiplying the number of engineers in Western Electric's research and development unit by a factor of five between 1910 and 1915. AT&T created the organization later known as Bell Laboratories with an ambitious research agenda. A 1911 report stated, "It was decided to organize a branch of the engineering department which should include in its personnel the best talent available and in its equipment the best facilities possible for the highest grade research laboratory work . . . A number of highly trained and experienced physicists have been employed, beside a group of assistants of lesser attainments and experience" (quoted in FCC, 1939, p. 187).

The third element of Vail's strategy was to embrace regulation. As discussed in Chapter 1, state regulation was initially developed for railroads and then expanded to other industries that appeared to be unsuitable for competition. Bell companies had earlier successfully used city franchise regulation to eliminate competition. For example, in the territory of Southern Bell Telephone Company, the company made private commitments to business organizations to secure their support for city regulations that allowed it to purchase the competing independent and obtain an exclusive city franchise for providing telephone service (Weiman and Levin, 1994). Vail recognized that bringing telephone service under the authority of the emerging state regulatory agencies could be a useful way to expand and protect monopoly provision of telephone service. He began advocating regulation in AT&T's 1907 annual report and continued seeking it in a number of public forums. In a later speech Vail stated, "I am not only a strong advocate for control and regulation but I think I am one of the first corporation managers to advocate it. It is as necessary for the protection of corporations from each other as for protection to, or from, the public" (Vail, 1915).

When Vail took over the Bell System in 1907, it appeared that the telephone industry was developing into unstable competition as noninterconnected companies sought competitive advantage in numerous cities. Noninterconnected telephone competition is competition "for the market" rather than only for individual customers. The value of a telephone network to a potential customer depends on the number of subscribers to that network with whom the potential new customer wishes to communicate. There is an incentive to compete intensely in the initial stage of development because the company with the largest subscriber base gains an advantage over companies with fewer subscribers and is likely to dominate the market. When there were two noninterconnected telephone companies, many businesses would subscribe to both companies in order to communicate with all telephone subscribers. Businesses often supported the Bell System efforts to establish protected geographic monopolies because they expected the price of monopoly telephone service to be less than the combined price of the multiple telephone subscriptions necessary to reach all customers under competition.

With the support of the Bell System, independent telephone companies, and many political leaders, telephone service was placed under the jurisdiction of many state regulatory commissions in the early twentieth century. Together with a widespread belief that large firms could enjoy economies of scale and produce more efficiently than small firms, there was also concern about the abuses of monopoly power. Regulated monopoly appeared to offer a solution that allowed the benefits of a single large firm while also allowing public input and control. Although the experience of the past century has greatly reduced the enthusiasm for regulation, most states chose regulated monopoly over competition at a time when there was considerable optimism regarding the social benefits of regulation.

Early regulation stabilized the industry structure and the price of telephone service. It ended the price wars between Bell companies and independents and their resulting threats to the financial stability of the companies. Regulation prevented new entry and froze the industry structure created by the interaction of the Bell System, the remaining independent telephone companies, and the Kingsbury Commitment. Although regulators supported geographical monopolies, they did not change the division of the country into Bell and independent territories. Early price regulation was very weak; considerable development of both regulatory techniques and legal authority was required before the formal rate case with established procedures became standard. Regulators did not have the legal or analytical ability to compute a "just and reasonable" price for telephone service on their own. They generally accepted the existing rates at the time regulation was imposed as meeting the typical statutory standard of just and reasonable. Yet they provided a forum for consumer complaints about increases in rates and made it more difficult for companies to change rates than without regulation. Thus with regard to both industry structure and prices, regulation gave a privileged place to the situation at the time regulation was imposed and protected that position against change. Moreover, consumers and producers gained property rights in the existing prices through regulation. Telephone companies could not be forced to reduce their price to meet competition because the regulators excluded competition. Consumers could not be forced to pay an increased price because of a decline in competition or a short-term spike in the cost of production. The financial historian of the early Bell System concluded that early regulation had little effect on total earnings: "For the system as a whole, from 1900 on through the period when the various States, one by one, gave their commissions regulatory power over telephone companies, the earnings continued at about the same rate" (Stehman, 1925, pp. 261–262).

Radio and Federal Regulation

The radio patent awarded to Guglielmo Marconi in 1896 led to the development of "wireless telegraphy" for ship-to-ship and ship-to-shore communication. Its importance for naval operations was quickly recognized, and initial installations of radio on British Navy ships began in 1899. The early Marconi radio put out a burst of waves of various frequencies. It could not be tuned to a single frequency and the waves could not carry voice signals, but the simple telegraph codes could be carried by radio. The Marconi Company dominated early radio service because of its patent position. The DeForest triode vacuum tube provided the crucial improvement necessary to carry voice over radio. In 1907, DeForest organized the DeForest Radio Telephone Company to develop wireless telephone service. He established a limited radio-telephone service between ships of the U.S. Navy, but the company failed after a successful Marconi Company patent infringement suit.

In 1916, a court ruled that the DeForest triode was an infringement on the "Fleming Valve" (a two-element "diode" vacuum tube controlled by the Marconi Company) if used in radio, but that Marconi's use of a three-element vacuum tube was an infringement on the DeForest patent (Reich, 1977, p. 216). Crucial patents held by General Electric and Westinghouse further complicated the patent interference problem. No company could utilize the best components known at the time in radio without interfering with the patents of another company. When the United States entered World War I in 1917, the U.S. Navy assumed responsibility for patent infringement and ordered the relevant companies to produce the best possible radio apparatus without regard for patent infringement. The patent pool created by the war emergency, together with heavy military demand for radio equipment, accelerated the development of vacuum-tube and radio technology. The navy took control of all radio stations above fifty watts and built many new stations on shore and on ships. The army also purchased extensive radio equipment, and the military trained 7,000 men in radio operations, providing an important source of postwar talent and interest in radio (Sterling and Kittross, 2002, pp. 48, 49).

The U.S. Navy supported a 1918 bill to make radio a government monopoly, but the bill did not pass. Continued U.S. concern with foreign control of radio (including concern that the British Marconi company might gain worldwide dominance in wireless communication) led to the creation of the Radio Corporation of America (RCA) in 1919. General Electric (GE) formed RCA as its radio operating subsidiary and purchased the assets of the American Marconi company on behalf of RCA. In order to alleviate the navy's concern about foreign control of radio, the initial RCA bylaws provided that at least 80 percent of its stock would be held by American citizens or U.S.-controlled corporations. In 1920 and 1921 patent cross-licensing agreements covering about 1,200 radio-related patents were signed among GE, RCA, AT&T, and Westinghouse. The licenses were used to divide the radio industry among the participants and create barriers to new entrants. AT&T received exclusive licenses for wire telegraph and telephone systems except for GE's right to establish private systems for itself and electric utilities. GE received an exclusive license for radio-telegraph operations (the then-dominant market for radio). AT&T was given exclusive rights to develop radio-telephones as a public network while GE received exclusive rights to develop radio-telephones for operation of electric utilities and communication among ships, airplanes, and automobiles. RCA agreed to purchase 60 percent of its radio apparatus from GE and 40 percent from Westinghouse (Reich, 1977; FCC, 1939, pp. 225–226; Sterling and Kittross, 2002, pp. 58–62).

The patent cross-licensing agreement assumed that radio would be used for point-to-point telegraph and telephone communication, not for broadcasting. The development of radio broadcasting during the early 1920s created conflicts among the patent cartel. AT&T attempted to take charge of broadcasting by setting up broadcasting stations, producing radios with fixed reception frequencies tuned to AT&T's stations, and interconnecting its stations with telephone lines to create a network. RCA challenged AT&T's actions as a violation of the patent cross-licensing agreement and won its case before an arbitrator. Rather than continuing to dispute how the wording of the earlier agreements should apply to the new and important broadcasting field, the parties negotiated new agreements in 1926 that clearly divided broadcasting among them. AT&T sold its broadcasting operations to RCA and agreed to stay out of broadcasting in return for exclusive rights to provide transmission of programs among network stations. The 1926 agreement applied the radio broadcasting boundaries to the foreseen but undeveloped television technology. The radio group received exclusive rights to sound-picture equipment connected with one-way radio (television broadcasting) while Bell received exclusive rights to sound-picture equipment connected with wire transmission (television network transmission to broadcasting stations)(FCC, 1939, pp. 228–230).

Radio transmissions utilized the electromagnetic spectrum and required coordination to allow communication without interference. Following a 1906 international conference on radio coordination, the United States passed the Wireless Ship Act of 1910 accepting the recommendations of the 1906 conference and requiring ships carrying more than fifty passengers to include radio apparatus. Two years later the United States passed the Radio Act of 1912. That law required all radio stations to obtain a license from the Secretary of Commerce that "shall state the wavelength or the wavelengths authorized for use by the station for the prevention of interference" (quoted in Sterling and Kittross, 2002, p. 42). The 1912 Act assumed point-to-point communication, but Secretary of Commerce (and later President) Herbert Hoover adapted its provisions to broadcasting in the early 1920s. The department created a radio broadcasting classification in 1921 and expanded the channels available as demand increased. By 1925 a total of 578 stations were broadcasting on frequencies from 550 to 1,365 kHz, essentially the current AM band. With the assistance of industry conferences called to coordinate radio issues, Hoover assigned licenses and prescribed time-sharing arrangements to avoid interference, stretching the authority of the 1912 Act (Benjamin, Lichtman, and Shelanski, 2001, p. 15).

Two 1926 court decisions created an incentive for radio broadcasting legislation. In *United States v. Zenith Radio Corp.*, a federal district court in Illinois limited the power of the Commerce Department to license broadcast radio, providing an opportunity for "wave jumpers" to broadcast on any frequency they chose and creating interference. Hoover did not appeal the decision in order to create pressure for Congress to enact a new law. Soon after the *Zenith* decision, Oak Leaves Broadcasting Station began broadcasting on a frequency that interfered with the *Chicago*

Daily Tribune's popular radio station WGN. The *Tribune* filed suit in state court and won a common law property right in its broadcasting frequency. The Cook County circuit court granted the *Tribune's* request for an injunction against the "wave jumper" and stated:

> Wave lengths have been bought and sold and broadcasting stations have changed hands for a consideration . . . The theory of the bill in this case is based upon the proposition that by usage of a particular wave length for a considerable length of time and by reason of the expenditure of a considerable amount of money in developing its broadcasting station and by usage of a particular wave length educating the public to know that that particular wave length is the wave length of the complainant and by furnishing programs which have been attractive and thereby cause a great number of people to listen in to their particular programs that the said complainant has created and carved out for itself a particular right or easement in and to the use of said wave length which should be recognized in a court of equity. (*Tribune Co. v. Oak Leaves Broadcasting Station,* quoted in Hazlett, 1990, p. 150)

The *Oak Leaves* decision provided a solution to the interference problems created by the *Zenith* decision. Even if the Secretary of Commerce could not license radio frequencies to prevent interference, the court's recognition of the right of an initial station to continue in operation without interference from a subsequent station would have eliminated interference problems if followed by subsequent courts. Broadcasters applauded the *Oak Leaves* grant of property rights in wavelength to first users, but worried that the combination of the two decisions would allow free entry into radio and reduce the value of their broadcasting rights. The 1925 Radio Conference had voted against expanding the broadcast band; broadcasters wanted to reduce the number of broadcast stations. Political leaders sought influence over the content of broadcasting, and they could obtain that influence more easily with government control of spectrum than with private property rights in spectrum. Immediately after the *Oak Leaves* decision, Congress passed a resolution asserting that private rights to spectrum would not be recognized and requiring broadcasters to sign waivers relinquishing rights to the spectrum.

With the support of the broadcast industry, Congress passed the Radio Act of 1927 (1927 Act). The 1927 Act created the Federal Radio Commission (FRC) with power to grant frequency licenses for a maximum period of three years to those who would use them in "the public interest." The law specifically prohibited private property rights in spectrum, overruling the common law presumption that property rights are acquired by use. Following the request of the commercial broadcasters, the FRC decided not to expand the range of frequencies designated for radio broadcasting. The FRC eliminated interference by creating regulations that favored the established commercial broadcast stations over potential entrants and noncommercial stations. The FRC interpreted its public interest mandate to distinguish broadcast license requests according to the content the station provided. It declared that there could be no stations oriented toward particular interests but that all must provide programming of general interest. It denied a request to expand coverage of a Chicago station that focused on programs of particular interest to organized labor, denied the renewal of a popular Los Angeles station where "Fighting Bob" Shuler vigorously attacked local corruption but was considered "sensational rather than instructive" by the FRC, and revoked the license of a Kansas station where John Brinkley's "astute combination of fundamentalist theology and medical information" made it the most popular station in the United States though not, however, appreciated by the FRC (Benjamin, Lichtman, and Shelanski, 2001, pp. 20–22). The FRC's content decisions were upheld by the courts, establishing the right of the regulatory agency to evaluate the broadcast messages in awarding licenses rather than focusing only on technical interference questions.

The 1927 decision to prevent private ownership of spectrum was very significant for the future development of radio services. The pre-1927 system had been developing as a system of technical control over interference through Commerce Department licenses together with ownership rights for incumbents by common law precedent. Continuation of that system would have provided wide scope for private enterprise to develop radio systems without government control over content. It would have been comparable to the nineteenth-century homestead approach to land in which farmers could acquire land without payment by moving to the frontier where there was government land available for homesteading. Those that chose to move to the frontier acquired full title to their land, including the right to sell it or convert it to nonfarm purposes, after living on it for the necessary number of years and fulfilling other requirements. Alternatively, a farmer could purchase land in the settled regions. Similarly, under the regime that was evolving prior to the 1927 Act, a spectrum user could "homestead" the spectrum by utilizing previously unused frequencies. Generally, that would have meant using higher frequencies with accompanying technical difficulties, just as nineteenth-century homesteaders generally had to move west beyond the fully settled regions. Alternatively, a spectrum user could have purchased rights from an existing user that had been licensed earlier and had acquired ownership rights through the application of common law principles.

The combination of the 1926 patent cross-licensing agreement and the 1927 Act established the structure of the broadcasting industry and protected it against major changes. The 1926 patent agreement provided a clear corporate boundary between AT&T (common carrier communications) and the radio companies (broadcasting). The 1927 Act formalized that industry division by preventing a broadcaster from participating in wired communications. Despite the explicit statutory denial of property rights in spectrum and the three-year license term, broadcasters gained the economic equivalent of limited property rights in their frequencies. License renewal requests were rarely denied, and broadcasters could sell their stations for a large premium over the value of the physical property so long as they followed the government's content regulations. While broadcasting licenses as such could not be sold, the licenses were effectively sold as a package with the broadcasting station because the regulators routinely approved requests to transfer a broadcasting license to the new station owner. Just as state regulation of telephone companies stabilized the industry and prevented new competition while imposing weak pricing limitations, federal regulation of broadcasting stabilized the industry and prevented new competition while imposing weak limitations on the content provided by broadcasters.

Early in the Roosevelt administration, a committee was set up under the Secretary of Commerce to consider alternatives (including government ownership) to the existing communications industry structure. The committee recommended continued private ownership of communications subject to stronger and more centralized regulation. President Roosevelt transmitted the committee's report to Congress in February 1934. Four months later Congress passed the Communications Act of 1934 (1934 Act), which followed the recommendations of the President and the committee. The 1934 Act created the Federal Communications Commission (FCC), made the FCC the successor to the FRC, and incorporated the statutory requirements of the 1927 Act into the new law. The FCC consisted of seven members (later reduced to five) who are appointed by the President and confirmed by the Senate. The commissioners serve for fixed terms and cannot be removed by the President during their term. Consequently, the commission is more independent than executive branch agencies that are under the direct control of the President. According to the 1934 formulation of radio spectrum statutory requirements:

> It is the purpose of the Act, among other things, to maintain the control of the United States over all the channels of radio transmission; and to provide for the use of such channels, but not the ownership thereof, by persons for limited periods of time, under licenses granted by Federal authority, and no such license shall be construed to create any right, beyond the terms, conditions, and periods of the license. (47 U.S.C. §301)

After the 1927 and 1934 Acts, it was still necessary for those who wanted new spectrum to move to "frontier" bands, but there was no automatic right to utilize new frequencies even if that use did not cause interference. The broadcasting concerns of the 1920s about excessive competition without regulatory controls on entry led to a rigid spectrum allocation and assignment system. An innovative radio-based service could not be offered unless the regulators first made a specific frequency allocation for its use. If that system had been in place at the beginning of broadcasting in 1920, it would not have been possible for the early broadcasters to experiment freely in order to find an economically feasible approach. Using the homestead analogy, spectrum policy under the FRC/FCC granted homestead rights for limited pieces of land, with each piece having a particular set of detailed requirements regarding the technology that could be used and the crops that could be grown. All new crops or technologies were prohibited unless specifically authorized.

The Communications Act of 1934 also supplemented state telephone regulation with federal regulation. Interstate telephone service had earlier been nominally subject to the Interstate Commerce Commission, but that agency had taken no regulatory action. The 1934 Act applied the provisions originally developed for railroad regulation to interstate common carrier communication services, with one significant exception. The courts had ruled that railroads became "interstate commerce" through interconnection with a railroad that crossed state lines, essentially defining the entire rail network as interstate and ending state railroad regulation. Because the telephone companies interconnected with AT&T's interstate long distance network, using the railroad definition of interstate commerce would have largely eliminated state telephone regulation. At the time only about 2 percent of calls actually crossed state lines, and the state regulators asked Congress to preserve their authority to regulate communications within their state boundaries. The 1934 Act preserved the authority of the state regulatory provisions by denying the FCC jurisdiction over "any carrier engaged in interstate or foreign communication solely through physical connection with the facilities of another carrier" (47 U.S.C. §152(b)(2)). Because the same equipment was used for interstate and intrastate service, the regulatory dividing line was vague and led to many disputes over jurisdiction between the state and federal regulatory agencies.

For many years the commission's primary attention was directed toward the politically sensitive task of assigning radio and television broadcasting licenses and establishing rules for the use of broadcasting stations. Telephone regulation remained primarily a state matter with limited attention from the federal commissioners who were appointed and rewarded according to their broadcasting decisions. The institutions of radio regulation were developed for radio broadcasting in the 1920s and 1930s and were adapted for television broadcasting in the 1940s and 1950s. Nonbroadcasting services requiring spectrum were a minor factor during the crucial institutional development period and were forced into the structure designed for broadcasting. Thus as new telecommunication technologies became available, the FCC attempted to fit the new services into a regulatory structure designed for railroads and radio broadcasting.

The First Information Revolution was created by a combination of government and private enterprise. The Post Office remained a government monopoly enterprise, and the government policy of low stable prices provided competition for other forms of communication. Telegraph and telephone services were developed privately but the companies sought regulation in order to limit entry and stabilize the industry. Radio broad-

casting also began as private enterprise and sought regulation to limit
entry and stabilize the industry. Regulation to limit competition and stabilize the industries accomplished for communications what many industries sought. Thomas McCraw writes with regard to the late nineteenth century:

> The rising productivity . . . often brought overcapacity. The response,
> among businessmen in every industrial nation, was to combine with
> one another in schemes designed to limit the total output of their
> plants, maintain the price levels of their goods, and discourage the en-
> try of new companies into their lines of business . . . [T]he immense
> capital investment represented by a large modern factory or string of
> factories raised the penalty for failure beyond anything [Adam] Smith
> could have contemplated . . . Thus industrialists felt a powerful urge to
> maintain a market for their products—if necessary by temporarily sell-
> ing below costs, if possible by cooperating with each other for the mu-
> tual protection of capital. (1984, pp. 66, 67)

The common concerns of late-nineteenth-century businessmen described by McCraw were accentuated in the railroad and telephone industries, with their large capital investments, economies of scale, and
importance in facilitating other forms of commerce. Thus while other
industries risked antitrust action for their efforts to fix prices and exclude competitors, the telephone industry gained that ability through
regulation while giving up some pricing freedom. Similarly, the broadcasting industry gained protection against entry in exchange for giving
up some freedom over the content it provided. Robert Horwitz describes
the stabilizing effect of telecommunication regulation as follows:

> The act [1934 Act] built upon the pre-existing institutional structures
> of each industry, and froze into law the industrial boundaries which
> had been cast by the 1913 Kingsbury Commitment and the 1926
> agreement between RCA and AT&T. The structure of the common car-
> rier system was determined first of all by the practical ability of West-
> ern Union and AT&T to establish dominance over their respective in-
> dustries. Following the *fact* of effective monopolization was the public
> policy assumption that telephone and telegraph service each consti-
> tuted *natural* monopolies . . . The place of broadcasting in the overall
> telecommunications system was defined by the division of industry
> consequent to the 1926 agreement between AT&T and RCA. Broad-
> casters would control the content of communication over the airwaves,

and would require licenses to gain access to the means of communication (a frequency) . . . A general governmental policy arose to keep telecommunications services *separated,* and telecommunications corporations in a single field of operation. (1989, pp. 123–125)

It is easy to criticize the practice of regulation; a vast literature elaborates on its shortcomings. A significant part of the remainder of this book will consider problems of regulated monopoly and why competition was added to facilitate the implementation of new technology. However, it is important to recognize that regulation is not merely a straw man to be knocked down. Regulated monopoly provided stable prices with benefits to both telephone companies and consumers. Regulated monopoly allowed telephone companies to make sunk cost investments with a long useful life with confidence that the investment and a "reasonable" return would be recovered from regulated monopoly rates. Depreciation schedules frequently extended to forty years, allowing lower prices than if risk premiums for new entry or obsolescence had been required. Political control of telephone prices gave consumers a voice in the operations of the monopoly telephone company and provided protection for businesses against opportunistic price increases after a business became dependent on telephone service.

The incentives for regulation flowed from two special characteristics of telephone service. First, there was no confidence that a competitive market could be sustained, or if sustained, that it would be efficient. The technology of stringing copper wires to each location appeared to be most efficiently accomplished by a single company. Early experience with competition was beneficial in expanding service to previously unserved areas and in reducing monopoly prices, but was criticized when direct competition required multiple companies to install wires on the same street creating congestion and duplication that appeared inefficient. Second, telephones were an infrastructure good that affected the choices of both businesses and consumers. In order to have confidence that investments could be made that were dependent on telephone service, it was necessary to have confidence that telephone service would be available in the future without any significant increase in price. People had that confidence in the government-operated Post Office, but could not have guarded against telephone company opportunism in an unregulated market after becoming dependent on the telephone for the conduct of their business.

The institutional structure of government regulation created a rigid interlocking structure of telephone company and regulatory practices that made adjustment to major technological change difficult. In order to fully implement the technologies of the Second Information Revolution, it was necessary to modify the institutions created for the earlier technology. Modification required overcoming opposition from beneficiaries of the earlier institutions. The creation of alternative institutions appropriate to the SIR has been a long and politically controversial process that is still unfinished.

3

Technological Origins of the
Second Information Revolution, 1940–1950

The technological foundation for the Second Information Revolution (SIR) was created through the intense research effort of World War II. The wartime research was aimed at immediate critical applications for the war effort, not at long-term changes in the economy. Despite the applied military orientation of the research, the mobilization of most of the country's scientific talent together with essentially unlimited funding and the novel character of several war projects led to the development of technologies with considerable civilian implications. The most important wartime technological contributions to the SIR were by-products or supporting technologies for the primary military mission of the research. Atomic weapons and code-breaking remained military technologies, but both required extensive computation that created the foundation for a civilian computer industry. Radar remained a military technology, but the understanding of how to utilize the high-frequency electromagnetic spectrum and the research on the properties of silicon crystals required for radar improvements provided a basis for civilian wireless communications and solid-state electronics.

While military-sponsored research created basic technologies that were later developed into the SIR, the military projects did not move directly into widespread civilian use. There was a vast gap between the price and performance requirements necessary to justify utilization under critical wartime urgency and the requirements necessary to justify utilization in a civilian application that could be accomplished with alternative methods. Extensive development, cost reduction, and the invention of additional supporting technologies and operational methods were necessary to bring the new methods into common use. Nevertheless, the military work was important for providing a technological foundation and a vision of fully integrated computer and communication systems for complex time-critical decisions. The early demand for that integration came in wartime fire control systems and postwar air defense systems, but the approaches could be applied to civilian operations after sufficient refinements and cost reductions. Such refinements and cost reductions were more difficult to achieve than early enthusiasts expected, but eventually were accomplished.

Radar

Military radar development created two conflicting results for the SIR. On the positive side, the generous resources of money and extraordinarily capable personnel devoted to radar development accelerated the technology for using high frequencies, expanding the effective wireless communication capacity of the electromagnetic spectrum. While the actual spectrum is a fixed resource determined by physical properties, the capacity of the spectrum to transmit communication is a function of the technology available to generate, modulate, receive, and amplify electromagnetic radiation of particular wavelengths. Because radar required wavelengths much smaller (or, equivalently, frequencies much higher) than the broadcasting bands used before World War II, much of the radar effort was devoted to developing methods of working with the necessary frequencies, thereby facilitating the use of those frequencies for communication. On the negative side, the military development of radar led to the military utilization and control of a wide range of frequencies. Once the military services developed equipment utilizing particular bands, there was a high cost of shifting spectrum to civilian uses and no clear institutional structure for evaluating the costs and benefits of reallocating spectrum. Even without the impetus of military work, the engineering methods for utilizing those frequencies would eventually have been developed in the civilian communications sector. Moreover, without the military utilization, a much wider range of frequencies would have been available for civilian communications as soon as the necessary equipment to manage them had been developed.

By the mid-1930s radio broadcasting and point-to-point radio communication were routine. Many observers had noticed detectable interference when large objects passed through the path of radio waves. In the United States naval researchers Albert Taylor and Leo Young observed the interference pattern of a ship on the Potomac River while conducting high-frequency radio communication experiments in 1922. Taylor and Young proposed a radio detection system for ships, but the concept was not developed. Later, the two men revived the concept for airplane detection and supervised the first U.S. radar test in 1934. Germany also conducted its first radar test in 1934, while Italy, the USSR, and Great Britain conducted initial radar tests in 1935. Each country believed that it had independently developed the concept of using radio waves to detect ships and aircraft, and conducted its tests under military secrecy.

Although several countries began radar tests at about the same time, Great Britain pressed the development more vigorously than the others because of its critical need for air defense warning. British war games following Hitler's takeover of Germany in 1933 showed that British air defenses were completely ineffective against a simulated German attack. The Air Ministry set up a committee led by Henry Tizard to survey scientific developments that might be useful to air defense. In response to committee inquiries, Robert Watson Watt, superintendent of the Radio Department of the National Physical Laboratory, prepared a February 1935 memo that provided calculations showing the feasibility of developing radio detection for airplanes. After a successful initial test was quickly put together from existing technology, the government established a research program to develop the technology and appointed Watson Watt to supervise the effort (Buderi, 1996, p. 59).

The initial British effort made rapid progress by applying known radio technology to the air detection problem. The researchers developed a ground-based warning system based on wavelengths of ten to thirteen meters (frequencies of 30 MHz to 23 MHz). The frequencies chosen were beyond those routinely used for broadcasting and commercial communication at the time, but did not require extensive new technology for transmission or reception. The effort quickly progressed from the initial concept memo and crude test in 1935 to the deployment of the first radar system in 1937. While the early British operational radar could detect planes at a distance of one hundred miles, it could only provide the altitude and location with a considerable range of error. The system was useful for providing early warning and directing pilots to the general location from which they could visually determine a more precise location during daylight, but it was of little assistance in defending against night attacks. Furthermore, the transmitters and receivers were both heavy and bulky, with the transmitting equipment weighing several tons and the large antennas mounted on 250-foot towers. More accurate and compact radar required shorter wavelengths, which would provide more precise resolution of the image and could also be received by a smaller antenna. However, producing high-power pulses at short wavelengths required the development of new technology rather than the adaptation of existing technology.

The British group was able to develop a prototype airborne radar at a wavelength of 1.25 meters (240 MHz), utilizing technologies under development for television prior to the outbreak of the war. When war began on September 1, 1939, the British government awarded radar research contracts to academic institutions and production contracts to industrial firms in order to accelerate the development and deployment of improved radar. The most critical single advance was the development of the cavity magnetron in early 1940 by John Randall and Henry Boot at the University of Birmingham physics department. Randall and Boot were able to combine concepts from two U.S.-developed radio generating devices, the magnetron and the klystron, to create the first device capable of generating high frequencies at high power. Both the magnetron and the klystron could generate high-frequency waves, but neither could produce high power. U.S. radar pioneer I. I. Rabi later described the cavity magnetron as a kind of whistle in which the size and shape of the cavities determined the output frequency (Buderi, 1996, p. 87).

The Randall/Boot cavity magnetron operated at ten centimeters (3,000 MHz or 3 GHz), and after early improvement the device was able to produce fifteen kilowatts of power, 1,000 times the power output of other devices capable of generating waves at that frequency. With Britain under critical war pressure in 1940, the laboratory-to-operation time for the cavity magnetron was drastically reduced over normal levels. The first successful laboratory test of the device occurred in February 1940, and by August of that year a refined cavity magnetron was incorporated into a working radar. However, the compressed development time also meant that the first working magnetrons still needed extensive improvements in order to operate in a routine military environment.

In August 1940, Winston Churchill approved a wide-ranging plan to share British military technology with the United States in order to gain U.S. assistance in producing critically needed items. Henry Tizard led the British Technical and Scientific Mission to the United States. The Tizard group brought drawings and samples of several critical technologies, including the cavity magnetron. Soon after arrival, Tizard met with Vannevar Bush, the chairman of the newly formed National Defense Research Committee (NDRC). Bush, an MIT electrical engineer with many accomplishments in analog computing, had secured President Roosevelt's approval in June 1940 to organize America's scientific resources for war while the conflict was raging in Europe but America was still officially nonbelligerent. Bush recruited MIT president Karl Compton, Harvard president James Conant, and Bell Laboratories president Frank Jewett for the committee, renamed the Office of Scientific Research and Development (OSRD) in 1941, and began organizing U.S. scientists for possible war research.

The British cavity magnetron was demonstrated at Bell Labs in October 1940, and tests confirmed that the device far outperformed other sources available to the United States. With support from Bush and Ernest O. Lawrence, inventor of the cyclotron and a Nobel prize winner, the United States decided to set up the Radiation Laboratory at MIT to develop radar technology under the direction and funding of Bush's committee (after mild protests from Bell Labs president Jewett who thought Bell Labs was a more suitable home for the project). Lawrence refused an offer to direct the lab but agreed to recruit top-level personnel for it. Vigorous recruiting by Lawrence and other leading physicists and a sense of war urgency because of Britain's dire straits in late 1940 resulted in the new laboratory beginning operations with some of the country's top scientists only a month after the decision to establish it. Five of the Radiation Laboratory's alumni were later awarded Nobel prizes.

The Radiation Laboratory began an ambitious research program, focusing first on air-to-air radar to guide fighter pilots against night bombers. After the Pearl Harbor attack on December 7, 1941, brought the United States into the war, the radar efforts at both the Radiation Laboratory and Bell Laboratories expanded and focused on U.S. rather than British war requirements. A particularly critical effort early in the war was designing an aircraft-based antisubmarine radar in order to combat the devastating German attacks on Atlantic shipping during 1942. The antisubmarine effort required higher frequencies than previously used in order to get good enough resolution to detect periscopes in the clutter of reflections from the ocean, a much more difficult problem than detecting airplanes. Later efforts focused on bombing radar and many other specific applications. Radar research results were immediately translated into production designs and installed on planes and ships for military operations. Approximately one-million radar sets in 150 different models were produced during the war. Most of the radar design work was done at either MIT's Radiation Laboratory or AT&T's Bell Laboratories and almost half of the radar sets were manufactured by AT&T's Western Electric, giving AT&T a strong base in both basic knowledge and production skills for microwave radio utilization (Bell Laboratories, 1978, p. 131).

Intensive research steadily increased the reliability of specific designs and pushed the frequencies higher and higher for better resolution. By the end of the war, three-centimeter radar (10 GHz) was common, and even higher frequencies were being used. Efforts to improve the accuracy of bombing radar late in the war by moving to one-centimeter waves (30 GHz) revealed physical limits on the march up the spectrum scale. Early experiments at MIT during the winter of 1944 were quite successful, but later in the year the performance dropped substantially. Extensive investigation showed that the high-frequency radiation was being absorbed by water vapor with little problem in the dry air of a Boston winter, but with increasing problems as summer rain and humidity increased. The water vapor problem was a serious obstacle for the planned use of the radar in the humid Pacific theater and effectively ended the one-centimeter radar as a World War II weapon (Buderi, 1996, p. 236).

Wartime radar research expanded the portion of the electromagnetic spectrum being used from 240 MHz to 10 GHz, a multiplier of forty. In the years of rapid advances, it appeared that the only limit on frequency availability was the development of appropriate technologies to generate and utilize higher and higher frequencies at adequate power. However, the water absorption problem demonstrated at the end of the war showed that severe natural limitations prevented the utilization of ever higher frequencies for wireless communications. While the immediate problem was simply the failure of one particular approach to improving bombing accuracy, that failure foreshadowed a much more serious problem of spectrum scarcity for wireless communication. That implication was not fully appreciated for many years, and much of the desirable communications spectrum was allocated to military uses or television broadcasting with little consideration for the economic trade-offs among various potential uses of the spectrum. Correcting errors from early dysfunctional spectrum management policies has been an important part of more recent efforts to facilitate the development of efficient communication systems.

The intensive wartime research on radar together with the mass production of radar equipment and its extensive utilization in war operations provided theoretical knowledge, experienced researchers and practitioners, and plentiful equipment for postwar developments in microwave communications. The military declared much of its radar equipment surplus at the end of the war, allowing universities and research centers inexpensive access to the equipment. The director of the Radiation Laboratory, I. I. Rabi, sought to place the wartime research knowledge in the public domain by publishing a twenty-seven-volume Radiation Laboratory Series (largely completed by the closing of the laboratory at the end of 1945) to provide details of the technology to anyone interested. Because personnel of the Radiation Laboratory and Bell Labs possessed most of the detailed knowledge of the microwave technology, Rabi was concerned that without an organized publishing program prior to the closure of the Radiation Laboratory, Bell Labs and its parent AT&T would appropriate the commercial benefits of the wartime research for themselves. Despite the public domain knowledge of microwave technology at the end of the war, the FCC's restrictive spectrum allocation policies allowed AT&T to gain almost exclusive control of commercial microwave communication in the early postwar period.

The Transistor

Silicon crystals were used in early twentieth-century radio receivers. Crystal receivers were inexpensive and popular with amateurs but were difficult to utilize in a reliable way. The "cat's whisker" had to be adjusted to precisely the correct spot (found by trial and error) on a crystal for success. Commercial radio companies turned to the more reliable vacuum-tube technology for reception and amplification. However, Bell Labs continued a small program in crystal research in hopes of producing a solid-state amplifier. Bell Labs director of research Mervin Kelly began building up the theoretical capabilities of the laboratories after a Depression hiring freeze was lifted in 1936, allowing the addition of MIT physics Ph.D. William Shockley. Kelly established a long-term goal of developing electronic telephone switching to replace the mechanical relays then used, and in 1938 set up a group to perform fundamental research on the physics of solid-state materials.

In early 1940, Russell Ohl was conducting experiments to improve crystal detectors. The high frequencies needed for radar were difficult to manage with the vacuum-tube technology of the day, and crystals appeared to be a feasible substitute if their characteristics could be controlled more precisely. Ohl found that certain samples of silicon showed a strong photovoltaic effect associated with the junction of two samples with different levels of impurities. With assistance from theoretical physicist Walter Brattain, Ohl defined "P-type" silicon for positive current flow and "N-type" silicon for negative current flow and defined the photoactive junction between the types as the "P-N junction" (Riordan and Hoddeson, 1997, p. 97).

As the radar cooperation with Great Britain developed in 1940, Bell Labs participated in improving the British silicon receivers by developing extremely pure silicon and then adding aluminum to generate reliable "P-type" receivers. After 1941 comparison tests of British and U.S. radar sets revealed that the British receivers using silicon crystals were superior to the U.S. receivers using vacuum tubes, the U.S. radar effort also sought to understand and refine crystal technology. However, Bell Labs did not share its knowledge of the P-N junction:

> Wartime urgency encouraged a remarkably open sharing of information among the expanding network of scientists and engineers working on crystal detectors— all, of course, under the dark umbrella of military secrecy . . . But Kelly embargoed any talk outside Bell Labs on one matter— the P-N junction. It was too important a breakthrough to bruit about. "I had to take the melts that were produced and cut the junctions out of them—cut the N-type material out of it and send the remaining P-type material to the British to fabricate," Ohl said. "We did not break the confidential basis of the company information and turn that over to the British." (Riordan and Hoddeson, 1997, pp. 102, 103)

Wartime research refined the techniques of producing effective microwave receivers using silicon and germanium doped with aluminum, boron, and other elements to precisely control the characteristics of the crystals, generating considerable knowledge of the properties of semiconductors through research directed toward improved radar sets.

In 1945, Kelly began planning the transition from wartime research and seeking ways to benefit AT&T from the research methods and technologies developed during the war. He reorganized the laboratory to create multidisciplinary research teams to perform fundamental research that had potential for commercial communications applications. Shockley was put in charge of a semiconductor research team that included Walter Brattain and new hire John Bardeen from the University of Minnesota physics department. The group explored the properties of silicon and germanium with various impurities in a search for a solid-state amplifier. The exploration included many experiments and extensive theoretical efforts to understand the underlying physics of the materials. In November 1947, Bardeen and Brattain achieved the first semiconductor amplification. While the 1947 success produced very limited amplification only at low frequencies, it pointed the way toward practical semiconductor amplifiers and led to increased efforts to develop both experimental improvements and theoretical understanding of the device. On June 23, 1948, Bell Labs presented the "transistor" to the military services. The Department of Defense considered, but did not formally request, classified status for the transistor. Bell Labs formally announced the transistor the next week.

The successful test of semiconductor amplification ended the previously good rapport among the research group in a struggle over credit for the obviously important device. Shockley wanted to write a broad patent application beginning with his theoretical ideas and continuing through the successful experiments of Bardeen and Brattain. However, a patent search turned up a 1930 patent (by J. E. Lilienfeld) on ideas similar to Shockley's, and the Bell patent attorneys decided to base the patent more narrowly on the experimental work of Bardeen and Brattain, leaving Shockley's name off the patent. Shockley then excluded Bardeen and Brattain from his ongoing research on transistors, causing Bardeen to leave Bell Labs and Brattain to join another research group. In 1951, Shockley's restructured research group succeeded in developing the "junction transistor," a substantial improvement over the 1948 Bardeen-Brattain "point-contact" transistor, and largely ended efforts to continue refining the Bardeen-Brattain device. Shockley, Bardeen, and Brattain shared the 1956 Nobel prize in physics for the invention of the transistor.

The first transistors were crude, difficult to produce, and unreliable. Further development was necessary before transistors could become a practical substitute for vacuum tubes. The production of reliable transistors required innovations in manufacturing techniques to allow the production of uniform crystals, precise control of impurities, and the attachment of wires to tiny surfaces. Tolerances much finer than established metalworking manufacturing were required, and slight variations in manufacturing procedures produced unworkable transistors. The military provided the first market for expensive early transistors. Whereas an early $20 point-contact transistor substituted for a $1 vacuum tube, the transistor responded without a warm-up period, required less power, and was smaller and lighter than the vacuum tube (Riordan and Hoddeson, 1997, p. 204).

Although the early transistors were not price-competitive with the mature vacuum-tube industry, there were far more opportunities for improvement in transistors than in vacuum tubes. By the time the transistor was invented, vacuum tubes had already undergone forty years of refinement since Lee DeForest's 1907 triode patent, and there were limited opportunities for further miniaturization and cost savings. In contrast, the solid-state transistor (and the integrated circuits that followed it) showed a remarkably high level of sustained reduction in size and price from the time of the initial invention to the present. Solid-state electronics became the driving force of the information revolution as the new devices progressed from a high-cost specialty item to a general substitute that largely eliminated the vacuum-tube electronics industry, and then to extremely low-cost integrated circuits that replaced numerous electrical and mechanical controls and allowed the creation of entirely new products.

Electronic Digital Computers

World War II and early postwar events created an intense demand for improved military computing and data processing capability. Three particularly important sources of demand that could not be satisfied with prewar technology included code-breaking, nuclear weapons research, and wide-area air defense. Code-breaking required analyzing large amounts of information. Nuclear weapons research required the computation of numerical answers to complex equations with many significant digits of accuracy. Air defense required fast real-time analysis of target information in order to transmit orders to defense units in time for them to be useful. Air defense also required extreme reliability to ensure that the computer was operating at the critical time period. The earliest electronic digital computers were developed in an effort to satisfy military requirements. More significantly, military requirements focused the interest of a substantial number of very capable individuals on the potential benefits and opportunities in automatic computation. After developing their skills on efforts to solve military problems, those individuals led the creation of a dynamic commercial computer industry.

By the beginning of World War II, analog computers were the most developed method of automatic computation. Analog computers were based on automating the operation of a slide rule. In 1873, Lord Kelvin built a tide predictor, possibly the first analog computer. Early analog computers were designed for a specific task, such as Elmer Sperry's 1916 battleship gunfire control system and the 1929 electrical current network analyzer used by Westinghouse to control its transmission network. Analog computers increased in flexibility through the research of MIT professor Vannevar Bush (later head of OSRD), who built a "differential analyzer" in 1930 to solve differential equations associated with electricity distribution and then a more general electrical analog computer in 1935 that could be programmed with punched tape (Beniger, 1986, p. 401).

A second method of automating computation was the development of electrical relay computers. AT&T considers George Stibitz's 1939 electrical relay computer (Bell Laboratories Model I) to be the first digital computer. AT&T had extensive experience in electrical relay technology for telephone switching and was able to apply that expertise to building a computing device. In Germany, Konrad Zuse also built an electrical relay computer in 1939. The most ambitious prewar effort to develop an electrical relay computer began with Harvard University instructor Howard Aiken's 1937 proposal. IBM agreed to fund and build the proposed machine. When completed in 1943 at a cost of $500,000, it was fifty-one feet long, contained 760,000 electrical components, and could multiply twenty-three-digit numbers (Beniger, 1986, p. 405).

Punch-card accounting machines also provided an important function that was later taken over by computers. Herman Hollerith originally developed punch-card machines for the 1890 census, and they were improved and produced by IBM for both business and government use. The creation of the Social Security system during the 1930s greatly expanded government record-keeping requirements and created strong demand for IBM's punch-card machines and techniques. The sorting and tabulating functions of early machines were enhanced by combining them with electric adding machines to automate a wide range of accounting functions. In 1933, Columbia University astronomer Wallace Eckert linked a variety of IBM machines to perform complex calculations, but the normal practice was simple computation on large amounts of data.

The three prewar approaches to computing represented three types of markets that continued distinct development even after all computing moved to electronic digital technology. The analog computers fulfilled a demand for process control. They required only small amounts of data as input and output and did not require extreme accuracy, but they had to respond in "real time." In Sperry's battleship fire control computer, for example, it was far more important to get useful immediate results than to get refined results at a later time. The IBM punch-card machines fulfilled a demand for company and government accounting and record-keeping. They required large amounts of data as input and output and generally had modest computational requirements. The electrical relay computers fulfilled a demand for scientific computation. They required only limited quantities of data as input and output, and time was not critical, but extreme accuracy was crucial. A slide rule or analog computer could provide a quick approximation, but only a digital computer designed for a large number of significant digits could provide adequate accuracy for complex scientific problems. The size and complexity of the Aiken/IBM machine were primarily caused by its requirement to accurately compute functions of numbers with many significant digits. When computing equipment was very expensive, it was efficient to design and build specialized machines for particular purposes. As the cost of computing declined, the specialized kinds of computers merged into a more uniform general purpose computer.

Code-Breaking Computation

The development of electronic digital computers during World War II began as a method of automating a portion of the intense effort to decipher enemy codes. The British intelligence services first developed an electromechanical device (with the assistance of mathematician and computer theoretician Alan Turing) called the bombe, and then a more sophisticated unit known as the Colossus. The Colossus was a mixture of electronic and electromechanical technology. The initial Colossus, with 1,500 vacuum tubes, went into operation in 1943. Ten enhanced models of the original machine, each with 2,400 vacuum tubes and 800 electromechanical relays, were operational in Britain at the end of the war, but the project remained secret for long after the war and was not included in early histories of the computer industry (Flamm, 1988, p. 39).

The U.S. Navy's code-breaking effort had access to British computing technology and also developed its own specialized computing machines. The Naval Computing Machinery Laboratory in Dayton, Ohio, employed 1,200 people at its peak and built over a hundred different types of computing devices. Engineers from many companies with experience in electronic circuitry were recruited for the laboratory. One of those, Ralph Palmer of IBM, led IBM's electronics laboratory after the war and recruited the technical experts that enabled IBM to transform itself from a producer of electromechanical machines to the leader in electronic computers.

At the end of the war William Norris and other computing experts from the laboratory formed Engineering Research Associates (ERA) with the support and encouragement of the navy. ERA's first business was developing special purpose cryptological machines for the navy, and in 1947 was awarded a contract to develop the Atlas, a general purpose electronic computer. ERA was given access to other government computing projects and asked to produce a survey of computing technology, facilitating sharing of ideas among groups developing the experimental postwar computers. When the Atlas was completed in 1950, it was the second operational stored-program digital electronic computer in the United States. An improved version of the Atlas was marketed commercially as the ERA 1103.

ERA was the dominant early computer producer, selling twenty copies of the ERA 1103 and receiving 80 percent of the revenue from computers sold in the United States through 1952 (Flamm, 1988, p. 46). ERA made an important contribution to the development of magnetic storage technology for computers, improving captured German magnetic drum technology to create an inexpensive but relatively slow central memory system. ERA used its magnetic drum expertise in many specialized cryptological machines, provided magnetic drums for other companies, and licensed its technology to IBM where it was used as the memory in IBM's popular early small computer, the 650.

Despite ERA's technical success and military contracts, it encountered financial difficulties and was purchased by Remington Rand (later Sperry Rand Corporation). The ERA engineers continued to develop cryptological and other military computers and commercial computers based on them. In 1957, William Norris (then the director of computer research for Sperry Rand) and other Sperry engineers formed Control Data Corporation (CDC). CDC's first products (the 1604 and 160) were derived in part from an innovative Sperry Rand computer built for the National Security Agency (NSA), the agency primarily responsible for the U.S. government's postwar cryptological work (Flamm, 1988, pp. 108, 109). CDC later became the industry leader in supercomputers, producing the fastest computers of the time primarily for use by the government.

Nuclear Weapons Computation

Demand for improved computing for nuclear weapons emerged early in the wartime effort to develop an atomic bomb, but electronic digital computers were not recognized as the solution until John von Neumann joined the ENIAC/EDVAC project (see below) and became a bridge between the University of Pennsylvania group and the secret atomic bomb group. When the United States established the Manhattan Project to develop an atomic bomb, it used a combination of outstanding mathematical expertise and mechanical computation devices to perform the necessary computation. The priority of the project allowed it to utilize the skills of the country's top mathematicians to devise solutions to the computing problems:

> Walking around the hastily built wooden barracks that housed the soul of the atomic bomb project in 1943 and 1944, a scientist would see dozens of men laboring over computation. Everyone calculated. The theoretical department was home to some of the world's masters of mental arithmetic, a martial art shortly to go the way of jiujitsu. Any

morning might find men such as [Hans] Bethe, [Enrico] Fermi, and John von Neumann together in a single small room where they would spit out numbers in a rapid-fire calculation of pressure waves . . . The scientists computed everything . . . first with rough guesses and then, when necessary, with a precision that might take weeks. (Gleick, 1992, p. 175)

Even with remarkable skills at mental computation, the project needed more precise answers for some problems than could be achieved with extensive knowledge of the mathematical functions and clever mental approximations. Mathematicians Richard Feynman and Nicholas Metropolis separated the problems into small components and developed an assembly-line method of computation that could substitute for a very slow electronic computer. They used large numbers of Marchant mechanical calculators, each operated by a person who performed a specific computation such as cubing a number. Cards with the output of one computation were passed to another operator to use as the input to another computation. The card flow among the calculator operators was controlled by the mathematicians who were essentially programming a computer by setting up the card flow to compute numerical simulations of the relevant equations (Gleick, 1992, pp. 179–181). The Los Alamos group also used innovative combinations of IBM electromechanical multipliers and accounting machines to supplement mental arithmetic and Marchant calculators, but the early code-breaking electronic digital computing innovations were not used in the wartime nuclear weapons research and appear to have been unknown to the Los Alamos group.

At the end of the war a high demand for sophisticated atomic weapon computation remained in order to refine the initial weapons and especially to evaluate the feasibility of a hydrogen fusion bomb. Scientists of the time knew that hydrogen fusion occurred in stars and could potentially be used as an extraordinarily powerful weapon, but did not know any practical way to ignite a sustainable fusion reaction. The feasibility of a fusion bomb depended on solutions to complex equations that could only be approximated numerically through extensive computation. A portion of the fusion problem was set up to run in the University of Pennsylvania's hardwired ENIAC while extensive efforts were made to build more capable electronic digital computers. The Los Alamos laboratory began building its own electronic digital computer (known as the

MANIAC) because as Carson Mark, head of the theoretical division, observed, "we really couldn't make any headway with what is called the main Super problem in a finite time with the kind of computing power [previously available]" (quoted in Rhodes, 1995, p. 383).

Progress toward an actual test of the late 1940s design for a "Super" (hydrogen) bomb was delayed while the researchers waited for the completion of the MANIAC and other computers under construction in order to test the theoretical feasibility of the design. However, delays in completing the new computers and the sense of crisis caused by the Soviet Union's successful atomic test in 1949 caused the researchers to undertake a computation based on mathematical sophistication and hand calculation:

> [Stanislaw] Ulam and [Cornelius] Everett had prepared calculations for the MANIAC earlier in 1949, but that machine was far from completion, as was John von Neumann's Princeton original. Now they undertook to calculate a simplified version of the problem by hand. At the same time, Los Alamos began preparing a simplified machine version that von Neumann could farm out to the ENIAC.
>
> The problem—whether a D + T burn would ignite a large mass of deuterium—required tracking the progress of thermonuclear reactions using Monte Carlo methods. "Each morning," Ulam recalls, "I would attempt to supply several guesses as to the value of certain coefficients referring to purely geometrical properties of the moving assembly involving the fate of the neutrons and other particles going through it and causing, in turn, more reactions." Ulam supplied his guesses in the form of random numbers which he generated by tossing one die of a pair of dice. (Rhodes, 1995, p. 422–423)

The two mathematicians worked with slide rules so long that Everett "almost wore out his own slide rule." Assisted by others using electric calculators, they labored for several months before concluding that the proposed design would not work.

In 1951, Stanislaw Ulam and Edward Teller developed a new approach to replace the earlier design that appeared infeasible. Refining the Ulam-Teller idea into a detailed design required extensive computations that stretched the capacity of the electronic digital computers then being completed. When the new Livermore Laboratory opened in 1952 as a second location for nuclear weapons research, mathematician Herman Kahn (associated with both Livermore and RAND) "applied

Monte Carlo techniques to calculations on the workings inside a hypothetical hydrogen bomb, especially the diffusion of heat and the collision of neutrons. At one point, Kahn had calculations on bomb designs plugged into all twelve high-speed computers then operating in the United States" (Kaplan, 1983, p. 221).

The initial ideas culminated in a successful thermonuclear device test ("Mike") on November 1, 1952, but the eighty-two-ton weight of the complex initial device precluded its air delivery as a weapon until further refinement (Rhodes, 1995, p. 495). The Mike test involved a task force of 11,000 people, generated a ten-megaton explosion, destroyed the island on which it was conducted, and vaporized 80 million tons of solid material that eventually fell as radioactive pollution around the world (Rhodes, 1995, p. 509). The extraordinary expense, complexity, and environmental degradation from building and testing thermonuclear devices made it necessary to use theoretical simulations of nuclear weapons refinements in place of actual tests whenever possible. Thus even after the initial thermonuclear explosions, the nuclear weapons laboratories retained a high demand for improved computing capabilities and provided support for multiple efforts to develop faster scientific computers.

The ENIAC and IAS Computers

During the 1930s the U.S. Army installed one of Vannevar Bush's differential analyzers at its Aberdeen Proving Grounds to calculate artillery firing tables. In 1939, the Moore School of the University of Pennsylvania utilized Bush's designs with their own modifications to build a differential analyzer for the army's Ballistic Research Laboratory and began training army personnel in computing. In 1942, faculty member John Mauchly submitted a proposal to the laboratory to build a digital electronic computer for ballistics calculations. Bush (then head of OSRD) opposed the project because he believed that advanced analog computers were more suitable for ballistics work than the proposed digital computer. George Stibitz (creator of the electromechanical relay computer at Bell Labs) also opposed the project because he believed that reliable electromechanical components were more suitable than the proposed faster but unreliable vacuum tubes. Despite the opposition of leading computer pioneers, the army funded the endeavor. The Moore School project, under the direction of Mauchly and graduate student J. Presper Eckert, created the ENIAC at the end of 1945 at a cost of $800,000. The ENIAC occupied 1,800 square feet, contained 18,000 vacuum tubes, and used 174 kilowatts of power (Flamm, 1988, p. 48). The ENIAC was a special purpose machine without a stored program. It could be laboriously programmed for different problems by changing the plug-board wiring.

Bush and Stibitz were correct in their 1943 assessment that wartime ballistics computation needs could be better met with the established analog and electromechanical technologies than with the innovative digital electronic computer. While the 2.5-year period between approval of the project and completion was very short compared to early postwar computer projects, it was too long to produce useful results during the war. However, the ENIAC was a crucial step toward postwar computer development. While the ENIAC was still under construction, the army issued a contract to the Moore School to develop an improved computer with more memory and more general programming capabilities, designated the EDVAC. John von Neumann learned of the project during the war (while primarily concerned with atomic bomb computations) and joined the discussions on the EDVAC design. Utilizing ideas developed by the ENIAC group, the prewar abstract conceptions of computing developed by Alan Turing, and his own ideas, von Neumann issued a report in April 1945 called "First Draft of a Report on the EDVAC." That report explained the logical structure of a general purpose digital computer and was so influential that standard computer designs are referred to as von Neumann architecture.

The EDVAC improvement to the ENIAC was never completed because the Moore School group split apart. Von Neumann returned to the Institute for Advanced Study (IAS) and set up a computer development project there, with funding from both the army and navy. Eckert and Mauchly argued with von Neumann over credit for the EDVAC design (only von Neumann's name was on the report but it utilized concepts developed by the working group) and argued with the Moore School over patent rights for their work. They left the Moore School in 1946 and set up a private firm to commercialize computer technology (later the Univac Division of Remington Rand). Other members of the working group moved to the IAS project, to the Eckert/Mauchly commercial venture, and to a new computer project at Burroughs.

The immediate postwar period brought a respite from military pressure and allowed normal academic research to resume. The computer technology was recognized as critical to national defense efforts and the military continued to fund its development, but there was time to develop the technology without having to produce an immediate working machine and without military secrecy. The IAS project became a major center of computer development in the United States, with careful development of the logical structure of the machine, extensive research at IAS and several collaborating institutions on the components of the computer, and publicly available papers on the progress of the machine over the six-year period (1945–1951) of its design and construction. The military funding contract called for sharing the IAS research and design results with five other government-funded computer projects that would build a computer based on the IAS design. Authorized copies included the MANIAC at Los Alamos and the JOHNNIAC at RAND, both used for nuclear weapons research. Several unauthorized copies were also built, including the BESM in Moscow, which was used for Soviet nuclear weapons research. Thus at the beginning of the Cold War, both the U.S. and Soviet nuclear weapons programs were supported by computing technology funded by the U.S. military and developed in an academic environment. IBM also hired von Neumann as a consultant and utilized some of the IAS project's results in the development of its first large-scale computer, the IBM 701, also known as the Defense Calculator.

The Whirlwind: Fast Real-Time Computation

The military also funded a major postwar computer research project at MIT that created the Whirlwind computer. While the Whirlwind project was not originally focused on air defense, it became the prototype for the AN/FSQ-7 computers at the heart of the SAGE air defense system, the world's first effort to create an integrated computer and communications system to manage complex geographically separated actions in real time. The Whirlwind project began modestly in 1944 when the Special Devices Division of the U.S. Navy established a research contract with the Servomechanisms Laboratory of MIT to design a general purpose aircraft simulator. The Servomechanisms Laboratory had been organized at MIT at the beginning of World War II to perform research on remote fire control for the defense of ships against aircraft attack, and by 1944 had a staff of one hundred working on war-related instrument problems. The simulator project was assigned to Jay Forrester, one of the assistant directors of the laboratory who had come to MIT in the fall of 1939 as a graduate student in electrical engineering.

Although the project began as an extension of previous laboratory projects utilizing mixtures of mechanical components and analog electronic computing devices, the design goals were beyond the capabilities of then-existing techniques. After Forrester visited the University of Pennsylvania to study the ENIAC design in 1945, he concluded that a switch to digital computation would generate more likelihood of success than the analog techniques he had been pursuing. In early 1946, Forrester and MIT obtained permission from the navy to expand the contract to include the research, design, and construction of a digital electronic computer and to delay the completion date until 1950. Because the Whirlwind was designed to simulate aircraft activities, it was critical that it process the information received and provide output immediately in a simulation of real aircraft performance. The desire for high speed dominated the Whirlwind design efforts and led to different design goals than those of other computers of that time, including utilizing parallel rather than serial transmission of information and searching for an internal storage mechanism that responded faster than the mercury delay line used in some early computers.

Forrester expanded his project team, including the recruitment of specialists on electronics from the radar project at MIT's Radiation Laboratory that was being closed down, and established an extensive research program to design the computer and develop the necessary components. The most significant component innovation from the project was the development of magnetic core memory. Several companies developed versions of magnetic core memory, but the design developed in the Whirlwind project by Jay Forrester, William Papian, and Kenneth Olsen (later founder of Digital Equipment Corporation) was faster and required less current than other designs and it was widely adopted (Redmond and Smith, 1980, pp. 181–185; Ceruzzi, 1998, p. 50). Magnetic core became the standard computer memory from the early 1950s through 1970. Whirlwind core innovations earned $22 million in patent royalties for MIT ($13 million from IBM alone, based on an expectation of installing twelve billion cores during the patent period), the highest royalties for any MIT patent and far more than the cost of the entire Whirlwind project (Buderi, 1996, p. 403).

Core memory was not fully developed when the Whirlwind began operation in 1950, and electrostatic storage tubes (adapted from radar innovations) were used at first. In 1950 an electrostatic storage tube cost $1,500 and could hold 256 bits of information. The initial memory was sixteen tubes (512 bytes in current terminology, though bytes were not used at the time), and it was expanded to eighty tubes (2,560 bytes) before being replaced by faster and more reliable core memory (Redmond and Smith, 1980, p. 185). The 1950 Whirlwind memory cost was $46,000 per kilobyte, requiring extreme efforts to economize on memory utilization. By late 2001 the price of memory had dropped to $.001 per kilobyte ($1 per megabyte), a price reduction factor of 46 million that is equivalent to a sustained price decline of 35 percent per year over the fifty-one-year period.

The ambitious research goals of Forrester and his large team were expensive and time-consuming, leading to conflicts with the navy over continued funding for the project. The original aircraft simulator goal was dropped, and the project focused on developing a fast real-time computer that could be utilized in a variety of projects. The Whirlwind project was much more expensive than other early military computer projects with a cost of $3 million by 1950, compared to $800,000 for the ENIAC and $650,000 for the von Neumann IAS computer (Redmond and Smith, 1980, p. 166). As navy investigators questioned the spending and design goals of the project and the navy threatened to stop funding the project, Forrester and his team developed multiple reports that provided an expansive vision of the benefits of high-speed computers for the military and the nation as a whole. The Whirlwind team, supported by MIT's administration, suggested that the computer technology they were developing could be utilized for "air traffic control, integrated fire control and combat information centers, interception networks, scientific and engineering research, guided missile offense and defense, and data processing in logistics" (quoted in Redmond and Smith, 1980, p. 117). They estimated that a full development of military computers including "auxiliary equipment, applications studies, field tests, and training of staff" would require fifteen years and cost $2 billion. While Forrester's team advocated preparation for a wide-ranging role for military computers to control complex real-time tasks, the navy's cost managers focused on the high cost and lack of specific purpose for the computer under construction. The navy was not convinced by Forrester's vision of future military computers but also was not willing to cancel a project that was nearing completion. It issued critical reports while continuing to fund the project at a level below Forrester's requests and suggesting that funding was unlikely to be continued for improvements to the Whirlwind.

The funding controversy disappeared in 1950 just before the Whirlwind began operating when MIT professor and U.S. Air Force scientific adviser George Valley chose the Whirlwind as the prototype for the SAGE air defense system computers (see Chapter 4). Valley received negative reports on the project from the Office of Naval Research that had been funding the project and was unimpressed with the behind-schedule and over-budget project. The navy considered Forrester's emphasis on high-speed operation unnecessarily expensive, but speed was critical for the proposed air defense system and the Whirlwind was the fastest computer then under construction. Robert Buderi describes Valley's evaluation of the project as follows:

> Valley was not immediately taken with Forrester or Everett [assistant director of the project], who . . . launched into their sales pitch with what seemed annoying cockiness. Valley recalled his exasperation: ". . . what a pair. They'd been put in charge of this and nobody'd ever reigned them in, or done anything. They were just off on their own spending money like it went out of style."
>
> [After reviewing documentation on the system over the weekend,] [o]n the following Monday he returned to the computer lab . . . When this second tour finished Valley confronted his hosts. "So, how much money do you need?" Forrester hesitated, but Everett jumped in and said they had to have $560,000 to stay afloat another year. Valley agreed on the spot, pending Air Force approval. (Buderi, 1996, pp. 367–368)

In March 1950, the air force took over the project. After successful tests of the computer in mock air defense applications, Forrester and the Whirlwind team were incorporated into the SAGE project and continued developing the technology for an improved real-time control computer that was first known as the Whirlwind II and later as the AN/FSQ-7. It was the largest computer project of the 1950s.

The development of radar, of the transistor, and of the electronic digital computer created the technical foundation for the Second Information

Revolution. By 1950 visionaries such as Jay Forrester were proposing methods of integrating computers and communications in order to achieve far better management of complex distributed operations than was possible with the telephone, telegraph, and mail service. However, that insight was only a vision in 1950 and could not be implemented for many years. Three different barriers to implementing the vision stood in the way:

1. Technical: Extensive further development was required before the new technologies could be utilized in a routine commercial environment. The initial technologies were unreliable and required expert intervention in order to function at all.
2. Economic: The new technologies of computers and transistors were far too expensive for routine replacement of earlier technologies. Only with great reductions in cost could the new technologies economically replace the older way of doing things and create large markets for entirely new products.
3. Institutional: The institutions and policies created during the FIR tended to limit the full exploitation of new technological opportunities. So long as the new technologies were specialized products with a military or limited civilian market, there was little conflict between the FIR institutions and the new opportunities. As the technical characteristics were improved and the price reduced, conflicts between new opportunities and old policies intensified and eventually led to a change in the institutions that facilitated the implementation of the new technologies.

It has frequently been observed that the initial research for a new product is a small part of the total cost of bringing a product to market. Expenditures for development, market research, and investment in production facilities and techniques tend to dwarf the initial research expenditures. Similarly, the roots of the SIR can be traced to innovations during the 1940s made under military pressure, but there was nothing easy or inevitable about the complex and lengthy process by which the products were refined and the institutional structures adapted to take advantage of the new opportunities.

4

The SAGE Project

During the 1950s the United States developed and deployed an ambitious air defense control system known as Semiautomated Ground Environment (SAGE). The SAGE project required the long distance transmission of radar signals to computers that analyzed those signals to help controllers guide interceptor aircraft and missiles toward invaders. The SAGE project was the first deployment of an integrated computer and communications system for controlling rapidly changing events over a wide distance. While integrated computer and communications control systems are routinely used at present, the SAGE system was far beyond the existing technology of 1950. It had precedents in the combat information centers used on World War II ships, but those analog computer-based systems operated on a much smaller scale with local communication throughout a single ship, rather than across the nation. The extensive research and development, liberal funding, and high national priority for the deployment of the SAGE project accelerated the required technology improvements. Many early individual computer specialists and computer companies gained their initial training and experience on the SAGE project, developing a critical base of human capital in computer hardware and software. It was IBM's first large digital computer contract and assisted IBM's transformation from the leading punch-card accounting machine company to the leading computer industry company.

The Department of Defense (DOD) shifted from generalized concern about inadequate U.S. air defenses to an intensive search for improved air defenses after the Soviet Union's successful detonation of an atomic bomb in August 1949. Air Force Chief of Staff General Hoyt Vandenberg and his scientific adviser MIT physics professor George Valley sought ways to improve air defense. In November 1949, Valley proposed the creation of a special committee to assess the vulnerability of the nation to air attack and to propose solutions. The proposal was accepted, and the Air Defense System Engineering Committee (also known as the Valley Committee) was formed with Valley as its chairman. The Valley Committee submitted an initial report in January 1950 and a more complete report in October 1950 noting that existing air defenses were completely inadequate and that a proper system needed "eyesight" and a "brain," that is, improved radar coverage and a method of rapidly coordinating the detection information and the interceptor information. The Valley report and other DOD studies caused the air force to ask MIT to establish a laboratory devoted exclusively to research and development for the design and construction of an air defense network (Redmond and Smith, 1980, p. 173). MIT agreed and established the Lincoln Laboratory in 1951.

Prior to the formation of the Lincoln Laboratory, Valley and other members of the committee had begun to consider the Whirlwind computer project (see Chapter 3) as a solution to the air defense "brains" problem. Immediately after the committee was formed, Valley examined the under-construction Whirlwind and began discussions with Jay Forrester on possible air defense use of the computer. The committee added funds to the dwindling navy support for the Whirlwind project during 1950 and then took over the project from the navy. The Whirlwind computer was greatly improved in 1953 when a magnetic core memory unit was substituted for the slow, expensive, and unreliable electrostatic storage tubes used earlier. After tests of the Whirlwind in air defense applications, the Whirlwind team began designing a successor computer based on the Whirlwind in order to serve as the brains of the new air defense system. The new computer was initially known as the Whirlwind II and later renamed the AN/FSQ-7 as it evolved into a production computer for the SAGE air defense system.

The SAGE project was an example of what Thomas Hughes calls the "military-industrial-university complex" (1998, p. 3). It was a complex research, development, and implementation project that required the development of new knowledge and its immediate application in a massive industrial project. That approach was pioneered by the atomic bomb and radar projects during World War II, both of which combined massive government funding with extensive university and industrial contracts devoted toward a single complex project. AT&T's regulated monopoly organization including Bell Labs and Western Electric provided an earlier similar approach with Bell Labs acting as an academic organization, Western Electric as an industrial organization, and the regulated monopoly operating companies providing guaranteed funding without dependence on the financial success of the new products. The SAGE project required unified control, but was not hierarchically managed in the then-standard military or industrial model. The great uncertainty in how to accomplish the task made it necessary to give individual groups considerable autonomy in developing their part of the knowledge, while coordinating the entire process to keep it focused on the goal and to solve interaction problems among the various groups.

The SAGE system incorporated multiple components that required research and development:

1. Advances in computer technology, especially core memory, in order to upgrade the Whirlwind into a faster and more reliable computer than any that existed at the time.
2. Development of methods of duplicating functions so that computer capacity would still be available when one portion of the system failed.
3. Experience in producing the computers in quantity, rather than one at a time by expert personnel for research purposes.
4. Development of extensive programming capability (largely ignored earlier) in order to develop the complex programs required.
5. Development of digital communications capability.
6. System management resources in order to integrate all of the various components together.

It does not appear that all of the tasks were accomplished well, but all of them provided learning experiences. Because the system was never utilized, it is unknown how much it would have contributed to defense against an actual attack. The system was designed to aid in defense against Soviet bombers carrying nuclear weapons, but by the time it was fully deployed the greatest threat was long-range missiles for which SAGE's ability to direct fighter aircraft and antiaircraft missiles was useless.

The initial design structure for SAGE was worked out in an MIT "summer study group." The summer study approach was initiated prior to SAGE as an effort to focus the attention of academic experts on a specific problem. Thomas Hughes traces the approach to the advice offered by the president of Bell Laboratories to the chief of naval operations on an earlier problem: "go to some place like MIT, since they have a lot of screwball scientists who will work on anything, and get a short study made" (quoted in Hughes, 1998, p. 25). When General Vandenberg asked MIT to establish a laboratory to develop an air defense system, MIT proposed that the air force first sponsor a summer study project to clarify the scope of the project. This "summer" study group (known as Project Charles) began in February 1951 and included an all-star cast, including F. Wheeler Loomis as chairman, Jerrold Zacharias, George Valley, J. C. R. Licklider (later of Arpanet fame), Jay Forrester, Edwin Land (founder of Polaroid), along with technical consultants John von Neumann and Jerome Wiesner and economic consultants Paul Samuelson, James Tobin, and Carl Kaysen (Hughes, 1998, pp. 26, 27). Following the Project Charles study, the air force awarded MIT a contract in September 1951 to establish Lincoln Laboratory, with study group leader Loomis as its director, Valley as director of the radar and communications division, and Forrester as director of the computer division. MIT requested and received air force assurances of steady long-term financing of the Lincoln Laboratory, including a commitment for $20 million in fiscal 1952 (equivalent to $115 million in 2001 dollars) and an expectation of continued funding at the $20 million per year rate (Hughes, 1998, p. 41).

In the spring of 1952, Forrester began searching for an industrial company to participate in the design of the defense computer. Bell Laboratories and RCA declined interest because of other commitments. Thomas J. Watson, Jr. (then president of IBM while his father remained CEO) has described his efforts to land the SAGE contract:

> The MIT engineer responsible for procuring the SAGE computers was Jay Forrester, an austere man about my age who was driven by a belief that computers could be made to do more than anyone thought . . . I thought it was absolutely essential to IBM's future that we win it. The company that built those computers was going to be way ahead of the game, because it would learn the secrets of mass production . . . I worked harder to win that contract than I worked for any other sale in my life. I was constantly making trips up to MIT. Forrester hemmed and hawed, but I finally told him that if he promised me the produc-

tion assignment, I would build him a factory without waiting for a contract . . . So he told me to go ahead. (Watson and Petre, 1990, pp. 230–233)

Watson's effort to land the SAGE contract was an outstanding use of his time. The SAGE contract produced IBM's first substantial revenue stream from digital computers. The contract began at $4.2 million in 1953 and peaked at $122 million ($632 million in 2001 dollars) in 1957. In the four-year period 1956–1959, the SAGE contract generated $412 million ($2.14 billion in 2001 dollars) in revenue for IBM (Computer Industry Census, 1971). The SAGE computers provided a guaranteed revenue source for developing the manufacturing techniques to make computers in quantity, and provided a direct source of technological expertise that was used in developing commercial computers. Thomas Watson, Jr., recalled: "[SAGE] gave IBM the giant boost I was after. Until the late '50s, SAGE accounted for almost half our total computer sales . . . it enabled us to build highly automated factories ahead of anybody else, and to train thousands of new workers in electronics" (Watson and Petre, 1990, p. 233).

The original SAGE plans called for thirty-two "direction centers," though only twenty-two were actually built. In order to provide continuous reliable operation (with an average downtime of only four hours per year), each center contained a pair of computers with the ability to switch functions between them and provide continuing computer power during breakdowns or maintenance. Each computer pair contained 50,000 vacuum tubes, occupied 40,000 square feet of floor space, used 3 megawatts of power, weighed 275 tons, and contained over 1,000 miles of wire and cable to connect its components (Hughes, 1998, p. 51; Buderi, 1996, p. 399). The last SAGE direction center was not shut down until 1984 when desktop computers had more capabilities than the AN/FSQ-7 monsters.

The successful IBM-Lincoln Laboratory cooperation did not come easily. Forrester and his team were favorably impressed with the IBM culture and attention to detail when they were evaluating companies:

Professional employees generally forswore alcohol in public settings and always dressed in trademark blue suits, white shirts, and dark ties. They were enthusiastic, professional, and expert in electronics and high-speed data processing, which fit in well with Lincoln's aims. Upon touring a manufacturing plant in nearby Poughkeepsie, the Whirlwind contingent found even assembly line workers neatly dressed and efficient. Factory floors seemed clean enough to eat off. (Buderi, 1996, p. 393)

However, once they began joint work, the different cultures of MIT and IBM clashed:

The Whirlwind clique, disdainful of outside expertise, oozed MIT cockiness. The straight-arrow IBM professionals tackled problems in manufacturing terms and found their partners tragically unversed in assembly line reality . . . The contract gave Forrester final say-so over all design changes. Yet he recalled battling Big Blue every step of the way. MIT would submit a blueprint, only to see IBM reconfigure it for manufacture. Forrester often changed it back. (Buderi, 1996, pp. 393, 394)

Thomas J. Watson, Jr., recalled:

Forrester was a genius at computer hardware, but he didn't appreciate how hard it is to set up a reliable production process. He thought we were handling the project all wrong . . . Forrester thought every engineering project needed a dictator, which was not the way our manufacturing men liked to work. His constant criticism made them angry and stubborn. (Watson and Petre, 1990, p. 232)

Despite the clashes, both parties had a strong incentive to make the partnership work, and top leadership insisted that the different perspectives and strong egos not derail the project. IBM sent representatives to Lincoln Laboratory where they gained insight into computer design work from the MIT experts. Lincoln sent representatives to IBM (including Kenneth Olsen, founder of Digital Equipment Corporation) where they learned manufacturing techniques from the IBM experts, and eventually mutual respect emerged.

The SAGE plans severely underestimated the effort required to develop the computer programs necessary for the project's success. There was limited experience with computer programming of any kind at that time, and no experience with programming the complex tasks required to implement SAGE. The engineers designing the system understood the problem of building reliable hardware that would perform at the desired level, but tended to assume that a general purpose computer could be easily programmed to perform any task within its hardware capabilities. Initially, Forrester's computer division was responsible for the programming, but as the scale of the programming increased, most of it was assigned to the RAND Corporation. RAND established a systems development division in 1955 to develop SAGE programming, but as the size of the task continued to grow, the RAND division became the independent System Development Corporation (SDC), which received a $20 million contract in 1957 to program SAGE and train personnel. By 1959 over eight hundred people were developing SAGE software (Hughes, 1998, p. 57).

The SAGE system provided the first computer programming training and experience for a large number of people along with the first experience in managing large software projects. Rather than economies of scale, there are diseconomies of scale in producing large software programs. Eight hundred programmers working on a single massive program cannot write as much code as if they were working on eight hundred small individual projects because of the large amount of time that must be spent coordinating approaches and ensuring that the various pieces of the program work together properly. The SAGE lesson on the diseconomies of scale in complex software has been relearned and reemphasized innumerable times throughout the history of the computer industry as more and more complex programs have been produced, often at greater cost and longer time than their designers expected.

The scale and complexity of the SAGE system led to problems in integrating and controlling the various components. Three different air force commands shared responsibility for the project, MIT's Lincoln Laboratory provided the primary research and design efforts, and IBM, AT&T, and over a hundred other companies provided equipment and services to the project, but there was no overall coordinating organization. MIT declined to allow Lincoln Laboratory to take overall control of the project as straying too far from its educational role, while both RCA and Bell Laboratories declined the coordination role because it came with a restriction on their participation in equipment contracts from the project. Eventually, a new organization was created, the MITRE Corporation, with a similarity to both RAND and SDC as a nonprofit organization carrying out federal contracts. MITRE was initially staffed by 300 people from the computer division of Lincoln Laboratory and funded with a $13 million air force contract (Hughes, 1998, pp. 62–64).

The SAGE system required extensive communication links in order to function:

1. Radar data collected at numerous sites required transmission to the designated direction center for processing in the AN/FSQ-7 computers.
2. Direction centers needed a web of fast voice communication links with other direction centers, air bases, and other military command and control points.
3. Aircraft in flight required radio links to ground controllers and connection of those radio links to the direction centers so that updated information processed at the direction center could be transmitted directly to pilots.

After evaluating the use of military-controlled radio links for all of the necessary communication, the designers concluded that telephone lines could provide greater security and reliability. Using telephone lines implied using the Bell System, and Bell Labs was enthusiastic about meeting the challenge. According to Robert Buderi, when George Valley met with Bell Labs vice president Don Quarles to seek his support for the project, Quarles "fairly glowed at the idea of sending radar data over Bell's phone lines" (1996, p. 370).

The Bell System formed the Air Defense Engineering Services organization, comprised of 1,300 people drawn from the research, manufacturing, and telephone operating components of the Bell System, in order to support the SAGE project (Bell Laboratories, 1978, p. 574). The most technically challenging requirement was the transmission of data from the remote radar sites to the direction centers. In the late 1940s, the air force had experimented with transmitting video images of radar screens using microwave communication links similar to those being developed for transmitting television programs among network stations. That approach required high bandwidth for transmitting a video signal, and the air force's Cambridge Research Laboratory found that it could greatly reduce the volume of information to be transmitted by digitizing the critical information (range and azimuth of all targets detected) and transmitting only the digitized information. While digital information had been routinely transmitted over wires for many years in the form of telegraph signals, the telegraph technology was too slow for the planned SAGE system. Teletypewriter circuits generally transmitted at 75 bits per second, and the SAGE specifications called for 1,600 bits per second with an error rate of one bit per 100,000 transmitted.

The goal of transmitting digital data over analog telephone lines designed to carry voice conversations induced extensive Bell Labs research to identify and remove impediments to the accurate transmission of digital signals over telephone lines. The SAGE data was carried over private lines (dedicated circuits between two points that did not go through a switch) between the radar sites and the direction centers, eliminating the noise generated by telephone switches. Bell engineers found that private line circuits contained a variety of possible sources of data errors, but that some of them could be eliminated by special conditioning of the dedicated lines. Bell chose a simple coding scheme that transmitted digital data by two-level frequency shifting, transmitting tones of 1,200 Hz and 2,400 Hz to represent the two states of digital signals. Both frequencies were within the portion of the frequency that is transmitted on voice-grade telephone circuits with the least distortion. The two-level "frequency shift keying" code allowed data transmission at the required SAGE speed with simple electronics and imperfect analog lines.

Even with the simple two-level code, the first data sets (Bell's term for the device that translated between analog and digital signals, now called a modem) contained 370 vacuum tubes. Increasing data transmission speed over an analog voice-grade telephone line required utilizing more complex coding schemes at the cost of more expensive electronics. Current modems transmit data over analog voice channels at thirty-five times the SAGE rate by using extensive electronics that would have been far more expensive than building additional transmission lines during the 1950s. Building on its SAGE experience, Bell introduced its first commercial data set in 1957 with a speed of 1,000 bits per second over conditioned private lines and later offered data sets that could transmit digital data over switched voice circuits (Bell Laboratories, 1977, p. 429; Bell Laboratories, 1985, pp. 703–747).

Bell also designed and installed an extensive private line system to provide voice communication in the SAGE system. The voice system utilized established technology together with innovations in the use of redundant geographically separate circuits to provide reliable service under adverse conditions. The system also included innovations in signaling and switching to provide more flexible command communications than could be provided by Bell's commercial services. While the

SAGE system had a less significant impact on the Bell System than on IBM, SAGE and other military contracts were an important impetus to the creation of data transmission services and to the expansion of Bell's long distance voice transmission capacity. At one point Bell's military communication lines had as much circuit mileage as the entire Bell System toll network (Bell Laboratories, 1978, pp. 575–579, 597).

The SAGE system has been described as "the best peace-time air defense system ever deployed" (Hughes, 1998, p. 64). It was an impressive technological accomplishment and outstanding learning experience, but how useful it would have been in an actual attack is open to question. It developed the essential components of an integrated computer communications system to manage geographically dispersed operations in real time. As Thomas Hughes states: "the project showed the world how a digital computer could function as a real-time information-processing center for a complex command and control system. SAGE demonstrated that computers could be more than arithmetic calculators, that they could function as automated control centers for industrial as well as military processes" (1998, p. 16). The multibillion-dollar cost of the complete SAGE system could be justified in the context of defending against bombers carrying nuclear weapons where a few minutes saved in directing defending aircraft and missiles could be critical to the outcome. However, it was far too expensive to adapt to civilian use because the benefits of improved management capabilities would be much less than the cost of the system.

In order to bring computer communications into widespread use, extreme reductions in cost were necessary. Those cost reductions occurred through innumerable specific innovations, but especially in the steady rapid decline in the size and cost of basic electronic components. As prices declined from $100 for high-quality early military transistors to a small fraction of a penny for transistors incorporated into an integrated circuit, computers, modems, and other electronic products became far cheaper and smaller, allowing them to be economically utilized in many applications. Reductions in size and power were also critical for making the systems economical because the 40,000 square feet of space and three megawatts of power required for an AN/FSQ-7 computer pair would have made widespread utilization infeasible even if the computer itself were free.

Because of the high cost of computer communications, the computer and communications industries of the 1950s and 1960s developed separately with little interaction. The SAGE style of human-to-computer interaction, with graphics displayed on a screen activated by a light pen, was also too expensive for widespread use. The computer industry developed around batch processing with input by punch card and output to printers, along with many efforts to economize on expensive computer processing power. That approach slowly gave way to widespread graphical interaction (with a mouse as a substitute for the SAGE light pen) as prices of computers and related equipment dropped far enough to make the additional convenience worth the increased computer power required.

I

The Separate Worlds of
Computers and Communications,
1950–1968

5

The Early Semiconductor Industry

The early semiconductor industry had a very high rate of innovation but almost no protection of intellectual property. The Bell System established the pattern with its nonrestrictive licensing of the fundamental patents, sharing of production technology with others, and absence of efforts to prevent its personnel from leaving to start new firms. Many companies entered into cross-licensing agreements with each other and freely shared information either through informal channels or through the movement of personnel. The industry was an unusual combination of cooperation and competition. It was highly competitive with multiple companies, low barriers to entry, and rapidly dropping prices. However, the crucial determinant of success was intellectual property, which was widely shared in a cooperative fashion. The industry was a mixture of the academic model (free sharing of research results) and the business model. That combination was facilitated by the early military market and the experience with combining academic and business characteristics in major World War II and Cold War projects. A similar combination of cooperative sharing of information and intellectual property combined with business competition appeared in the development of the Internet.

The Creation of a Competitive Market

The invention of the point-contact germanium transistor in 1948 was the product of a long program of basic research in semiconductor properties at Bell Labs directed toward providing the necessary technology for direct dialing of long distance telephone calls with operator assistance. However, the early development of the transistor industry was dominated by military concerns. The first transistors were too expensive to compete with vacuum tubes in most commercial applications but were immediately recognized as a significant military technology. William Shockley served as a military adviser while continuing to lead the Bell Labs transistor research group. His visit to a Korean battlefield in 1950 convinced him that his ongoing work on a new "junction transistor" could be used to create a mortar proximity fuse that would be useful in the Korean War (Riordan and Hoddeson, 1997, p. 187). Shockley accelerated the Bell Labs effort to complete the junction transistor and announced it in July 1951, ending efforts to continue refining the 1948 point-contact transistor. With the creation of the junction transistor and the development of manufacturing techniques to overcome the many problems encountered in producing the earliest transistors, transistors were soon used in many electronic devices.

At first, Bell Labs disclosed the physics of the transistor, but not the manufacturing processes, to a selected set of defense contractors. Bell was working closely with the military services, attempting to be responsive to military concerns to limit information about the transistor processes while avoiding formal limits on the use of the information. The Joint Chiefs of Staff requested Bell Labs "to guard the special manufacturing processes so essential to the success of the transistor development and production with all possible care short of actual military classification," while Bell managers "were staunchly opposed to classification of the junction transistor" and believed that "both the company and country had more to gain by publicizing the breakthrough" (Riordan and Hoddeson, 1997, p. 196). By the end of 1951 (after the patent on the Shockley junction transistor was issued), the argument was settled in favor of disclosure rather than secrecy. AT&T began licensing the transistor patents for a $25,000 initial fee. It provided technical manufacturing information to licensees (at first only to firms from the United States and other NATO countries) during 1952 and allowed licensees to tour the Western Electric transistor manufacturing facilities. Bell also provided written materials on manufacturing processes to licensees that, though initially classified, were later published and known informally as "Mother Bell's Cookbook" (Riordan and Hoddeson, 1997, p. 197).

The 1951–1952 decisions to license the transistor patents and disseminate technical information on manufacturing techniques had important implications for both the Bell System and the future semiconductor industry. Strict controls would have preserved the transistor market for Bell so long as its patent claims were upheld and other companies were not able to invent around its patents. The strength of Bell's patent claims, however, was uncertain. Bell patent lawyers had denied Shockley's proposal to write a broad patent application on the initial transistor because they thought it would not be granted and instead wrote a narrow application on the specific experimental work of John Bardeen and Walter Brattain. Even with the narrow patent application, two claims were denied because of similar previous work by others.

If Bell could have obtained a broad controlling patent on semiconductor amplification similar to its 1876 controlling patent on voice telephone service, it would have had an extraordinarily valuable new franchise. On the other hand, narrow specific patents were of much lower value because new technology quickly replaced older products. For example, complete control of the 1948 point-contact transistors would have been of limited value when they were replaced by the 1951 junction transistors. While Bell led the way in both the initial invention and the development of manufacturing techniques for the transistor, there was no reason to believe that other research groups and companies would not be able to duplicate Bell's success. According to one estimate, an Army Signal Corps–funded germanium research project at Purdue University was only six months behind the Bell Labs semiconductor research in 1948 (Riordan and Hoddeson, 1997, p. 162).

Bell's opportunity to maintain complete control of the transistor technology was further limited by the political situation. The Department of Justice filed an antitrust suit in 1949 that accused the Bell System of illegally using its integrated structure to foreclose competition in telephone equipment, and any effort to limit transistor manufacturing to Bell's subsidiary Western Electric could potentially have bolstered the DOJ antitrust claims. With the Korean War in progress and allegations of Communist spying and infiltration of the U.S. government receiving wide publicity, an AT&T effort to restrict a potentially vital defense technology for its own profit could have been devastating. In order to be confident of the supply of transistors before designing them into military equipment, the Department of Defense wanted multiple suppliers. The DOD helped finance transistor production facilities at Western Electric and several other companies in order to ensure adequate supplies.

AT&T's liberal transistor licensing policy was generally followed by other companies that made transistor innovations. Companies frequently offered licenses to their innovations in exchange for licenses to the innovations of others. Despite the large number of patents granted on semiconductor technology, the innovations were almost public domain property because of easy availability of licenses. Any company could get access to the best technology available at the time and develop its own improvements to that technology. Companies retained an incentive to innovate because of the short-term advantages that they could gain before their innovations were widely copied. The free sharing of technology in the early semiconductor industry was a sharp contrast with the early radio and vacuum-tube electronics patent litigation and resulting deadlock. With easy access to semiconductor patent licenses, there were no significant barriers to the creation of new semiconductor companies. The most significant requirement for a new semiconductor company was the recruitment of highly skilled personnel, and they moved quite freely among companies. Capital requirements were modest at the beginning but increased over time as semiconductor manufacturing became more complex.

With the licensing of transistor patents, dissemination of technical information, military financial support for development and manufacturing, an extensive price-insensitive military market for improved transistors, and many opportunities for technical improvement, the semiconductor industry exploded far beyond Bell Labs-Western Electric control. The many financial and technical opportunities in the new field, along with personality conflicts, induced repeated movement of key personnel to new companies and prevented any single company from controlling the rate at which semiconductor innovations were introduced to the market.

In 1952, the small military electronics company Texas Instruments (TI) obtained a transistor patent license, and four of its representatives attended a Bell symposium on transistor manufacturing where they met Gordon Teal. Teal had developed the critical process of growing large crystals of extremely pure germanium, working on the process at first with borrowed space on nights and weekends because Shockley and other Bell Labs leaders thought it had no potential. After Teal's germanium crystals substantially improved the early transistors, he turned his attention to the much more difficult problem of growing large crystals of pure silicon. Experts of that time understood that silicon transistors would have better performance than germanium transistors and that silicon was a cheaper material, but silicon's high melting point and propensity to absorb impurities from the container in which it was melted made the fabrication of a silicon transistor a difficult technical problem.

At the end of 1952, Teal joined Texas Instruments as director of research and recruited a number of scientists to continue the silicon research he had begun at Bell Labs. In the spring of 1954, Teal's group succeeded in developing a silicon transistor. Texas Instruments rushed it into production in order to satisfy a military market that was willing to pay $100 for each of the new silicon transistors (compared to $16 for germanium transistors at that time) because of their ability to operate under conditions of heat and humidity that caused germanium transistors to fail. While TI pursued the high-end military market for expensive silicon transistors with tolerance to temperature extremes, it also during 1954 pursued the low-end market by seeking to reduce the price for germanium transistors from $16 to $2.50 in order to produce a consumer radio. The first transistor radios were marketed in late 1954, and production expanded rapidly during 1955. TI became a major transistor supplier for established radio producers (Riordan and Hoddeson, 1997, pp. 206–213).

Shockley himself had become dissatisfied with his rewards at Bell Labs. While he received scientific recognition and prizes, he did not obtain either a leading management position or royalties. After failing to secure a position on the terms he requested from either academic institutions or companies, he decided to set up his own company. As he wrote to a friend at the time, "Think I shall try to raise some capital and start on my own . . . it is obvious I am smarter, more energetic and understand people better than most of these other folks" (quoted in Riordan and Hoddeson, 1997, p. 232). In 1955, Shockley received financial support from Arnold Beckman (formerly professor of chemistry at CalTech and head of the successful scientific instruments firm Beckman Instruments) and strong encouragement from Stanford's dean of engineering, Frederick Terman, who asked him to set up his firm near the Stanford campus. Shockley began recruiting a team of star scientists for the new research-oriented firm, including Robert Noyce, an MIT-educated physicist then working at Philco, and Gordon Moore, a CalTech-educated physical chemist then working at the Johns Hopkins Applied Physics Laboratory. Soon after the company was formed, Shockley (along with Bardeen and Brattain) was awarded the Nobel prize in physics for the invention of the transistor, increasing his fame and ability to attract top scientific talent to the Shockley Semiconductor Laboratory. However, Shockley's scientific and recruiting abilities were not accompanied by strong managerial skills, and the company fell into disarray.

In September 1957, eight of Shockley's top scientists resigned as a group after discussions with Beckman and Shockley had failed to satisfy their grievances. The next day, the "traitorous eight" (Shockley's term for them) signed an agreement with Fairchild Camera and Instruments that called for Fairchild to provide $1.5 million in financing to set up a new semiconductor company. Fairchild retained the right to purchase the scientists' interest in the new company for $300,000 each, and Fairchild exercised that option two years later (Jackson, 1997, p. 21). The Fairchild agreement was intermediate between an ordinary employment agreement and the later development of true venture capitalists. It provided substantial incentives for the founders to develop a profitable company but no guaranteed right to an ongoing equity stake in the company. The Soviet Sputnik launch the month after the former Shockley scientists formed Fairchild Semiconductor began the space race and created a new government market for high-priced innovative electronic components. In contrast to the unprofitable Shockley Semiconductor Laboratory, which focused on long-range research, the new Fairchild Semiconductor quickly moved into manufacturing and began earning profits by the end of 1958.

Shockley continued to be more successful at recruiting capable scientists and conducting research than in managing a company, and his company continued to lose personnel (to Fairchild and others) and money. After Beckman decided against suing Fairchild for utilizing intellectual property developed at Shockley, he sold Shockley's company to Clevite Transistor in 1960. Clevite was also unable to make a profit on the Shockley enterprise, and Shockley left the company to become Professor of Engineering and Applied Science at Stanford (Riordan and Hoddeson, 1997, p. 277). While his own company was never financially successful, it was a critical force (along with IBM's San Jose Laboratories) in establishing "Silicon Valley" as the center of technological innovation in electronics and computers. Even Shockley's management difficulties helped develop other companies as he recruited and then drove away exceptionally capable people who formed new companies and continued electronic progress. Twenty-five semiconductor companies in the San Francisco Bay area have been considered descendants of the original Shockley company (Walter-Carlson, 1974, pp. 5420, 5433).

Japan began transistor research in 1949 in laboratories associated with Nippon Telegraph and Telephone Corporation (NTT), a public corporation until partial privatization in 1985, and the Ministry of International Trade and Industry (MITI). Hitachi, Toshiba, and Nippon Electric Corporation also began semiconductor research but did not seek licenses from Bell Laboratories. Instead Hitachi and Toshiba gained rights to Bell's semiconductor patents indirectly through a patent licensing agreement with RCA that also included a transfer of RCA's monochrome television technology and RCA technical assistance (Flamm, 1996, p. 42). The RCA agreement gave the companies access to Bell patents because of RCA's cross-licensing agreement with Bell. In 1954, MITI approved Bell Labs licenses for Sony, Toshiba, Hitachi, and Kobe Kogyo. Thousands of Japanese engineers traveled to the United States to attend electronics conferences and tour manufacturing plants and were generally given free access to information.

The Japanese companies focused on developing the consumer market for transistors, especially in radios. NTT labs produced a prototype transistor radio in 1953, and Sony offered a successful commercial transistor radio in 1955. Japanese transistor production accelerated from 6 million units in 1957 (21 percent of U.S. production) to 87 million units in 1959 (106 percent of U.S. production). Toshiba was the leading Japanese transistor producer in 1959 with 26 percent of the Japanese market. Over half of the Japanese transistors of the late 1950s were used in radios, and 77 percent of the Japanese transistor radios were exported in 1959 (Flamm, 1996, p. 47). Japan's early transistor success was based on the low Japanese wage rates of the time that created cost savings in the labor-intensive production of low-quality germanium transistors. As higher-quality silicon transistors dropped in price during the early 1960s, the United States regained the lead in total production from Japanese companies in 1961 and maintained the lead until 1968 when Japanese companies again surpassed U.S. companies in total transistor production (Flamm, 1996, p. 47).

Innovation and the Integrated Circuit

The Bell System continued to make crucial contributions to the rapidly improving semiconductor technology after its invention of point-contact and junction transistors. In the 1952–1956 period, the Bell System obtained 192 of the 490 patents granted on semiconductors (39 percent), while RCA received 103 (21 percent) and GE received 54 (11 percent). Companies with experience in making vacuum tubes obtained 84 percent of the semiconductor patents in the 1952–1956 period, while semiconductor companies with no previous experience in making vacuum tubes (including IBM, Texas Instruments, Motorola, and Hughes) obtained the remainder (computed from Tilton, 1971, table 4-2, p. 57). The Bell System's share was much smaller in what John Tilton classifies as "major innovations" during that time period. Of the nine major innovations Tilton cites, Western Electric is credited with the process of oxide masking and diffusion and is credited jointly with Texas Instruments for the "diffused transistor" that resulted from that process (Tilton, 1971, pp. 16–17).

Another way of assessing the credit for early improvements is to note that the two innovations with the most significant impact on the future development of the semiconductor industry were Texas Instruments' 1954 silicon junction transistor and Western Electric's 1955 diffusion process. The diffusion process was developed from research sponsored by the U.S. Army Signal Corps, which funded about half of Bell's transistor research in the years 1953–1955 (Flamm, 1996, pp. 31–32). According to Kenneth Flamm, the diffusion process was the first method for producing high-frequency transistors:

> The two principal methods of creating junction transistors involved adding the impurity while growing a single silicon crystal (grown junction transistors) or melting silicon materials already treated with impurities into one another (alloy junction transistors) . . . The diffusion process worked by exposing a semiconductor substrate to a carefully controlled atmosphere of heated, gaseous impurities, which diffused into the surface of the substrate. Very precise control of the composition and thickness of the impurities in the silicon could thus be achieved, and the operating frequencies of the new transistors so produced jumped by two orders of magnitude. (1996, p. 32)

Bell continued to receive many semiconductor patents in the years after 1956, but its share of total patents declined from almost 40 percent in the early years to 10 percent in the mid-1960s. The number of patents obtained by firms without vacuum-tube experience jumped from fifteen per year in the early period to 250 per year in the mid-1960s (Tilton, 1971, p. 57).

Bell's production of semiconductors was a far smaller share of the total market than its innovative contributions. According to John Tilton's estimates, Texas Instruments was the leading semiconductor producer in the late 1950s with 20 percent of the total market, while Bell was the sixth-ranking producer with 5 percent of the market (1971, p. 66). As a result of the 1956 consent decree (see Chapter 7), Bell was restricted to producing semiconductors for its own use and for the government, but the company did not consider that restriction a major change to its pre-decree practice. Texas Instruments and other companies without vacuum-tube experience were able to use the Bell innovations through patent licensing and personnel movement and were more aggressive in developing efficient mass-production facilities for transistors.

Shockley developed a device similar to an integrated circuit (the "Shockley diode") during 1958, but it was difficult to produce in a reliable manner and did not become a commercial success. At about the same time, Jack Kilby of Texas Instruments sought ways to produce all circuit elements (transistors, resistors, and capacitors) out of silicon so that they could be built from a single silicon chip. At that time, resistors and capacitors commonly used cheaper material, but Kilby recognized that the key to further circuit miniaturization was building all elements from the same material. On September 12, 1958, Kilby obtained a crude integrated circuit from a block of germanium and on February 6, 1959, TI filed a broad patent application for the integrated circuit.

Physicist Jean Hoerni of Fairchild developed an important manufacturing improvement in 1958 (the "planar" process of using silicon dioxide to protect sensitive junctions) that greatly increased yields (Riordan and Hoddeson, 1997, p. 263). Hoerni, Fairchild Director of Research Robert Noyce, and Director of Production Engineering Gordon Moore were all part of the "traitorous eight" that had left Shockley as a group. Robert Noyce recognized early in 1959 that he could use Hoerni's silicon dioxide process to provide integrated connections among components built on a single chip. The standard procedure at that time consisted of forming multiple transistors on a single chip of silicon, slicing the individual transistors from the chip and then wiring together transistors and other components to create the desired circuit. Using the fine layer of silicon dioxide as a protecting insulator, Noyce found that he could build "wires" of fine lines of molten metal during the manufacturing process and connect them by making a hole in the silicon dioxide layer and depositing a metal contact. After further work, Fairchild filed a patent application on July 30, 1959, for Noyce's version of the integrated circuit. Fairchild knew of the TI patent application filed five months earlier and consequently focused its application narrowly on the manufacturing techniques developed at Fairchild for integrated circuits.

The first integrated circuit patent was granted on April 25, 1961, to Noyce, apparently because the more narrowly focused application was easier to evaluate and approve than the broader and earlier Jack Kilby/ Texas Instruments application. By March 1961 Fairchild had made enough progress in the difficult manufacturing techniques for integrated circuits to introduce its first set of integrated circuit products. The space race continued the earlier defense emphasis on low weight and low power consumption for electronic devices. Civilian space applications and military missile applications (especially the Apollo and Minuteman II guidance computers) provided an eager market for expensive early integrated circuits. Texas Instruments began selling integrated circuits in October 1961, and Motorola, Westinghouse, General Electric, and Teledyne (among others) began developing integrated circuit products (Riordan and Hoddeson, 1997, pp. 260–273). While defense and space applications adopted integrated circuits rapidly, the commercial computer, telephone, and electronics market moved much more slowly into integrated circuits. Where size, weight, and power consumption were not critical advantages, discrete components on a circuit board retained price and reliability advantages during the first few years of integrated circuit production.

Falling Prices, Rising Output

The table provided shows the quantity and prices of germanium and silicon transistors produced in the United States from 1954 to 1969. Because of their much lower price, germanium transistors dominated the early market even though they were inferior to silicon transistors. The alternative to transistors was triode vacuum tubes. Vacuum-tube sales rose to almost 400 million in 1950 and remained between 350 and 500 million in each year from 1950 through 1966 when they began a sharp decline. The average tube price was $.65 in 1950 and $.68 in 1966, with minor variations during the intervening years (computed from Electronic Industries Association, 1979, p. 88). Vacuum tubes were cheaper than germanium transistors until 1963 and cheaper than silicon transistors until 1966, the year that marks the rapid decline of vacuum-tube sales.

In the late 1950s low-quality transistors were substituted for cheaper vacuum tubes in portable radios because of their low weight and power consumption while computers and televisions continued to use the cheaper vacuum tubes. In the early 1960s high-quality transistors were substituted for cheaper vacuum tubes in computers because of their power consumption and reliability advantages while televisions continued to use vacuum tubes. By the late 1960s high-quality silicon transistors were cheaper than vacuum tubes and generally replaced tubes except in limited applications where the special characteristics of tubes retained advantages.

The average price of silicon transistors was cut in half between 1954 and 1960 (from $23.95 each to $11.27 each), an average price decline of 12.6 percent per year. Those were years of low production (from

U.S. factory transistor sales and prices, 1954–1969

Year	Germanium		Silicon	
	Quantity (millions)	Price ($)	Quantity (millions)	Price ($)
1954	1.3	3.56	0.02	23.95
1955	3.6	2.88	0.09	20.44
1956	12.4	2.34	0.42	19.94
1957	27.7	1.85	1.0	17.81
1958	45.0	1.79	2.1	15.57
1959	77.5	1.96	4.8	14.53
1960	119.1	1.70	8.8	11.27
1961	177.9	1.14	13.0	7.48
1962	213.7	0.82	26.6	4.39
1963	249.4	0.69	50.6	2.65
1964	288.8	0.57	118.1	1.46
1965	333.6	0.50	274.5	0.86
1966	368.7	0.45	487.2	0.64
1967	270.3	0.43	489.5	0.58
1968	199.3	0.41	684.1	0.44
1969	208.5	0.37	934.5	0.37

Source: Electronic Industries Association, *Electronic Market Data Book* (Washington, D.C.: Electronic Industries Association, 1979), p. 107.

insignificant in 1954 to 8.8 million units in 1960) with sales to military and other quality-conscious but price-insensitive users. Silicon transistor production was dwarfed by the 200 million germanium transistors and 400 million vacuum tubes produced in 1960. From 1960 to 1966, the number of silicon transistors sold grew by 66 percent per year (from 8.8 million to 487 million per year) while the price declined by 48 percent per year (from $11.27 each to $.64). During the next six-year period (1966–1972), the rate of silicon transistor growth in production and rate of price decline slowed. The number of silicon transistors grew at 15 percent per year while price declined at 14 percent per year, leaving total revenue from silicon transistors only slightly higher in 1972 than in 1966.

The basic pattern of silicon transistor prices and production is comparable to the trajectories of other new products, but with higher rates of growth and price decline than with most other products. There is frequently a period of low production and high prices following the innovation (1954–1960 for silicon transistors), followed by a period of rapid growth and substantial price declines as the product gains acceptance in the mass market and efficient manufacturing facilities are developed (1960–1966 period), and then a slowdown in growth and price reductions as the product matures (1966–1972 period).

The unique aspect of semiconductor development is the continuous improvement in integrated circuits that has allowed a high rate of technological progress to be sustained over a long period of time. While price reductions for individual transistors came much more slowly in the late 1960s than the early 1960s, the effective price for transistors continued to drop rapidly as the price of integrated circuits (containing multiple transistors along with other circuit elements) was reduced and more elements were included in an individual circuit. Continuous progress in manufacturing miniature circuits allowed doubling the number of components contained on a single chip every eighteen months, a proposition first developed by Gordon Moore of Shockley-Fairchild-Intel and known as Moore's Law. By 2000 Intel's Pentium IV microprocessor chip contained 42 million transistors, reasonably consistent with a Moore's Law prediction extrapolated from 1960s integrated circuits.

The cost of manufacturing individual chips remained approximately constant over generations of chips at corresponding points in their production cycle. The cost of each new generation of circuits begins high and declines over time, but at the time of maximum production the cost of a new generation is approximately equal to the cost of the previous generation at its time of maximum production. The combination of Moore's Law and constant production cost per chip implies a reduction in the price per transistor embedded in an integrated circuit of 46 percent per year, approximately the same rate as the 48 percent per year price decline during the six-year period of maximum price reduction in discrete silicon transistors. One study of semiconductor memory prices for the period 1972–1988 showed a price decline of 42 percent per year (Flamm, 1996, p. 10). The long-term computation of computer memory price changes discussed in Chapter 3 found a memory price 46 million times higher in 1950 than in 2001, equivalent to a continuous price reduction of 35 percent per year over the fifty-one-year period that included semiconductor and other memory technologies.

6

The Early Commercial Computer Industry

The most significant beneficiary of the progress in semiconductors during the 1950–1968 period was the computer industry. Electronic digital computers advanced from experimental status to routine and indispensable components of scientific research and business operations during that time period. As in semiconductors, there were no dominating patents that significantly influenced the development of the industry. Computer central processing units consisted almost entirely of electronic components and therefore advanced in lockstep with component progress.

A functioning computer required far more than the central processing unit (CPU): it required memory, input and output devices, data storage, programming, and knowledge of how to apply the computer power. The growth of the computer industry also required substantial restructuring of business operations in order to best utilize the new capabilities for managing information rather than computation only. The supporting technologies advanced along with electronics improvements, causing a dramatic drop in the effective price of computers. Three different computations of the rate of price decline based on different indices of computer power yielded price reductions ranging from 23 percent per year to 27 percent per year during the 1954–1967 time period (Brock, 1975, pp. 78, 79). The rate of price decline in computers was somewhat lower than the 35–48 percent per year reduction in semiconductor prices discussed in Chapter 5 but unusually high compared to most other technologically progressive products.

Vacuum-Tube and Transistor Computers

The established business equipment companies first developed the commercial computer industry. After leaving the University of Pennsylvania in 1946, J. Presper Eckert and John Mauchly established the Eckert-Mauchly Computer Corporation to develop and sell a successor to the ENIAC. They obtained a contract from the Census Bureau for what became the Univac I (with stored programming in contrast to the ENIAC's external wired program, and magnetic tape instead of punch cards for data storage), followed by contracts from Prudential Insurance and other government and commercial customers. However, the high development costs, multiyear development period, and limited venture capital available at that time created financial difficulties for the company. Remington Rand, IBM's only competitor in punch-card accounting machines and also a producer of typewriters and other business machines, purchased the Eckert-Mauchly company in 1949.

Remington Rand completed the Univac in 1951 and delivered the first machine to the Census Bureau. The next year the company purchased the financially struggling Engineering Research Associates (ERA), the cryptological computer firm that had developed the Atlas and the ERA 1103 computers. Remington also hired General Leslie Groves, the wartime director of the atomic bomb program, giving the company prestige and contacts to accompany its new computer product line (Flamm, 1988, p. 107). While Remington Rand received a great deal of favorable publicity for its leading role in the computer industry, its early computers did not produce much revenue or transform the decentralized management structure of the conglomerate. Although Remington was the leading commercial and scientific computer company in 1954 (but not the leading military computer company), the company received only $4.9 million from the Univac and ERA computers while receiving five times as much revenue ($24.4 million) from keypunches and other data entry units (Computer Industry Census, 1971). The two computer product lines obtained from the Eckert-Mauchly and ERA acquisitions remained relatively independent of each other and of the rest of the company. Remington Rand's salesforce for punch-card accounting machines remained separate from and competitive with the computer salesforce. The company did not embrace the opportunities for rapid continuous innovation in computers, and the company's lead was soon lost to technologically superior products.

IBM did not view electronic computers as a profitable business at first, but experimented with computer innovations to support its image as a technologically progressive company. In 1947, IBM built the Selective Sequence Electronic Calculator (SSEC) as an improved sequel to the Harvard Mark I. The SSEC was a huge hybrid of electromechanical and electronic components. IBM installed the SSEC on the ground floor of IBM headquarters in Manhattan where it could be seen from the sidewalk and offered its use for free to solve scientific problems (Watson and Petre, 1990, pp. 190, 191). Thomas Watson, Jr., recalled his first reaction to examining the ENIAC with IBM's executive vice president, Charles Kirk, in 1946: "I couldn't see this gigantic, costly, unreliable device as a piece of business equipment. Kirk felt the same way. On the train from Philadelphia back to New York, he said, 'Well, that's awfully unwieldy. We could never use anything like that.' We both agreed . . . this ENIAC was an interesting experiment way off on the sidelines that couldn't possibly affect us" (Watson and Petre, 1990, p. 136). IBM's commercial interest in computer technology increased when the company began offering a vacuum-tube calculator at $550 per month and found demand far higher than expected.

When the Korean War began in June 1950, IBM sought to contribute to the war effort and found strong military demand for computing power. The company decided to build a large-scale general purpose computer, first known as the Defense Calculator and later as the IBM 701, in part as a patriotic gesture. John von Neumann served as a consultant to IBM, and the IBM 701 was closely related to von Neumann's IAS computer (Flamm, 1988, pp. 52, 53). The expected $3 million development cost and $8,000 per month rental price were far higher than previous IBM projects, but IBM found that it generated substantial orders for the machine even before a prototype had been produced. Thomas Watson, Jr., was particularly impressed by the strength of the new market when higher than expected costs for developing and producing the new computer caused the company to double the price initially quoted to customers: "To my total amazement, we managed to hang on to as many orders as we'd started with. That was when I felt a real *Eureka!* Clearly we'd tapped a new and powerful source of demand. Customers wanted computers so badly that we could double the price and still not drive people away" (Watson and Petre, 1990, p. 228). IBM also began developing a business-oriented computer (the Tape Processing Machine, or IBM 702) to respond to the risk of losing its largest punch-card accounting customers to the Remington Rand Univac.

In 1955, IBM hired Emanuel Piore, formerly chief scientist at the Office of Naval Research and a leader in its computer and electronics programs, in order to develop a long-term research program and expand IBM's scientific capabilities. Piore established a comprehensive program that included fundamental research on computer-related technologies and applied research for particular products. IBM's internally financed research and development spending jumped from under 15 percent of earnings to over 30 percent of earnings. Kenneth Flamm states:

> Some knowledgeable observers date IBM's shift to a business strategy explicitly based on a continuous investment in research, incorporated into a steady stream of new, technology-intensive products that were more advanced than those offered by its competitors, to the transition between the Watsons in the mid-1950's . . . IBM was one of the first companies to analyze correctly the nature of a high-technology, research-intensive business in an area of continuous rapid technological progress. IBM's strengthened research organization was an important first step toward dominance of the computer industry. (1988, pp. 84, 85)

When IBM recognized that its 702 business-oriented computer was losing customers to Univac, it accelerated its planned upgrade schedule and introduced the improved 704 (scientific) and 705 (business) machines as replacements for the 701 and 702. Both the 704 and 705 used the core memory pioneered in the Whirlwind project and then being produced by IBM for the AN/FSQ-7 computers in the SAGE project. With the rapid replacement of its first large-scale computers, IBM gained a technological lead on the Univac at the cost of revenue that could have been earned from continued rental of the 701 and 702 computers. In 1958, IBM began delivering the high-speed 709 to replace its mid-1950s machines. IBM provided three generations of vacuum-tube computers during the 1950s, quickly translating technological innovations into products and creating confidence that customers could commit to IBM computers and expect the company to provide improved products in the future. IBM had extended its long-standing practice of renting rather than selling punch-card machines to its new computer business. Renting shifted the risk of obsolescence from its customers to IBM. Customers did not need to evaluate the probability of a new computer reducing the value of their investment because they could trade their existing model for the enhanced model when it was available. With a small installed base of computers and many opportunities for growth, IBM was willing to replace computers that had only been rented for a short time in order to establish its position in the computer market.

In 1954, IBM introduced the small-scale business-oriented 650 computer with a rental price of $3,250 per month. The 650 combined IBM's established skill in punch-card accounting machines with its developing electronic expertise. The 650 memory was a rapidly rotating magnetic drum (developed from technology licensed from ERA) that was slower but more reliable and cheaper than the memories of the large-scale 701, 702, and Univac. The IBM 650 provided a popular bridge between the earlier punch-card accounting machines and the later more sophisticated computers. It used punched cards as input and a printer as output, as in the earlier electromechanical accounting machines, but with a much more flexible central processor. It became the first mass-produced computer (over 1,000 produced) and helped maintain the loyalty of IBM's established punch-card accounting machine customers. The IBM 650 also played an important educational role because IBM donated the computer or provided it for a minimal price to universities that agreed to offer computer courses, providing many students with an introduction to computers (Ceruzzi, 1998, p. 44).

Many other companies entered the vacuum-tube computer industry, but none of them were able to develop a successful long-term business with sustained technological progress. In many cases a company was based on an innovative computer that met a specific need (aircraft design, for example) but was not able to provide upgrades and enhancements to maintain its position in the market. IBM gained a dominant position by 1956 and maintained it through the 1970s. By 1956 the IBM 650 system alone was producing almost as much revenue as all of Remington Rand's computer products. All of the commercial products were eclipsed by the SAGE contract, which produced $93 million for IBM in 1956, compared to $15 million for the IBM 650, $16 million for the IBM 700 series, and $16 million for Remington Rand's 1100 and Univac series of computers (Computer Industry Census, 1971).

While the SAGE contract was critical to IBM's technological expertise and revenue during the 1950s, IBM was unusually successful in translating its military experience into commercial products. It was able to combine its sales orientation and punch-card accounting position from the pre-computer age with its military contract and a newly created internal research capability to reach a dominant position in the commercial computer industry. IBM's close relationships with commercial customers kept it focused on developing an entire system (CPU, input-output devices, programming, and support) that would be useful to customers with limited computer expertise. IBM developed important peripheral technologies, including upgrades to older punch-card and printing products and completely new products such as the 305 disk drive that provided access to nonsequential data and was first used by United Airlines for reservations.

While transistors were available throughout the 1950s, they were too expensive to compete with vacuum tubes for most computer applications. In the late 1950s the average price for germanium transistors was about three times the price of vacuum tubes while the price of silicon transistors was over twenty times the price of vacuum tubes (see Chapter 5). After some experimental and special purpose computers produced by Bell Labs, Lincoln Laboratory, and others, transistor manufacturer Philco produced the first general purpose transistor computer under contract for the National Security Agency (NSA) and offered a commercial version of that computer in 1958 (Ceruzzi, 1998, p. 65). While the Philco transistor computer was successful, Philco was not able to sustain the necessary upgrades to remain competitive. RCA and other companies entered the computer business, while existing computer companies announced new transistor models. Transistor prices remained higher than vacuum-tube prices at the time most computer companies switched to solid-state components, but it was clear that transistors would soon be cheaper and the transistor computers provided advantages in size, power consumption, and reliability over vacuum-tube computers.

IBM signed a contract with Texas Instruments for high-volume transistor production in order to convert from vacuum tubes to transistors, with a volume discount pricing plan and an expectation that IBM would use most of the output of a new Texas Instruments transistor plant (Watson and Petre, 1990, pp. 295–297). IBM began deliveries of the high-speed vacuum-tube 709 in 1958 and only one year later transformed it into the transistorized 7090, first to meet a military contract requirement and then for general sale. The 7090 and the further improved 7094 became the standard large-scale computers of the early 1960s. IBM also created an extremely successful transistor successor to the 650 with its 1401. While the 1401 contained a limited processor, it was supported by extremely capable peripheral equipment including the 600-line-per-minute 1403 printer. Ten thousand 1401 systems were installed (Ceruzzi, 1998, p. 75). Some were used as stand-alone installations to replace punch-card or manual accounting systems that required simple computations on large amounts of data. Others were used as supporting systems for large computer installations such as the IBM 7090/7094 systems in which a 1401 would transfer data from punched cards to magnetic tape and from magnetic tape to printers. With that arrangement, the fast, expensive computer could be used more efficiently by reading data in from tape and writing its output to tape without wasting time waiting for the much slower data transfer rates of punch cards or printers.

The System/360 and IBM Dominance

IBM's early computer line (including both vacuum-tube and transistor computers) had evolved from efforts to optimize designs for specific needs of various segments of the market. While IBM offered a large number of computers and peripheral devices, the machines were not compatible with each other. Each computer family remained an isolated island with its own processor, peripheral devices, machine architecture, and software. A growing company could not easily shift from a small IBM computer to a larger computer because such a shift required new software that was generally written by the company for its own applications at great expense. The isolated nature of the various systems prevented IBM from obtaining all of the potential economies of scope from supplying a wide range of computers.

In 1961, IBM concluded that the incompatibility between its computers was limiting its options. IBM engineers developed plans for a full line of new computers that would be compatible with each other, but not with the existing machines. The goal was to create a standard architecture, software system, and peripheral interface to span the entire line, with prices ranging from a low-end $2,500 per month to a high-end $115,000 per month. A new family of peripheral devices was designed for attachment to any of the processors, providing far greater flexibility for customers and eliminating the need to design specific peripheral devices for each machine. The machines were designed with the same basic instruction set so that customers could use the same application software when they upgraded to a higher model processor. The System/360 was announced in 1964 and deliveries began in 1965.

The System/360 concept represented a major change from the early design goals of IBM and other computer producers. Rather than designing each piece of hardware to optimize its performance on a particular kind of problem, the designers accepted somewhat lower hardware performance in order to attain compatibility and conserve on the software and expertise required to use the computer. That evolution was attractive to customers because of the falling price of computer hardware relative to software and labor costs. The high price of early computers made it desirable to maximize the benefits of expensive computer hardware even despite incompatibility among various computers and high labor costs. The System/360 line abolished the earlier practice of designing separate computers for business and scientific use and substituted a more flexible design that could be used for either. It created a standardized interface for attaching peripheral devices (tape and disk drives, printers) to the CPU, allowing users to choose among the wide array of peripheral devices offered with the 360 line in order to customize their system to expected needs.

The technology of the System/360 was derived in part from an earlier very large-scale computer (the IBM 7030, also known as the STRETCH) that IBM had developed under contract for both the NSA and the Atomic Energy Commission (AEC). Both agencies demanded the most powerful computers possible, but the NSA's needs were similar to business users (analysis of large quantities of data) while the AEC's needs were similar to scientific users (rapid computation with high accuracy). IBM combined those two markets in the 7030, which was the world's most powerful computer when it was delivered in 1960. IBM also began producing its own components for the 7030 (after using outside suppliers for its vacuum tubes and early transistor computers) and continued that practice with the System/360, becoming one of the largest semiconductor producers in order to supply its own needs. IBM used an early form of integrated circuit for the System/360 that combined the characteristics of discrete components on a circuit board and later monolithic integrated circuits. According to Thomas Watson, Jr., IBM chose to produce its own circuits rather than rely on outside suppliers because it believed that much of the design function of a computer would eventually be contained in an integrated circuit and that it needed to supply the circuits in order to retain control of the computer design (Watson and Petre, 1990, p. 350).

One significant technical innovation in the System/360 was the use of microprogramming. A "machine language" command in the basic instruction set did not directly activate electronic circuitry as in earlier computers. Instead, the instruction was interpreted into more basic machine commands through a specialized microprogram that applications programmers could not access. Microprogramming reduced machine performance compared to direct execution of commands, but it provided improved compatibility. Different-size computers could use the same instruction set, allowing application programs to be moved among them without reprogramming, because the microprograms in each machine could interpret the same instruction into the different electronic circuitry of the various machines. Microprogramming also allowed the 360 computers to "emulate" earlier computers. The 360 was incompatible with IBM's earlier computers; with emulation, a microprogram would interpret the instruction set of another computer, allowing programs written for that computer to be run without change on the 360. Emulation was particularly important in providing an upgrade path from IBM's popular 1401 computer to the smaller 360 models (360/30 and 360/40) because it allowed those models to run 1401 programs much faster than the 1401 itself (Ceruzzi, 1998, pp. 145–150).

The System/360 was enormously popular from the time of announcement, with 1,100 orders in the first month and orders continuing at higher rates than IBM had expected. Even as delivery schedules slipped and the complex operating system software was delayed, the orders continued to pour in to IBM. The success of IBM's salesforce in promoting the virtues of the new line created a crisis within IBM as the company struggled to expand production and complete the promised software. Completion of the promised operating system was extremely difficult. By 1966 IBM had 2,000 people developing the operating system, and the final cost was $500 million, the largest single cost in the System/360 program (Watson and Petre, 1990, p. 353).

IBM overcame the initial problems and began a period of extraordinary growth based on the success of the System/360. IBM's revenue from all computer products and services increased from $1.5 billion in 1964 (the year of the System/360 announcement) to $4 billion in 1968 (Computer Industry Census, 1971). It maintained high steady profits despite rapid growth and conservative accounting, with an average after-tax return of 17.6 percent on stockholder equity between 1965 and 1968. The company's internal assessments showed that it had a market share of approximately 74 percent of "systems and peripherals" during the 1965–1968 time period while a computer industry census using a very broad definition of data processing revenue (including software companies and special purpose computers) showed IBM's market share rising from 41 percent in 1965 to 49 percent in 1968 (Brock, 1975, p. 21; Computer Industry Census, 1971).

The System/360 induced far more companies than before to install computers and thoroughly established IBM's position as the dominant general purpose computer company in the world. Other computer companies either sought compatibility with the System/360 standards (such as the RCA Spectra line) or focused on a particular area in which the general nature of the 360 computers left an opening: Control Data focused on supercomputers, General Electric on time-sharing, Digital Equipment on minicomputers. IBM's success also created concerns among foreign governments about its dominance. While several countries made important contributions to experimental computers, only the United States developed a substantial early commercial computer industry. According to one count, the United States had 5,400 electronic digital computers in use in 1960, seven times the combined total number of computers for the United Kingdom, France, West Germany, and Japan (Flamm, 1988, p. 135). As computers developed from experimental status to a critical component of business, science, and military operations, many countries became concerned about the dominance of the United States in general and IBM in particular. According to Kenneth Flamm, "Computers became a symbol of a perceived lag in national firms' ability to produce the technology-intensive goods at the leading edge of economic growth. IBM's announcement of the System 360 in 1964 was the symbolic act that roused governments to act, and in the middle years of the 1960s all foreign countries with significant computer industries promoted programs to stimulate their competitiveness" (1988, p. 133).

The European efforts to develop "national champion" computer firms to compete with IBM and other U.S. companies were not especially successful, but Japan did develop a strong computer industry. The strength of domestic computer industries was significant in later debates about liberalizing the telecommunication industry. Liberalizing essentially meant making the telecommunication industry more similar to the computer industry. In the United States early moves toward liberalization affected the boundary line between AT&T and IBM, both politically connected American firms with no presumption that one should be favored over the other. In countries already concerned with American dominance in computers, there was further concern that liberalizing telecommunication could subject another critical industry to American dominance. Those concerns were most thoroughly developed in an influential French analysis in the 1970s that proposed government monopoly telecommunication systems as a bulwark against IBM's increasing dominance of information technology (Noam, 1992, pp. 64, 65).

Alternatives to IBM Computers

While IBM's systems approach to marketing computer equipment and its System/360 series of computers established IBM's dominance of the computer market, it did not control all parts of the market. IBM's focus on compatibility and standardization among its computers of different sizes made it easy to retain customers as their needs changed but also imposed additional cost. For example, the "channels" that managed input and output functions allowed the attachment of a wide range of peripheral equipment to each model yet were more expensive than alternative architectures for the smaller models. Similarly, IBM's practice of providing extensive "free" service and software with its machines was an effective marketing technique for placing computers in companies with limited computer expertise, but it caused IBM's cost to be well above the cost of supplying the machines alone. IBM's full-service and compatibility strategy consequently left openings for companies to specialize in particular segments of the overall market that were not fully satisfied with IBM's approach. Moreover, IBM had no legal or regulatory privileges that allowed it to exclude other companies from the market. While many mainstream business people never seriously considered alternatives to IBM equipment (a common statement was "no one has ever been fired for buying IBM"), there were enough users with special needs to support multiple financially successful alternatives to IBM. The significance of the alternative approaches increased over time. As IBM's later upgrades maintained compatibility with the System/360 and continued to use major portions of the System/360 architecture, IBM eventually lost its dominance to products more closely aligned with new design concepts and technological opportunities.

In the early 1960s IBM's competitors were known as the "seven dwarfs" (Burroughs, Sperry Rand, NCR, Control Data, Honeywell, General Electric, and RCA). Except for Control Data, they generally followed a strategy similar to IBM with a series of computers, associated peripheral equipment, software, and services marketed to a wide range of potential users. Control Data concentrated on offering the most powerful computer possible to sophisticated scientific users (including the atomic weapons laboratories) who generally wrote their own software and needed little support from the company. It was successful in that specialty, and its 6600 and later 7600 easily outperformed any other computer in the world at the time of their introduction. After CDC's top designer, Seymour Cray, left in the 1970s to establish his own company, Cray Research took the lead in a supercomputer market of diminishing importance. The other dwarfs provided successful particular products and some competitive pressure on IBM, but were not able to develop a sustained profitable strategy and either left the computer business or developed a particular niche of the market.

The future structure of the computer industry was much more significantly influenced by the minicomputer segment of the market than by the strategy of the seven dwarfs. At first the minicomputer segment appeared to be a minor specialty area and was often not even included in analyses of the computer market, but the minicomputer producers created a competitive market with easy entry, rapid adoption of component innovations, and pricing based on the cost of each feature requested. The minicomputer approach provided a sharp contrast to IBM's strategy and eventually eroded IBM's control of the market.

The minicomputer segment of the computer market was pioneered by Digital Equipment Corporation (DEC) and further developed by many other companies. Kenneth Olsen helped develop core memory as part of the MIT Whirlwind project, learned computer manufacturing from IBM as a Lincoln Laboratory SAGE liaison, and supervised the development of the innovative 1957 transistor TX-0 computer at Lincoln Laboratory.

In 1957, Olsen and other members of the TX-0 team left Lincoln to establish DEC. The new company began with a $70,000 investment from American Research and Development Corporation, a venture capital firm established by Georges Doriot. General Doriot had been the director of U.S. Army research and development during World War II and was then a Harvard Business School professor who wanted to promote the commercial applications of technology developed for the military services (Ceruzzi, 1998, p. 127; Scherer, 1999, p. 73). DEC was profitable from the beginning, and after its initial public offering in 1966 it accounted for almost 75 percent of the value of the forty-five companies in American Research and Development's portfolio (Scherer, 1999, pp. 74, 75). DEC's extraordinary return on a small investment contributed to the rise of venture capital firms that specialized in financing technology entrepreneurs, an important institutional innovation that freed later firms from having to sell their intellectual property to large established firms.

DEC completed the PDP-1 in 1959, a commercial machine with many similarities to the Lincoln TX-0. The DEC machines were called programmed digital processors instead of computers in order to emphasize that they were different from the computer industry dominated by IBM and other large business machine companies. DEC sold its computers (in contrast to IBM's rental policy) and published detailed information about the computer (in contrast to IBM's proprietary control of information). The price of the PDP-1 and later DEC computers was far lower than the price of IBM machines with equivalent performance, but DEC provided only the computers rather than a complete system and support. The DEC computers consequently operated in a different market segment than IBM and were not directly competitive. Customers who wanted a complete solution to their computing needs (including most businesses in the era of limited computer experience and expertise) found IBM's bundled package attractive. Technically sophisticated customers (including companies that wanted to build computer processing into other products) found DEC's approach attractive with its a-la-carte pricing and detailed information that allowed them to pay for exactly what they needed and to customize the computer to their particular requirements. DEC emphasized low-cost operations—setting up its headquarters in an old wool mill, printing its technical manuals on newsprint, and providing few services to its customers.

The first PDP-1 went to the Cambridge, Massachusetts, consulting firm of Bolt Beranek and Newman (BBN) at the request of J. C. R. Licklider, who had learned to use the successor of the TX-0 while at Lincoln Laboratory and later played a key role in the early Internet. The PDP-1 allowed a programmer to interact directly with the computer, and the BBN installation received extensive experimental use:

> The presence of the PDP-1 and the work Licklider was doing with it attracted a number of leading computer scientists to BBN. The firm had also become well known as a place whose hiring philosophy was to recruit MIT dropouts. The idea was that if they could get into MIT they were smart, and if they dropped out, you could get them cheaper . . . People at BBN kept the computer going day and night doing interactive programming. They even built a time-sharing system around it, dividing the screen for four simultaneous users . . . The richly academic atmosphere at BBN earned the consulting firm a reputation as "the third university" in Cambridge. (Hafner and Lyon, 1996, pp. 85, 86)

The early BBN experience with the DEC PDP-1 was far removed from the typical business experience with an IBM computer. Instead of tightly controlled access and a structured system for producing regular reports needed by the company, the BBN computer was used for experimentation by a wide variety of people looking for interesting things that could be accomplished by the new machine. Rather than DEC providing software and training, the customer developed new applications for the machine. The BBN environment became a model for the later Internet approach of allowing many different users to contribute to the technology and gradually improve it.

DEC began deliveries of the PDP-8 in 1965, the same year that IBM began deliveries of the System/360. The PDP-8 was a fast, inexpensive small computer that introduced the age of personal computing and accelerated the use of computers as controllers in many different kinds of processes. It was initially sold for $18,000, less than one month's rental on most models of the IBM System/360. Fifty thousand PDP-8s were sold, five times the level of IBM's popular 1401 system. The PDP-8 had only a 12-bit word length in contrast to the 32-bit word length in the IBM System/360 series. The short word length made accurate computation and memory addressing difficult, but simplified the logic and reduced the cost.

DEC and its customers developed many innovative ways to effectively utilize the PDP-8 despite its limitations. The PDP-8 came with the then-new Teletype Corporation Model 33 as an input and output device, and could be used with an inexpensive small tape drive that used small reels of tape called DECtape. The Teletype 33 could send and receive data directly to and from the computer, it could print, and it could punch paper tape. It became the standard early terminal for direct interaction with computers before CRT terminals were common, and its keyboard layout and special characters influenced many later terminals (Ceruzzi, 1998, p. 133). The PDP-8 provided many computer experts with experience utilizing an inexpensive computer with limited capabilities. While the PDP-8 was difficult to program, it was frequently used with a single program as a special purpose computer incorporated into industrial control processes. A separate company would purchase the computers from DEC, provide the specialized programming and the other needed parts, and sell the assembly to a customer for a particular purpose. The PDP-8 was the inspiration for Intel's 1971 microprocessor that created a small general purpose machine as a substitute for specialized chip designs.

DEC also introduced the large PDP-10 in 1966, an important early time-sharing machine. IBM's System/360 was designed for batch processing rather than time-sharing. Time-sharing sought to provide direct user interaction with a large computer while not wasting expensive computer time in waiting for a user to type commands. Time-sharing required a complex operating system that could keep track of multiple jobs and shift computer resources to them as needed, and early developers encountered considerable difficulties in making time-sharing systems work well. Many universities installed DEC PDP-10s to allow students direct access to the computer through teletypes rather than indirect access by submitting decks of punched cards for input and receiving printed output at a later time. A number of companies also set up commercial time-sharing services by purchasing a PDP-10 and offering customers access for a fee. A vast number of students got their first introduction to computer programming on a PDP-10, including future Microsoft founders Bill Gates (then in the seventh grade) and Paul Allen (then in the ninth grade) when their school obtained a teletype connection to a PDP-10 in a commercial time-sharing service. After attempting to run programs that crashed the computer, the young computer enthusiasts were invited to help document bugs in the operating system in exchange for free computer time (Wallace and Erickson, 1992, pp. 20, 29).

DEC was not the only minicomputer company or time-sharing computer company. Other important early time-sharing computers were developed by General Electric and Scientific Data Systems. IBM added a time-sharing computer to the System/360 family and built time-sharing capability into its successor computers, but many academic and research institutions found the DEC and Scientific Data Systems machines better suited to their needs. After DEC engineer Edson DeCastro decided that DEC was moving too slowly in developing a 16-bit minicomputer, he and two others left the company to create Data General in 1968. Data General announced the Nova in 1968 and its upgrade, the Super Nova, in 1971. Both machines incorporated the latest semiconductor technology. The Nova was the first commercial computer to use "medium scale integration" integrated circuits with increased density. The Super Nova was the first commercial computer to use semiconductor memory in place of magnetic core memory. The extremely rapid progress in the highly competitive semiconductor industry allowed firms such as DEC and Data General access to more advanced components than those used by the vertically integrated IBM, with corresponding cost savings. One internal study at IBM in 1969 estimated that IBM's component technology lagged one to two years behind the open-market technology despite extensive research and large-scale production (Brock, 1975, p. 194). The inexpensive small computers using the latest component technology gradually expanded their share of the total computer market as users developed the necessary expertise and software to substitute for IBM's full-service approach, but they did not become a dominant force until they were connected into networks.

7

The Regulated Monopoly Telephone Industry

From 1920 through 1968 the integrated Bell System dominated the telephone industry with 85 percent of the telephones and the only long distance network. A large number of independent telephone companies provided local telephone service in small towns and rural areas and connected with the Bell long distance network to allow nationwide access to their subscribers. The independent telephone companies and the Bell System were cooperating geographical monopolies, not competitors. Each telephone company served a defined geographical area, and state regulatory commissions generally prohibited any other company from providing telephone service within that area. The Bell System had a complex corporate structure that included the corporate holding company AT&T, the interstate long distance provider AT&T Long Lines, the subsidiary Bell operating companies, the research arm Bell Telephone Laboratories, and the manufacturing subsidiary Western Electric.

The Bell operating companies were constituted as distinct companies within each state (such as the Indiana Bell Telephone Company and the Illinois Bell Telephone Company) and were regulated by the respective state utility commissions. AT&T Long Lines was regulated by the Federal Communications Commission, and Western Electric was an unregulated manufacturing company. However, the lines of regulatory authority were vague and overlapping. While Western Electric was unregulated, the prices charged for the equipment that Western Electric supplied to the Bell operating companies became regulated "cost" to the operating company, and consequently the regulators had an interest in the reasonableness of the Western Electric prices. The operating companies used radio licenses for part of their operations, and radio was licensed at the federal level. Furthermore, the interstate revenue was

112

shared with the operating companies through a complex process of sep-arations and settlements that assigned a portion of the operating com-pany cost to the interstate jurisdiction and therefore brought the operat-ing companies under federal as well as state regulation.

The various regulatory authorities generally followed a "rate of re-turn" or "cost-plus" form of regulation. The essence of that regulation was the determination that total revenue was equal to the cost of provid-ing service, including a "reasonable" return on invested capital. Cost was measured by the accounting cost of actual expenditures, not by a benchmark measure of the expected cost to provide service given the current technology and efficient techniques. Because telephone service was capital-intensive, a substantial part of the total cost was directly re-lated to capital equipment: depreciation, maintenance, and return on capital. Consequently, an increase in capital required to provide tele-phone service generally translated into higher prices, which in turn caused regulators to be skeptical of new capital installed. Regulators generally had oversight authority regarding major investment plans and were obligated to allow adequate rates to cover the capital expenses once they were authorized.

Considerable concern was also expressed about potential duplication of capacity, excess investment, and retirement of plant while it was still capable of providing service. Hence the safe course through the regu-latory process was to follow a conservative investment strategy, only building when demand was clearly available to justify the new facilities. The regulatory structure was designed for a stable capital-intensive busi-ness with little, if any, concern for promoting technological progress. There was an implicit presumption that substantial economies of scale existed, and therefore that the most efficient operation would occur with a single company while duplicate companies risked the possibility of ex-cess authorized investment with the accompanying increase in revenue requirements.

At the beginning of the computer era, AT&T and IBM were the mas-ters of electromechanical relay technology for telephone switching (AT&T) and punch-card accounting (IBM). Both built experimental electrical relay computers and initially advocated the slower but reliable and mature relay technology over the faster but unreliable and new elec-tronic computer technology. IBM transformed itself in the early 1950s by creating new laboratories and developing a frequently upgraded series of electronic computers. In contrast, AT&T did not undertake any major transformation in the postwar period. It grew rapidly and updated its production technology, but it remained essentially the same company with the same standardized products and operating procedures.

AT&T and its regulators viewed telephone service as a unique market with specialized equipment requirements that were best provided by its manufacturing subsidiary Western Electric, rather than viewing telephone equipment as one part of the rapidly changing electrical and electronic equipment market. AT&T was not required to adopt new technology in order to protect existing markets, nor did it attempt to enter new markets except to supply specialized military needs. It developed the transistor as a research project to supply long distance service without operator intervention and produced an early experimental transistor computer, but did not attempt to develop a strong commercial position in either the semiconductor or computer industries. The incentives for AT&T and for IBM to implement new technologies were very different. IBM could undertake risky projects and enjoy a high return if they were successful, or it could follow a conservative strategy and risk losing its position in the market to a more innovative firm. Either approach to technology carried risks for the firm. If AT&T failed to implement new technologies, its core market position was protected through regulation and network interconnection effects. If it undertook risky projects, it would receive criticism from regulatory authorities for failures (for increased cost of new technology or especially for service failures due to new technology), but could not receive financial rewards for success.

AT&T established a conservative engineering approach to managing telephone service. The company performed innovative research in Bell Labs and frequently advertised its research accomplishments, but only incorporated new products into the network after exhaustive testing. Moreover, it used severe reliability and longevity standards as benchmarks for evaluating new products. For example, central office switches were designed to have only two hours of downtime over a forty-year period (Bell Laboratories, 1982, p. 425). While such reliability and longevity were impressive accomplishments that kept some telephone switches in service for over half a century, the Bell System standards slowed the utilization of new opportunities created by advances in semiconductors and computers.

Local residential service was generally provided on a flat-rate basis with a fixed monthly fee and no additional charges for conversations. The flat-rate price structure was first used to avoid the high cost of manually recording and charging individual calls, but it became a politically popular rate structure protected by the state regulatory commissions. Toll calls included both short calls handled by the local operating company that went outside the "local calling area" to an adjacent town and long calls that were passed to AT&T's toll network. By 1950 telephone users (including both business and residential) averaged just under four local calls per day and about one toll call per week.

Telephone prices remained very stable throughout the 1950–1968 period. The average base rate for a residential access line increased from $4.29 in 1950 to $5.61 in 1968. The AT&T toll rate for a ten-minute two-hundred-mile daytime call remained constant at $2.20 from 1943 through 1969, while the toll rate for a short call increased and the rate for a ten-minute nationwide call dropped slightly from $6.70 to $4.90 (FCC, 1999a, pp. 95, 96). The telephone service component in the consumer price index increased by 15 percent between 1950 and 1968 while the overall consumer price index increased by 44 percent, leaving a 20 percent decline in real telephone prices after adjusting for inflation. The index of local telephone service prices rose by 23 percent over the period while the index of toll prices remained almost constant (FCC, 1999a, pp. 97, 98).

The percentage of U.S. households with telephone service increased from 61.8 percent to 88.5 percent between 1950 and 1968 while the average daily conversations increased from 171 million to 427 million, a compound annual growth rate of 5.1 percent (U.S. Census, 1975, p. 783). The book cost of telephone plant (original cost of equipment) rose from $10.7 billion in 1950 to $48.9 billion in 1968 (FCC, 1974, p. 14), a compound annual growth rate of 8.4 percent. During the same period, local service revenue rose from $2.1 billion to $7.7 billion while toll service revenue rose from $1.2 billion to $6.8 billion (FCC, 1974, p. 14), a compound annual growth rate of 7.2 percent for local service and 9.6 percent for toll service. The book cost of telephone plant was 3.2 times total service revenue (toll plus local) in 1950 and 3.4 times total service revenue in 1968.

The number of telephone operating company employees increased from 565,000 to 734,000 between 1950 and 1968, a 1.5 percent annual rate. The number of telephones per employee increased from 68 to 130, while the book cost of plant per telephone increased from $270 to $508. After adjusting for inflation, the constant-dollar book cost of plant per telephone increased by 25 percent over the period, a modest shift toward more capital-intensive production of telephone service. A 1971 classification of the telephone operating company labor force showed that it was dominated by construction, installation, and maintenance employees (32 percent), telephone operators (24 percent), and clerical employees (22 percent), with professional and semiprofessional employees only constituting 11 percent of the labor force (FCC, 1974, p. 17). The employee numbers do not include employees of Western Electric or Bell Labs.

Antitrust and the 1956 Consent Decree

The U.S. Department of Justice (DOJ) filed a Sherman Act antitrust suit against AT&T and Western Electric in January 1949 charging Western Electric and AT&T with a conspiracy to restrain trade and charging Western Electric with monopolizing the market for telephones and related equipment. The government asked for an end to AT&T's ownership of Western Electric, the dissolution of Western Electric into three companies, and an end to all restrictive agreements among AT&T, the Bell operating companies, and Western Electric. According to the DOJ, the contracts among the various units of AT&T constituted a price-fixing conspiracy and an aid to Western Electric's monopolization of the telephone equipment market. The antitrust suit sought to separate regulated telephone service from the unregulated supply of telephone equipment as had already been imposed in electric utilities. The FCC had examined that question earlier and had rejected the recommendation of its staff that it propose legislation to require separation of the telephone equipment and service markets. After the FCC rejected the staff recommendation, one of the senior staff members moved to the DOJ and became the lead attorney in the DOJ case that sought to implement the FCC staff recommendation through antitrust action.

AT&T responded that the unified operation of research and development, manufacturing, and provision of service was necessary for effective telephone service. The company denied that a market for telephone equipment existed and therefore Western Electric could not monopolize that market. According to AT&T, Western Electric was the "supply arm" of regulated telephone service and was indirectly regulated through the ability of regulatory commissions to challenge Western Electric prices, in contrast to the DOJ view of Western Electric as an unregulated monopolist of the telephone equipment market.

Soon after the suit was filed, the U.S. government asked AT&T to take over management of the production of atomic weapons at Sandia Laboratories. The beginning of the Korean War in June 1950 intensified AT&T's defense responsibilities. After AT&T informed the Department of Defense that its efforts to defend itself against the antitrust suit would detract from its military commitments, the Secretary of Defense requested that the Attorney General postpone the case for the duration of the Korean War. After the Eisenhower administration took office in January 1953, AT&T successfully sought Department of Defense support for dismissing the suit. The Secretary of Defense wrote to the Attorney General:

> Currently, Western has orders for equipment and systems for the armed services totaling over $1 billion . . . The pending antitrust case seriously threatens the continuation of the important work which the Bell System is now carrying forward in the interests of national defense. This is for the reason that the severance of Western Electric from the system would effectively disintegrate the coordinated organization which is fundamental to the successful carrying forward of these critical defense projects, and it appears could virtually destroy its usefulness for the future . . . It is therefore respectfully urged that the Department of Justice review this situation with a view of making suggestions as to how this potential hazard to national security can be removed or alleviated. (U.S. Congress, 1958, pp. 2029–2031)

The Attorney General refused to dismiss the suit but agreed to settle it with restrictions that did not hamper AT&T's established business practices. According to the account of AT&T's general counsel regarding his private meeting with the Attorney General:

> I then made a number of statements about the injury the case threatened to our efficiency and progress as a communications company and to our contribution to the national defense, [and] told him . . . that we were hopeful that he would see his way clear to have the case dropped . . . He asked me whether, if we reviewed our practices, we would be able to find things we are doing which were once considered entirely

legal, but might now be in violation of the antitrust laws or question-
able in that respect . . . [H]e thought that we could readily find practices that we might agree to have enjoined with no real injury to our
business . . . [He said] it was important to get this case disposed of. He
said the President would understand this also and that if a settlement
was worked out he could get the President's approval in 5 minutes.
(U.S. Congress, 1958, pp. 1953–1955)

Following the Attorney General's suggestion, AT&T and the DOJ began
negotiations that led to the consent decree of 1956. The consent decree
allowed the existing arrangements among the various companies of the
Bell System to continue but restricted the scope of the Bell System to regulated activities and required liberal licensing of Bell System patents.

AT&T was "enjoined and restrained from engaging, either directly, or
indirectly through its subsidiaries other than Western and Western's
subsidiaries, in any business other than the furnishing of common carrier communications services" with minor specified exceptions. Similarly, Western Electric was "enjoined and restrained from engaging, either directly or indirectly, in any business not of a character or type
engaged in by Western or its subsidiaries for Companies of the Bell System" with certain exceptions, including the right to make any equipment for the U.S. government. The restrictions confined AT&T to regulated services and Western Electric to making equipment for those
regulated services, producing a closer tie between AT&T and the regulatory authorities than had previously existed. AT&T's conception of
Western Electric as a captive supply arm of a regulated utility rather
than a general manufacturing company that monopolized the telephone
equipment market was endorsed by allowing the continuation of
AT&T's ownership of Western Electric, but restricting Western Electric
to producing the type of equipment used by Bell operating companies.

The decree also required AT&T to license all of its patents at a "reasonable royalty" (with provisions for the court to set the royalty if the
parties could not agree) and to provide technical information along with
patent licenses on payment of reasonable fees. AT&T patents that had
been included in a cross-licensing agreement among AT&T, General
Electric, RCA, and Westinghouse were required to be issued royalty-
free to anyone except the parties to the cross-licensing agreement. That
cross-licensing agreement had been used to create product boundaries
and avoid direct competition among the parties and had previously

come under antitrust attack. The licensing provisions were in accord with the conception of the Bell System as a regulated monopoly rather than a market-controlled company. Within the regulated arena, the regulators controlled entry "in the public interest" and thus there was no need for patent protection against competition. Because, according to the consent decree, Bell could not enter unregulated businesses, compulsory licensing of the patents was a method of making the technology available to industries outside of the scope of regulation.

The most significant AT&T patents at the time were those related to transistors, including the original patents and patents on improvements and manufacturing processes. AT&T was already licensing the transistor patents at the time of the decree, but licensees had no guaranteed right to continue in the transistor business or to obtain Bell System technical information. Transistor licenses were issued for four years with a right for either party to terminate the license with one year's notice after the initial period. Bell provided technical information to licensees but did not give them a legal right to obtain the information. After the consent decree, transistor licenses were granted royalty-free under the patents existing at the time of the judgment and at a royalty rate of 2.5 percent of the selling price for transistors using patents issued after the date of the decree. The royalty was reduced or eliminated if the licensee controlled patents that it licensed back to Bell. Licensees were guaranteed the right to technical information for a specified set of fees. The most significant change in the transistor patent licenses was the grant of a legal right to participate in the transistor business on a continuing basis. The post-decree schedule of payments was a modest modification of the pre-decree schedule, but the post-decree licensees could make long-term research and investment decisions without concern that a change in Bell System licensing policy would eliminate the value of those investments. (Sample transistor licensing agreements are reprinted in U.S. Congress, 1958, pp. 3261–3344.)

The 1956 consent decree marked an important change in the Bell System strategy. During its first eighty years, the Bell System used patents to establish the monopoly, prevent entry, and establish industry boundaries. The consent decree's restriction of AT&T to regulated activities essentially accepted the company's position that regulation was a substitute for antitrust. AT&T gave up the ability to protect its market power through patents and entry into other markets but gained the freedom to continue operating as a dominant integrated firm in the regulated markets. It thus became dependent on regulatory decisions for protection from competitors and for the scope of its activities.

AT&T's decision to accept the consent decree rather than risk the divestiture of Western Electric from the operating companies was also a commitment to "old technology" rather than "new technology." AT&T abandoned the right to fully participate in the new computer and semiconductor industries and chose instead to strengthen its control of the telephone market based on electromechanical technologies. AT&T continued to develop computer and other electronic technologies through Bell Labs and Western Electric but with a focus on the specialized needs of the telephone business. A sharp distinction developed between the kinds of electronic equipment utilized in central office switching and the kinds of equipment developed and sold on the open market. The telephone business was far larger than the computer business in 1956 and it had many specialized needs, but the DOJ-AT&T choice to use the regulatory boundary as a corporate boundary prevented AT&T's management decisions from being tested in the open market. Within the regulatory boundary, AT&T had a monopoly and outside the regulatory boundary AT&T was prohibited from operating. Thus there was little incentive for either AT&T or other firms to develop the equipment and operational procedures necessary to utilize more general computers for telephone switching, and the telephone technological trajectory became separated from the unregulated electronics and computer technological improvements.

Microwave Technology and Potential
Long Distance Competition

Long distance telephone service remained an effective AT&T monopoly from the earliest days of the Bell patent monopoly through the 1950s. As early as the 1878 patent negotiations with Western Union over the conflicting patent claims, Bell manager Theodore Vail recognized the potential competitive importance of control over long distance lines. Vail refused Western Union's request to settle the outstanding disputes by assigning local rights to Bell and long distance rights to Western Union, even though long distance telephone service was not technically feasible at that time. Vail also reserved long distance rights to the parent company when licensing local operating franchises under the patent monopoly. During the competitive era (1894–1907), the inability of the independent telephone companies to develop an effective competitor to Bell's established long distance network left them limited to local service. The Kingsbury Commitment of 1913 allowed all companies to interconnect with the Bell long distance network and eliminated efforts to develop a competitive network.

Despite the effective Bell monopoly, no formal government policy either in favor of monopoly or against monopoly in long distance service was adopted. The Bell monopoly was implicitly endorsed by the many different policy actions related to long distance that never sought to eliminate the long distance monopoly. The antitrust action settled by the Kingsbury Commitment sought interconnection rights but not a competitive network. The state regulatory commissions sought a portion of the long distance revenues for the local companies, but accepted the existing market structure. The Communications Act of 1934 prescribed regulation for "every common carrier engaged in interstate or foreign communication by wire or radio" but provided no explicit discussion of the desired market structure. The early FCC accepted the existing monopoly without either formally endorsing monopoly as in the public interest or making any effort to create competition.

The simultaneous development of television and microwave transmission technology in the years immediately following World War II provided a potential competitive threat to AT&T's control of long distance transmission services. During the 1930s AT&T had developed patent and business agreements with RCA, GE, and Westinghouse in which AT&T provided all transmission of radio network programs among broadcast affiliates but agreed not to provide radio broadcasting services or radio receiving sets. Those companies expected the same arrangements to continue when television broadcasting became commercially viable. Experimental television broadcasts were provided during the late 1930s, but efforts to develop commercial television were halted during World War II and resumed at the war's end. Television transmission requires far higher capacity than radio transmission, and television programs could not be transmitted among network affiliates using AT&T's prewar long distance facilities. AT&T had planned a major expansion of network capacity using coaxial cables that would be capable of carrying television signals or many simultaneous telephone conversations.

The massive wartime radar research advanced technologies that could be utilized to provide a microwave radio-based alternative to AT&T's planned coaxial cable network for transmitting video signals. Microwave radio was capable of transmitting the high bandwidth necessary for video signals, and much of the technology was in the public domain as a result of government radar development and the extensive publications issued by MIT's Radiation Laboratory. Microwave radio transmission could be implemented with line-of-sight relay towers spaced twenty to thirty miles apart, eliminating the requirement for a continuous right-of-way and facilitating new entry. However, microwave required frequency allocations from the Federal Communications Commission. The FCC freely granted experimental licenses for the required frequencies, but deferred the question of permanent licenses and operating rights until the technology was more fully developed. Philco achieved the first operational domestic microwave link when it completed a Washington-Philadelphia line in the spring of 1945. Western Union opened a Philadelphia-New York line soon afterward as the first step in a planned nationwide network. Raytheon also planned an extensive network for television transmission while IBM and General Electric planned a microwave business data transmission network.

Bell Labs had earlier built an experimental microwave communications system capable of carrying eight simultaneous conversations. The system was used to create telephone links across the Rhine River during the invasion of Germany in early 1945 and was adapted for commercial use in 1946 to provide service between Los Angeles and Santa Catalina Island, but it did not have enough capacity to carry a television channel. At the end of the war Bell Labs initiated a high-priority project to develop a microwave system capable of transmitting television channels. In late 1947, the experimental multihop wideband system known as the TD-X was completed between New York and Boston. It was first used for free experimental transmission of television programs and put into regular tariffed service in May 1948. The TD-X system used klystrons to generate and amplify the signals in the 4-GHz band. Information was carried through frequency modulation on a bandwidth of four megacycles, allowing the transmission of a television program or 480 simultaneous telephone conversations.

While the TD-X system was under development, AT&T initiated an ambitious research project to develop a coast-to-coast microwave relay system. The TD-X system could not be simply extended with multiple towers because the klystron tubes created distortion that was amplified over the many relay stations required for a nationwide network. In order to generate the required frequencies with acceptable distortion, Bell chose a new vacuum-tube triode then under development at Bell Labs that required extraordinarily precise spacing. The new "TD-2" system was completed between New York and Chicago in June of 1950 and extended to San Francisco in September 1951 in time to allow the nationwide transmission of President Truman's opening address to the Japanese Peace Treaty Conference (Scherer, 1960).

AT&T successfully used a combination of its own development of the microwave technology and restrictive FCC spectrum licensing policies to protect itself against the developing competitive threat from microwave. AT&T argued that the microwave frequencies should be reserved to common carriers and that the noncommunications companies that had received experimental licenses should not be eligible for permanent licenses. The FCC adopted AT&T's position and restricted microwave licenses to common carriers in its 1948 microwave licensing decision. At that time, AT&T still lacked the necessary facilities to provide television network transmission among all requesting broadcast stations. Consequently, the television networks were authorized to build temporary microwave networks to meet their own needs but were required to abandon their private facilities when common carrier facilities became available (Beelar, 1967, pp. 29–32).

AT&T's 1948 video transmission tariff included a strict noninterconnection policy that prohibited both direct physical connection of facilities and anything that created the equivalent of interconnection such as receipt of a program in the studio over Bell lines and filming it from a television monitor for retransmission over non-Bell lines. AT&T testified that it intended to create a monopoly and that "competition with the Telephone Company in the intercity video field is not in the public interest" (FCC, 1949, p. 13). When AT&T refused to deliver a program to NBC in New York because NBC planned to transmit the program to Philadelphia using Philco facilities, Philco filed suit against AT&T. The court deferred to the FCC, saying that in order for the court to have jurisdiction, "there must be some vice in the regulation other than unfairness, unreasonableness or discrimination," which were issues properly left to the FCC (U.S. District Court (E.D., Pa.), 1948, p. 397).

After a twenty-month FCC investigation of the AT&T interconnection prohibition, the FCC concluded that interconnection should be required with the temporary broadcast company systems but not with common carriers (FCC, 1949). Thus the private systems were allowed interconnection but denied permanent operating licenses while common carrier systems were allowed permanent operating licenses but denied interconnection rights. The FCC's restrictive licensing decision of 1948 and decision in 1949 not to require interconnection with permanent facilities effectively ended the development of competition in video transmission services. AT&T expanded its previous monopoly of voice transmission and radio broadcast network transmission to include video broadcast network transmission and established control of microwave transmission technology.

While the FCC prohibited microwave competition with AT&T, some private microwave systems continued in locations where AT&T did not build adequate facilities. AT&T's tariff structure during the 1950s caused users with a high volume of communication among a few locations to pay far more than the cost of self-supply of that service through microwave. Several large companies (including both potential users and equipment supplier Motorola) pressed the FCC for broader authorization of microwave systems. AT&T argued that private microwave should be limited to areas where common carrier facilities were not available and should be abandoned when common carrier service became available. They argued that frequencies were scarce and could be most efficiently used by common carriers. The Electronic Industries Association (representing microwave manufacturers) presented a very detailed engineering study to the FCC that indicated an opportunity for a twentyfold increase in the then-current number of microwave stations without interference even in the most congested areas. In 1959, the FCC concluded that adequate frequencies were available for both common carrier and private microwave systems and that therefore private systems should be licensed, a decision known as "Above 890" because it was concerned with allocations of frequencies higher than 890 MHz (above the frequencies allocated to UHF television).

The Above 890 decision did not authorize new companies to enter the communication business in competition with AT&T but only allowed individual users to build systems for their own use. The case was decided as a frequency allocation issue and not as a matter of competitive policy. In frequency allocation questions the key factual issue is the availability of frequencies. Because the data showed that adequate frequencies were available, the FCC granted increased license rights but did not formally consider the question of how that might affect long distance service.

AT&T responded to the decision allowing private microwave systems by filing a new price structure (known as the Telpak tariff) that largely eliminated the incentive for any company to build a private system where AT&T facilities were available. The new price structure replaced the previous flat-rate structure (where multiple private lines were charged by simply multiplying the number of lines times the rate per line) with extensive volume discounts reaching up to 85 percent for bundles of 240 lines. For a set of 240 lines over a distance of one hundred miles a customer would have paid $75,600 per month under the old rates and $11,700 per month under the new rates. The old rates were four times Motorola's estimate of the cost of a comparable private system, while the new rates were 30 percent below that cost estimate (Brock, 1981, pp. 202–210).

AT&T's volume discounts for private lines increased the incentive to use private lines over switched services. Many large companies established systems of private lines as a replacement for switched voice service. The largest of these new systems was the federal government's Federal Telecommunications System (FTS), which established an extensive system of private lines connected by switches to provide the equivalent of switched long distance service communication among government agencies. The very low prices for bulk private lines compared to either individual private lines or switched service encouraged large organizations to develop sophisticated internal communications systems. Initially those systems were primarily voice, but were later developed as data communications systems as well.

While many companies that had considered utilizing private microwave were pleased to take service from AT&T under its discounted Telpak tariff as a substitute, the equipment manufacturers viewed the price response as AT&T's method of reversing their victory in obtaining spectrum for private microwave systems. The equipment manufacturers protested AT&T's volume discounts on private lines before the FCC. The FCC had not previously been required to make detailed cost allocation judgments or to evaluate the rate structure in detail; thus it did not have the staff expertise and operating procedures to evaluate the competing claims. Because of the FCC's inability to fully resolve the issues, AT&T's right to have its tariff go into effect unless found unlawful prevailed initially and the rates became widely utilized. The FCC's investigation of the Telpak rates bogged down into an extraordinarily complex and lengthy proceeding that extended almost twenty years after the authorization of private microwave systems. The extended proceedings favored AT&T because it was allowed to implement the tariff and slow the spread of private microwave for many years before the FCC found the rates illegal. However, the FCC's inability to make a decision also encouraged the Department of Justice to look more closely at the competitive problems of the industry rather than deferring to an apparently inept FCC that lost credibility as the "expert agency" managing telecommunication policy.

Throughout the 1950–1968 period, AT&T continued its control of long distance services and strengthened that control through the addition of video network transmission services and the decline of Western Union's telegraph service as an alternative to long distance voice communication. AT&T successfully defended its position against potential new microwave entrants through the 1948 FCC restrictive licensing policy, utilizing its freedom to refuse interconnection to exploit the advantages of being the largest carrier in a network industry, and the Telpak volume-discounted prices to reduce the incentive to build private microwave systems after the licensing restrictions were relaxed.

AT&T continued to expand its long distance capacity through a combination of microwave (60 percent of channel mileage by the early 1970s) and coaxial cable, together with some use of older technologies such as open-wire and cable-pair systems on low-density routes. The capacity of a coaxial cable pair was increased from 600 voice conversations in 1946 with repeaters spaced every eight miles to 3,600 voice conversations in 1967 with repeaters spaced every two miles as improved electronics allowed the use of higher frequencies. Similar but less dramatic improvements were made in microwave relay systems (Bell Laboratories, 1977, pp. 327–340). Microwave radio was the lowest cost technology for moderate densities but the increasing capacity of coaxial cable and the ability to place multiple coaxial cable pairs in the same conduit made coaxial cable the cheapest technology for very high-density routes. Coaxial cable's apparent economies of scale also supported Bell's argument that long distance service was a natural monopoly that could be most efficiently provided by a single carrier.

Central Office Switches

The essential structure of the local network was a twisted pair of copper wires that connected the customer's telephone instrument to the telephone company's central office switch. Calls that did not originate and terminate at the same central office required connection to an outgoing trunk line that led to the terminating office. In 1950, many of the central offices in smaller communities consisted of manual switchboards. For lines connected to those offices, the customer gave the operator the name or number of the desired party and the operator connected the incoming and outgoing lines by plugging in a cord.

Most customers were served by central offices that contained step-by-step switches. The step-by-step system was invented in 1889 and utilized in many independent telephone companies before the Bell System began using it in 1919. The switch was a "direct progressive control system" in which each digit dialed by the customer creates physical movement of a contact through the switching system. There was no standard dialing sequence; the number of digits varied by the size of the community. Thus for a community served by a switch of 1,000-lines capacity, there would be a three-digit sequence, and each digit would cause the switch mechanism to move toward the outgoing line. It was a simple and extremely reliable switch designed for small and moderate-size offices. For the largest offices in major cities, the Bell System installed another type of electromechanical switch (the Panel Switching System) that was easier to expand to large groups of lines (Bell Laboratories, 1977, pp. 236–238).

Step-by-step switches helped shape the telephone company response to the new opportunities created by the rapid decline in the cost of computers and electronic components. The reliable long-lasting switches provided economical basic telephone service, but with little flexibility to add new features. They required a rigid numbering system that associated each number with a physical wire and each office with a particular prefix, making geographical number portability impossible. The Bell

System continued to develop its expertise at refining electromechanical relay systems rather than moving quickly toward electronic computer switching. Furthermore, state regulatory commissions discouraged the replacement of step-by-step systems with more expensive electronic switches that could provide new services. Step-by-step switches served a peak of 24.4 million Bell System lines in 1973, fifty-four years after the Bell System began using them. At that time more Bell System lines were served by step-by-step switches than any other type of switch (Bell Laboratories, 1982, p. 34). At the beginning of 1976 there were 6,060 step-by-step systems in place compared with 2,700 of the next most popular switch (No. 5 crossbar), but the higher average size of the crossbar systems meant that they served slightly more total lines (Bell Laboratories, 1977, p. 234). While the total number of lines served by step-by-step systems declined during the late 1970s as central offices were upgraded to more modern switches, the systems remained an important part of the telephone network until the late 1980s when many were replaced by digital switches without going through the intermediate generations of switch technology.

The persistence of step-by-step technology through most of the twentieth century severely limited the flexibility of telephone engineers in designing new approaches to telephone transmission. New approaches were designed to be compatible with all of the switches in the network, and thus there was a process of incremental improvements to a very old model of telephone calling. It was not possible to follow IBM's approach of the early 1960s in designing a complete new family of computers without regard for compatibility with old models. IBM undertook business risk by the noncompatibility strategy (mitigated by the production of emulators that allowed the System/360 computers to run programs designed for earlier machines), but faced no legal or regulatory barriers to its strategy. There is no evidence that AT&T had any interest in making a wholesale replacement of its old technology, but the state regulators would not have allowed it to do so if it had tried.

At the end of World War II automatic switching of local calls was common on step-by-step and panel switches, but long distance switching was performed at manual toll switchboards. A customer dialed a long distance code to connect to the toll office and then multiple operators would participate in setting up the call, one for each toll-switching center through which it passed. The first step in automating that process was to introduce "operator dialed" toll calls in which the initial toll operator set up the call by dialing rather than speaking to other operators.

Operator dialing (and later customer dialing) required a standardized numbering plan. An AT&T task force created the plan of using three-digit area codes and seven-digit numbers within area codes that remains the standard addressing method in the United States and Canada. The initial proposal included seventy-eight U.S. and eight Canadian area codes, most of which covered an entire U.S. state or Canadian province. The transition to standardized all-digit dialing was slow (extending from the initial area code plan in the 1940s to 1979) and was accompanied by considerable political controversy as subscribers objected to dialing a larger number of digits and to having favorite office names replaced by numbers. The transition also required extensive technical adjustment to the many different kinds of dial equipment in use. In particular, the many step-by-step offices could not accept ten-digit numbers. That problem was solved by modest modifications to the older offices and the introduction of a "1" before a toll call to indicate that the call should be passed to the toll office (with either an operator or a more sophisticated switch) rather than being processed by the originating step-by-step office (Bell Laboratories, 1982, pp. 122–125, 177).

AT&T's first major upgrade to step-by-step switching systems was the No. 1 crossbar. The crossbar switch was an electromechanical switch, but separated the control function from the actual switching function. That separation allowed more flexibility in adding features to the system as well as increasing the efficiency of control functions that could be used during the call setup process and then released during the duration of the call. The crossbar development began in 1934 with the first installation in 1938 and gradually increased to peak service in 1970 (Bell Laboratories, 1982, p. 73). The No. 1 crossbar system was primarily used in large cities for both central office and tandem switching. A modified version (the No. 2 crossbar) was developed in 1940 for smaller offices but was abandoned after it turned out to be more expensive than step-by-step switches for those offices. However, AT&T's continued desire to develop a successor to the step-by-step switch led to the successful No. 5 crossbar switch, first installed in 1948. The No. 5 crossbar contained more complex electrical relay circuits than previous switches and was designed to accommodate longer dialing sequences in preparation for interstate dialed service. The complex No. 5 crossbar was initially more expensive than the step-by-step system it replaced, creating resistance to implementation. The AT&T official history states:

> Like most new switching systems the initial installed price was higher than expected. Within the first four years a considerable joint effort of Western Electric and Bell Laboratories greatly reduced the price difference between No. 5 crossbar and the step-by-step system . . . Training proved somewhat of a stumbling block, since a more complex system was being introduced into areas that to that time had been exposed only to the simplicity of the step-by-step system. As a result, Bell Laboratories, for the first time, organized and provided instructors for a school for telephone company instructors. New documentation was devised to simplify the understanding of the complex circuits. (Bell Laboratories, 1982, pp. 166, 167)

New No. 5 crossbar switches were installed between 1948 and 1976 (Bell Laboratories, 1982, p. 169), a twenty-eight-year period that contrasts with the typical four-to-five-year period of installing new computers of a particular type during that time. While new electromechanical No. 5 crossbar switches were being installed, computer technology progressed from the experimental precommercial period through vacuum tube, transistor, and integrated circuit generations.

Bell System engineers began a research program on electronic switching in the immediate postwar period but did not begin formal development of a central office electronic switch until 1958. The design of the first central office electronic switch (the No. 1 ESS) was completed in 1962, and general installation of the switch began in 1967 after exhaustive testing in the laboratory and field trials (Bell Laboratories, 1982, pp. 260–261). The No. 1 ESS followed the crossbar switch distinction of separating control functions from the actual switching of calls. Control functions were performed by a special purpose stored-program computer, using a special memory designed at Bell Labs rather than the standard computer core memory. The program (known as a "generic") contained a number of variations in order to provide special features at some offices and not at others.

The actual switching of telephone calls in the No. 1 ESS was performed by a nonelectronic "ferreed switch." Bell had begun development of electronic switching, but had encountered difficulty because of the compatibility requirements with many older standards developed for the electromechanical era:

One of the major limitations in electronic network elements had been their inability to directly handle some of the conventional telephone signaling and test voltages and/or currents. For example, in crossbar switching systems a telephone is rung by connecting its loop through the switching network to a ringing generator. The ringing signal required to operate the bell is nominally 86 volts r.m.s. at 20 hertz superimposed on 48 volts dc. To collect or return coins, a 130-volt dc signal is sent through the network to coin telephones. Test circuits also require electrically transparent dc connections through the switching network to the customer's loop. (Bell Laboratories, 1982, pp. 244, 245)

While it would have been possible to facilitate true electronic switching by designing a new line of telephone instruments, Bell resisted any plan that would require new telephone instruments in order to avoid the one-time costs. No single-switch proposal justified the cost of changing telephone sets:

[Solving the voltage problem by] changing the station sets . . . has been explored several times. A low-level ac signal from the central office may be amplified at the station with dc loop power to generate an audible tone. Although such stations may be only slightly more expensive than existing ones, the total expense for a changeover would be substantial. A cutover strategy would be required that would assure continuity of service, and each station would require at least one field visit.

The new line of equipment would also complicate Western Electric manufacture, stocking, and repair operation . . . So far, no new switching system has been able to justify the massive turnover of station equipment necessary to avoid high-power alerting. (Bell Laboratories, 1977, pp. 457, 458)

The ferreed switch consisted of small reed switches arranged in matrices with control wiring that was operated electronically, but "provided metallic contacts which could handle the wide range of existing signaling and test voltages and currents without special circuitry" (Bell Laboratories, 1982, pp. 245, 246). Thus the switch itself continued to provide the original function of a patch cord in creating a complete electrical circuit between the originating and terminating telephone, while the control function utilized a stored-program electronic computer. The No. 1 ESS was gradually modified to increase its capacity and flexibility and to move it closer to mainstream computing technology. The special memory was replaced by standard magnetic core memory in 1971 (about the time commercial computers were abandoning magnetic core for semiconductor memory), and magnetic core memories began to be replaced by semiconductor memory in 1977 (Bell Laboratories, 1982, p. 295).

Terminal Equipment

Terminal equipment, also known as customer premises equipment (CPE), translates between voice or data and the electrical signals that transmit information between the user and the central office switch. It is distinguished from other parts of the telephone network by being dedicated to a single customer while the other network components are shared. Terminal equipment can be simple (an individual telephone or modem) or complex (a large PBX serving many extension telephones). The telephone companies considered terminal equipment an intrinsic part of the network under the ownership and control of the telephone company with strict limitations on the rights of subscribers to use the equipment in any way inconsistent with telephone company expectations.

Early telephone instruments were permanently mounted fixtures with the electrical components contained in a large wooden box along with batteries to provide power for the telephone (sometimes called "coffin telephones"). As common battery power was gradually introduced throughout the telephone system (power supplied from the central office over the telephone lines), the ornate handcrafted wooden fixtures were replaced by much more compact mass-produced metal and later plastic telephones.

Bell introduced the "500" telephone set in 1949 as a standardized rotary-dial telephone set. The model 500 was an extremely durable telephone and a durable design; it remained in production for thirty-five years with only minor refinements (Mountjoy, 1995, p. 157), and many of the telephone sets remain in use today. The ringing volume could be adjusted but not turned off. The Bell System asserted that the customer had an obligation to answer the telephone and should not be allowed to ignore incoming calls. An upgraded version of the model 500 was introduced with Touch-Tone service in 1963. The Touch-Tone version contained the first electronics in a standard telephone set in order to create the tone signals. Touch-Tone service was offered at a premium price and required a service call to replace the dial telephone with a push-button telephone (Bell Laboratories, 1977, pp. 408, 409, 456).

The model 500 telephones were designed for long life, rough use, and standardized installation procedures when all phones were hardwired by telephone company personnel:

> [the telephone set] must be designed to operate under severe extremes, from inside a cold storage warehouse to the sunny windowsill of a humid, un-air-conditioned house in Florida . . . [T]he set must be sufficiently rugged to withstand . . . being knocked off a table onto a concrete floor . . . The design should take into account . . . more than 100 million installed stations, 100,000 installers and repair personnel, and 75,000 trucks. Without simplicity and commonality in design, the large numbers of plant personnel can lead to inefficient installation and repair of low production units. (Bell Laboratories, 1977, pp. 408, 409)

Even by the mid-1970s Bell Labs noted that electronic components were rare in standard telephones: "Today, the use of electronics in the telephone is limited to the TOUCHTONE dial and to low-volume, special-purpose station equipment. At present, electronics are too expensive to replace internals of the existing general purpose 500 set" (Bell Laboratories, 1977, pp. 410, 411).

The most complex customer premises equipment was private branch exchange (PBX) switches. Large customers used a PBX to switch among extension telephones and to connect extension telephones with the telephone company central office. A PBX was essentially a small telephone company central office switch with modifications to fit the internal needs of an organization. PBX technology followed a similar pattern to central office switches, progressing from manual to electromechanical to electronic switches. AT&T introduced its first electronic PBX (No. 101 ESS with an initial capacity of 200 lines) in 1963 after the central office No. 1 ESS design was completed but before it was installed. AT&T continued to supply most of its customers with manual and electromechanical PBXs throughout the 1960s.

The long life of both customer telephones and switching equipment complicated the introduction of new technology or services. Innovations in terminal equipment were slowed by the need for compatibility with older central office equipment. For example, the Touch-Tone push-button signaling could not be used directly with step-by-step offices, and could only be introduced in areas served by newer offices or in offices with auxiliary equipment to translate between Touch-Tone signals and the dialing pulses required for step-by-step switch operation. Both technical compatibility considerations (signaling, voltages) and procedures and personnel training designed to serve particular kinds of equipment limited innovation:

> Each new design of plant equipment must be compatible with older equipment, with the building environment, and with personnel and administrative procedures conditioned by the older equipment. Inter-office transmission systems interface with switching systems, and switching systems interface with loops and stations. Signal levels, time intervals, and sequences at the interfaces must correspond. New designs also may be restricted by building characteristics such as floor loading, frame height, temperature variations, or electrical induction . . . Standardization of interfaces, environments, and operations allows smooth introduction for new equipment, but by the same token, sometimes restricts the economies and service features that a new technology might realize . . . The biggest challenge of a new service feature is to retrofit it into old plant without losing money. (Bell Laboratories, 1977, p. 456)

AT&T played a key role in the invention of important technologies for the Second Information Revolution, but did not implement them widely in its telephone network. The computer and semiconductor industries developed largely separate from AT&T, while the telephone business remained tied to the electromechanical technology of an earlier era. The institutional structure provided both the incentive and the ability to remain with conservative technology. The regulatory pressure for low prices, slow depreciation, and reliable basic service encouraged a conservative technology approach. The rate-of-return system prevented AT&T from reaping the rewards of risky innovative technologies. Consumer complaints magnified through the regulatory agencies encouraged compatibility with earlier generations of equipment and discouraged risk taking. Regulatory boundaries, particularly after the consent decree of 1956, created incentives for AT&T to focus on the regulated business and not to develop major positions in newly developing industries.

While the regulatory structure discouraged risk taking and the introduction of new technologies, it also protected AT&T against potential competitors who might utilize the new technologies to attract favored customers. Competition was specifically prohibited in many states and was implicitly prohibited in interstate services. Thus there was no market test of whether or not AT&T's decisions and the regulator's decisions regarding appropriate technology were the ones customers desired after knowing the alternatives available to them.

The interlocking system of AT&T, the regulatory structure, and long-lived capital investment appeared impervious to change, but the rapidly declining price of basic electronic components created more and more pressure on the system. Telephone technology and prices became increasingly separated from the technology and prices that would have resulted from a competitive market. That difference created increasing tension between the structure upheld by AT&T's market power and regulatory fiat and the structure that would have been created by market-oriented policies. The pricing policies of AT&T and the regulators masked the substantial reduction in the underlying cost of long distance telephone service during the period, while tying AT&T, the independent telephone companies, and the state regulators into a single structure resistant to change. The FCC stood somewhat outside of that structure. Its political imperatives were generally derived from broadcast rather than from common carrier issues and therefore the staff had greater freedom to pursue its own policies. As senior FCC staff members began experimenting with small changes in the regulated monopoly policies, they initiated a series of conflicts that eventually resulted in substantial changes in the industry structure and institutional framework for communications.

II

Boundary Disputes and
Limited Competition,
1969–1984

8

Data Communications

As discussed in Chapter 6, the unregulated computer industry developed independently of the regulated communications sector. There was minimal interaction between the two sectors and no pressure to change the regulated monopoly structure to accommodate the rapidly growing computer industry. Most computer systems were self-contained batch processing systems. While there was extensive internal communication among the boxes comprising the computer system (transferring data from a tape drive to the CPU and from the CPU to a printer, for example), that internal communication had no interaction with the telephone network nor did it follow telephone standards.

Only a small portion of the computer industry required interaction with the telephone system. Following the pioneering examples of the SAGE air defense network and the SABRE airlines reservation system, some companies set up data communications systems to allow remote terminals to interact with a central database. Those systems connected the remote terminals to the central computer through analog AT&T private lines designed for voice transmission. Private lines bypassed the switch with its associated potential for adding noise to the line. AT&T provided the early modems to convert between the digital computer signals and signals that could be carried over the voice-grade line, and sometimes AT&T provided special "conditioning" to the lines used for data in order to improve their performance.

The separate worlds of regulated communications and unregulated data processing began to collide on a regular basis beginning in the late 1960s. The growing popularity of time-sharing computers created demand for routine combinations of communication lines and computers. Computer users sought specialized equipment and greater flexibility

139

from the telephone companies and complained that AT&T's slow intro-duction of standardized products and tight control of the network failed to meet their needs. AT&T supplied the modems and the teletype termi-nals for many early time-sharing systems, but unregulated computer and electronics companies could also produce computer terminals and mo-dems, raising questions about the boundary line between regulated communications and unregulated data processing. Computer users questioned the suitability of AT&T's monopoly analog voice network for data transmission and raised doubts about whether AT&T's long-standing monopoly of long distance service should continue to be sup-ported by regulatory policy.

The early time-sharing computers were developed in an effort to give individual users direct interaction with the computer at a time when large computers were much cheaper per unit of operation than small computers. An alternative route to interactive computing was opened by Intel's invention of the microprocessor in 1971 and rapid improvements in microprocessors during the 1970s. As the improving microprocessors and complementary products were built into personal computers and workstations, desktop computers replaced computer terminals attached to a distant large computer. While many tasks could be accomplished with stand-alone desktop computers, much more could be done if the computers could communicate with each other and with databases. As desktop computers were linked by local area networks (LANs) and those LANs were linked to larger private data networks and later to the public Internet, an extensive data communications infrastructure devel-oped outside of the regulated common carrier infrastructure dominated by the telephone companies. The communications-intensive "client-server" model of data processing, with computer power at each user lo-cation linked to other users and numerous information servers, began to replace earlier approaches to data processing and developed its own communication standards and procedures without regard to telephone company practices.

The development of data communications networks created an incen-tive to reform the regulated monopoly structure of telephones. Com-puter users had specialized needs that were not easily satisfied by stan-dard products and services offered by the telephone companies. The FCC's effort to accommodate those specialized needs caused reexamina-tion of the assumptions supporting regulated monopoly. Rapid technological progress in computers and data communications as compared to telephones raised questions about AT&T's portrayal of itself as a highly progressive company.

Reform efforts were complicated by the fact that substantial portions of the telephone network appeared to be a natural monopoly and by the cross-subsidies among various telephone services that made a direct comparison of costs between AT&T and its competitors difficult. Moreover, the FCC's attempts to introduce limited competition in telephone terminal equipment (Chapter 10) and long distance service (Chapter 11) were criticized by state regulatory authorities who believed that the regulated monopoly structure should be maintained and used their power to block or slow the FCC's changes. The Department of Justice (DOJ), for its part, also criticized the FCC's actions because it believed that the FCC was too supportive of AT&T's continued dominance and too timid in introducing reforms. With the divestiture of AT&T (Chapter 12), the DOJ used its antitrust power to impose more radical changes than the FCC desired. The result of the conflicting goals and actions of the state regulators, federal regulators, the DOJ, and the courts was a policy of mixed competition and monopoly regulated by federal and state jurisdictions with close attention to revenue flows and continued subsidies to favored companies and services. While the compromise policy that evolved from the actions of the multiple power centers lacked a coherent intellectual foundation, it did provide much greater opportunity for innovative approaches to communications than the earlier unified regulated monopoly.

While data communications provided an incentive to liberalize the telephone monopoly, early steps toward liberalization in telephones were critical to the further development of data communications. The freedom of computer users to attach terminal equipment of their choosing to the telephone network, to combine computer processing with telephone lines in order to create enhanced communications, and to use newly constructed competitive long distance networks for transmitting computer data boosted data communications in the United States ahead of countries that retained a tightly controlled monopoly telephone network. As innovative new capabilities based on combinations of computer industry and communications industry capabilities became recognized as important sources of improvement for the overall economy, political support for the regulated monopoly approach to communications dwindled in favor of policies that utilized at least partial forms of competition.

Packet-Switching and the Arpanet

As with many innovations, packet-switching developed from the efforts of multiple independent thinkers. One important line of theoretical reasoning came from Paul Baran, who joined the computer science department at RAND in 1959. RAND was deeply involved in developing strategy for fighting nuclear wars and had long been concerned about the vulnerability of the nation's communications system to a Soviet first strike. Severely disrupted communications would limit the ability of U.S. forces to respond to an attack. Baran considered designs for a survivable communications system, reasoning from analogy with the brain's neural network and its ability to bypass dysfunctional areas. That analogy suggested a network with redundant connections, but such a network would differ substantially from the analog telephone network of the time. Although the telephone network had been built with survivability in mind, it was largely based on hierarchical switching approaches in order to minimize the number of switches.

Baran conceived of a distributed network with no hierarchy. Each node would be connected to a set of additional nodes and would contain a computer with routing tables to transmit messages. Similarly, messages would be broken up into blocks that could be independently routed over the network and reassembled at the final destination point. Baran's theoretical scheme contained the major elements of packet-switching in a distributed network. He worked on the project from 1960 to 1965 and developed extensive papers on how such a network would function, but his proposal was not implemented (Hafner and Lyon, 1996, pp. 53–64). Baran later described his motivation and concept as follows: "[I]f you had an attack—and not very many missiles—aimed at our strategic forces, it would take out the telephone system without even aiming for it . . . The problem was that the telephone system was centralized. You had a hierarchical switching system . . . It was all analog transmission in those days, and you couldn't go through more than five links before the quality was unacceptable" (Brand, 2001, pp. 149, 150).

According to Baran, the air force (RAND's sponsor) wanted to build the system and asked AT&T to do it, but AT&T did not think the plan would work and declined. Although the air force was interested in proceeding without AT&T, it was not allowed to build a communications system on its own. Meanwhile, Baran and others at RAND did not believe that the Defense Communications Agency (DCA) would make a serious effort to implement the new concept; they were concerned that if DCA attempted to build a system and failed, packet-switching would not receive further consideration for a long time (Brand, 2001).

In 1965, Donald Davies of the British National Physical Laboratory (NPL) independently developed the concept of packet-switching as the solution to an entirely different problem. While Baran was concerned with transmitting data over a degraded network, Davies focused on providing an efficient transmission method for the "bursty" character of data transmission. Ordinary telephone channels provide an open path for the duration of the conversation, but data communication tends to come in random intervals, with a need for rapid data transmission at one time followed by substantial dead time of no transmission. Davies worked from analogy with the early time-sharing computers that allowed many users to share the capacity of a large computer by allocating each a slice of time in a regular manner. Davies proposed to break up messages into small units that could go independently through the network and then be reassembled. Each user could consequently share a high-capacity channel and could receive rapid data transmission of messages so long as the channel was not too crowded. Davies designated the units "packets" because of their similarity to small packages. Davies's term was widely accepted, and the approach became known as "packet-switching." Davies's group built the first packet-switching network on a small scale with short lines at the NPL (Hafner and Lyon, 1996, p. 106).

A third motivation inspired the initial packet-switching efforts of the Advanced Research Projects Agency (ARPA) of the U.S. Department of Defense. ARPA financed basic research with potential military applications and developed close ties with major universities. During the early 1960s, ARPA funded a number of university computer programs, with special emphasis on developing early time-sharing computers. Although time-sharing allowed multiple users to access a machine, there was no convenient way to share expensive specialized resources among the various ARPA-funded sites. In 1966, ARPA allocated an initial $1 million to develop an experimental data network that would facilitate sharing computer resources and hired Lincoln Laboratory computer expert

Larry Roberts to direct the effort. Roberts connected the project to the extensive interrelated computer expertise of MIT, Lincoln Laboratory, and the consulting firm Bolt Beranek and Newman (BBN) in Cambridge, Massachusetts.

While at first the ARPA effort was unaware of either Davies's or Baran's work, Roberts soon learned of it and incorporated their insights into the developing plans for the network. At the suggestion of Bob Kahn (an MIT professor then working at BBN), the initial experimental network was planned to connect distant computers. Kahn believed that the problems of building a long distance network utilizing telephone company facilities were quite different from those of a short distance network such as the one Davies built at the NPL. Although funded by the DOD, the ARPA network plans were developed in an open academic forum with extensive input by leading academic computing experts. Just as the early military-funded but widely publicized computers developed at the Institute for Advanced Study and MIT provided critical expertise to a wide range of computer pioneers, so the ARPA-funded network experiments developed extensive intellectual capital for later network innovations.

The ARPA group decided to solve the problem of communication among incompatible computers by constructing a data network that terminated in identical controllers at each node. Each site would then be responsible for building an interface between the controller and the computer utilized at that site, with a different interface required for each different type of computer. That approach simplified the network design by allowing the network to communicate among the controllers without concern for the capabilities or standards of the main computer at the site. It also relieved the main computer of the resource burden of directly managing the communications and provided a communication path among incompatible computer formats by translating all network messages into a common format used within the network.

In the summer of 1968, graduate students from the planned first four host sites began meeting to consider how to develop host-to-host protocols. The ARPA specifications called for the network to transmit packets of information among the controllers but did not specify the method for the host computers to carry on useful work with each other. The graduate students called themselves the Network Working Group and began distributing minutes of the meetings as documents titled Request for

Comments (RFC). Hafner and Lyon describe the group as "an adhocracy of intensely creative, sleep-deprived, idiosyncratic, well-meaning computer geniuses" (1996, p. 145). Their unofficial RFCs became a critical means of communicating ideas and reaching consensus on computer networking standards. The Network Working Group completed specifications for the Telnet protocol that allowed remote log-in to a host computer over the network and for the host-to-host protocol that became known as the Network Control Protocol by 1970, and the File Transfer Protocol (FTP) slightly later. With no formal membership or authority, the group of computer experts continued to propose a wide variety of networking standards through the RFC process. When enough people found the proposed standards useful and incorporated them into their own work, they became de facto standards without a formal approval or enforcement process.

After detailed design planning, ARPA issued a contract in early 1969 to BBN to build and program four controllers (known as Interface Message Processors) and create a four-node network. BBN modified a Honeywell 516 minicomputer to create the controllers and developed the necessary program to manage communications among the nodes. The first node was Leonard Kleinrock's Network Measurement Center at UCLA, which included graduate students Steve Crocker, Vint Cerf, and Jon Postel who played major roles in the development of computer networking. The four-node network was completed at the end of 1969 and expanded with additional nodes during 1970 to create a nationwide network (known as the Arpanet) that primarily linked Massachusetts sites (Harvard, MIT, BBN) with California sites (UCLA, UC at Santa Barbara, RAND, SRI).

By 1971 the Arpanet was considered stable enough for routine operation rather than experiments only, but was lightly used with only about 2 percent of its capacity utilized. The original ARPA goal of promoting computer resource sharing remained elusive. Despite the network connection, it remained difficult to conduct effective computer work on distant sites. However, the network facilitated communication among the computer science faculty and students who had access to it. The FTP protocol allowed the transfer of program and other files among computer centers and was also used for the first e-mail. In 1973, 75 percent of the Arpanet traffic was e-mail, and this induced numerous protocol and programming innovations to simplify the first awkward procedure for e-mail communication. As the network matured, DARPA (successor to ARPA) decided that it should not continue to manage an operational network. When AT&T declined interest in taking control, the network was transferred to the Defense Communications Agency in 1975, marking the end of its role as the focus of academic experiments in networking and the beginning of routine packet communication over a wide area.

Network Protocols and Interconnection

By the early 1970s a number of packet-switched data networks were under construction or in operation, each with different design goals and technical specifications. Each network formed a closed universe with no way to send messages across networks. Representatives of various networks formed the International Network Working Group with Stanford professor Vint Cerf (formerly a graduate student working on the first Arpanet node at UCLA) as leader in order to explore ways of connecting the networks. After playing a major role in the design of the Arpanet for BBN, Bob Kahn joined ARPA and began developing a radio-based mobile packet network for military uses. It had a different structure than the Arpanet, but Kahn wanted to connect the networks so that the mobile network could access resources from the Arpanet computers. During 1973 Cerf and Kahn worked together to create an inter-networking protocol, aided by a number of Stanford graduate students and other network experts. The Cerf and Kahn ideas were published in 1974, and after further refinement were implemented as the TCP/IP protocol (Transmission Control Protocol/Internet Protocol).

The Cerf-Kahn TCP protocol encapsulated messages received in multiple formats in a standard "envelope" with a specified addressing structure. The gateways between disparate networks could then read the standardized addresses in order to forward the message correctly, without requiring the messages themselves to be in a standard format. The TCP protocol also revised the error-handling structure of the Arpanet. The Arpanet considered the network responsible for reliability and built extensive acknowledgement and error correction mechanisms into the controllers at each network node, allowing the host computers to assume that messages had been correctly transmitted. The TCP protocol borrowed an idea from the French Cyclades network and from the Hawaiian radio network Alohanet in which error correction was entirely the responsibility of the host computers. The network was assumed to be unreliable, and hosts were responsible for repeating the packet transmission if there was no acknowledgement of correct transmission (Hafner and Lyon, 1996, p. 227).

The transfer of error correction responsibility to the edges of the network (the hosts) allowed the interconnection of disparate networks with varying levels of reliability. So long as networks were responsible for the accurate transmission of packets, it was crucial that all component networks of the larger network conform to particular reliability standards. With the network built on an assumption that internal links might not be reliable, it was possible to link up networks of varying reliability and allow the host error correction mechanisms to request retransmission of packets not accurately received.

The change in error handling was a significant conceptual shift with far-reaching consequences for the developing Internet. It recognized that the packets could be duplicated essentially for free and that it might be more efficient to retransmit some messages rather than to ensure error-free handling across the network. The economically efficient solution is to choose a level of reliability in which the marginal cost of an error is equal to the marginal cost of adding reliability to the network to prevent that error. The Arpanet approach assumed that the cost of an erroneously transmitted packet was high and consequently made an effort to ensure that the packets were transmitted correctly. The TCP approach assumed that the cost of an erroneously transmitted packet was low if the host could recognize the error and request retransmission. To use a shipping analogy, the Arpanet approach assumed that the contents of the containers were valuable and therefore it was worth some expense to ensure that the containers were handled carefully and delivered without damage. The TCP approach assumed that the contents of the containers could be replaced at minimal cost and that the goal was to maximize the number of undamaged containers transmitted while providing replacements for any damaged in transit.

Telephone networks placed the intelligence and control in the center of the network. Initially, that role was played by human operators who manually set up and broke down circuits, and later by increasingly sophisticated automatic switches. Terminal equipment was simple (a voice telephone in most cases), and the customer's options for use of the network were limited by the capabilities built into its central office switches. Similarly, the early Arpanet was centrally managed from the BBN headquarters. In contrast, TCP moved the intelligence of the network to the edges under the control of individual end users while limiting the network itself to the simple transmission and routing of packets. The TCP/IP protocol allowed the Internet to develop without central management. Individual networks with varying standards and degrees of reliability could be attached to it, and individual applications could be developed to add value to the network without changing the fundamental network control. The simplicity of the network created by the encapsulation procedure, as well as the "best efforts" approach rather than guaranteed delivery, provided an open platform that was able to easily accommodate major changes in the volume of network traffic and in the type of services provided over the network.

During the 1970s the TCP/IP approach to data communications was only one candidate among many possibilities. Major computer manufacturers created their own proprietary standards to facilitate networking among users of their brand of equipment. IBM's Systems Network Architecture (SNA) and Digital Equipment Corporation's DECnet were the two most important of these standards. The major telephone companies sought to develop a data networking approach that would not be dependent on the computer manufacturer's standards. The standards body of the International Telecommunication Union (ITU), the CCITT, began developing an international standard for data communications under the leadership of telephone companies from Canada, France, and Britain along with the U.S. company Telenet that was started by BBN to commercialize its Arpanet experience. The initial x.25 standard was approved by the CCITT plenary meeting in 1976. It was adopted by Telenet, Canada's Datapac, France's Transpac, Japan's DDY, and the British Post Office's PSS by 1980 (Abbate, 1999, p. 154). U.S. representatives sought approval of TCP/IP as an international standard but were unsuccessful. Despite the official CCITT standard, many networks could continue using TCP/IP because most countries did not require compliance with CCITT standards. Both standards were created at roughly the same time and before extensive data networks existed, so that there was not a problem of switching a large installed base from one to the other. They developed along separate lines with the CCITT approach utilized primarily by telephone companies to provide public data networks and the

TCP/IP approach utilized primarily by computer users to attach their computers or local area networks to the wider Internet.

The CCITT's x.25 data networking standard was patterned after telephone company practice. It created "virtual circuits" through the network rather than merely transporting packets of information. It was designed as a public data network that could be interconnected to other public data networks using the x.25 protocol, but could not easily accommodate the interconnection of private networks. The assumption was that users would connect computer equipment to the public x.25 data network in a similar manner to the way in which they connected voice terminal equipment to the public voice-grade networks. Error control was the responsibility of the network provider. It was assumed that packets would flow across an x.25 network in an error-free manner, and that if two x.25 networks were interconnected, the respective networks would each ensure that the transmission was reliable. Thus a host computer (a customer of the network) would have no control over the reliability of the network and would simply subscribe to the most appropriate service available from the data communications utility.

The x.25 approach was a challenge to both the computer manufacturers and to the Internet community. It was an effort to take control of data communications away from the proprietary standards of the computer manufacturers. The proprietary standards could take advantage of the particular characteristics of a specific brand of equipment and also create a network effect with that brand. Because a brand's equipment was most suited to its proprietary standards, there was an incentive to limit purchases to one brand. Insofar as one company could gain initial dominance in networking with a proprietary standard, it could potentially gain greater long-term control over the networks as individuals sought compatible equipment in order to be able to interconnect with the brand. The initial incentive for the creation of x.25 was Canada's effort to find an alternative to IBM's SNA for its public data network in order to avoid locking users into IBM equipment.

Rather than computer company-controlled proprietary protocols or telephone company-controlled x.25 networks, the TCP/IP protocol for the Internet provided a method of interconnecting networks without any central control or limits on the characteristics of the constituent networks. Neither the telephone companies nor the computer companies expected a network to operate reliably on a large scale without central control. Their dispute centered on the identity of the controlling party, not on the question of whether central control was needed. The TCP/IP approach gradually won over the others because it was consistent with the general direction of technology and with wide incentives for individual innovation. Neither the computer manufacturer's proprietary protocols nor the telephone company x.25 protocol allowed the easy connection of private and public networks. The proprietary protocols worked adequately for private systems utilizing the particular manufacturer's equipment, but they did not easily integrate disparate networks and equipment types.

TCP/IP also gained an advantage from the availability of free Unix operating systems with TCP/IP support, creating an incentive for academic computer centers to utilize Unix and TCP/IP. Unix was developed at Bell Labs as an internal program to facilitate file sharing in the early 1970s. It was written in the C programming language and originally planned for DEC's small PDP-11. The PDP-11's limited capabilities inspired Unix's creators (Ken Thompson and Dennis Ritchie) to keep the program small and efficient. Because it was written in C rather than assembly language, it was relatively easy to adapt Unix for non-DEC computers that had a C compiler. AT&T did not sell the program commercially (and couldn't under the 1956 consent decree restrictions) and instead offered it to universities for a nominal license fee. The Unix license also gave universities rights to the source code, allowing them to modify and improve the system for their own purposes. Unix was greatly expanded through the work of many different students at various universities in order to make it a more complete and useful operating system. In contrast to corporate control of commercial software, the early Unix work at universities was an important model for freeware and collaborative improvements to a program. Many versions of Unix were available, and students could add improvements and offer the modified Unix to others.

The University of California at Berkeley first obtained a Unix tape in 1974 and installed it on several campus computers. Graduate student Bill Joy, along with a number of others, put extensive effort into improving Unix, and in 1978 began offering tapes of the improved Unix that became known as Berkeley Unix. In 1980, ARPA recommended Berkeley Unix as a common standard and supported Joy's effort to incorporate support for TCP/IP into Berkeley Unix. The freely available Berkeley Unix with TCP/IP was quickly adopted by numerous academic computer centers and became the standard operating system software for the emerging Internet (Ceruzzi, 1998, pp. 282–285).

Local Area Networks and Ethernet

In the early 1970s, the Xerox Palo Alto Research Center (Xerox-PARC) began researching ways to inexpensively link multiple small computers within a building to a single expensive printer. Xerox was developing an early personal computer, but printers of the time were far too costly to dedicate to a personal computer economically. Robert Metcalfe was an early Arpanet participant, and in 1969 while a student he helped develop the link between MIT's DEC PDP-10 and the Arpanet (Ceruzzi, 1998, p. 291). Metcalfe joined Xerox-PARC in 1972 and began working on an inexpensive and flexible way to link small computers with a shared printer. The Arpanet approach to networking (which required dedicated small computers to handle communications at each node) was far too expensive to meet the Xerox requirements.

As part of his Ph.D. dissertation Metcalfe had closely analyzed the Hawaiian radio-based network Alohanet. The Alohanet was designed to provide inexpensive packet communication by radio among seven computers on four islands. Using a radio system designed for taxi dispatch, it allowed all sites to utilize the same frequency. Packets, however, could be lost because of interference when two computers broadcast a message at the same time on the same frequency. Consequently, it was the responsibility of the host computers to be certain that the messages were received properly. A receiving computer broadcast an acknowledgment when it received a message; if the sending computer did not receive the acknowledgment, it resent the message after a random interval designed to reduce the probability of another interference failure.

Metcalfe envisioned a fast form of the Alohanet over a local area in which signals on a coaxial cable were substituted for radio signals in the air. All computers on the network would be attached to a single coaxial cable without a switch, and computers could be added or subtracted from the cable without changing the overall network configuration. Any computer could transmit whenever the cable was not occupied, and if two attempted to transmit at the same time, they each waited a random interval and tried again. The system was named "Ethernet" in honor of its debt to the Hawaiian radio system, which transmitted radio waves through the "ether." Metcalfe wrote a theoretical description of the proposed system in 1973, including an analysis that showed it should be able to handle very high-speed data. Metcalfe and David Boggs built a working model the next year and achieved a speed of 3 megabits per second, far faster than the 56 kilobits per second Arpanet or the voice-grade modems available at the time (Ceruzzi, 1998, p. 292).

In 1979, Digital Equipment Corporation, Intel, and Xerox worked together to create a standardized form of Ethernet. That agreement removed control of Ethernet from any one manufacturer and prevented conflicts in communication over similar but not identical versions of Ethernet. Digital accepted Ethernet as the standard way to connect its small computers (the VAX models) into local networks. Xerox's personal computer was not successful, and the company failed to profit from its network innovation. Metcalfe left Xerox to form 3Com Corporation and facilitated the popularization of Ethernet by providing a variety of networking products.

Ethernet was by no means the only LAN protocol, but its simplicity and the wide availability of inexpensive products to create an Ethernet allowed it to become the most commonly used protocol. Ethernet's most significant competitor was IBM's Token Ring protocol. In a Token Ring LAN, the computers are connected in a ring. A special message called a token is passed from computer to computer. When a computer receives the token, it transmits one frame of data (if it has data to send) and passes the token to the next computer. As with an Ethernet, each computer on the LAN receives all data but discards all except what is addressed to that computer. As the token passes around the ring, each computer gets a turn to transmit data. The potential collisions on an Ethernet are avoided on a Token Ring because only one computer at a time is allowed to transmit data (Comer, 1997, pp. 63, 64).

LANs developed as a private communication device internal to a particular institution. They did not require public charters, rights-of-way, or permission of telephone companies or regulatory authorities. LANs created the data communications equivalent of the development of independent local telephone companies at the beginning of the twentieth century. The original independent local telephone companies were small-scale islands that were not connected to each other through a long distance network. However, they established local electrical communication and provided the basic infrastructure for larger-scale networks when they were interconnected through the AT&T long distance network. Similarly, LANs connected local computers and established both the experience and the infrastructure for data communications with distributed intelligence. The LANs generally operated at high speed and experimented with numerous different configurations of workstations and servers. While the competitive threat of independent telephone companies was overcome by connection to AT&T's monopoly long distance network, LANs could be connected through a number of different Internet backbone providers to provide an unregulated worldwide network.

Packet-switching is an example of what Clayton Christensen calls a "disruptive technological change" (1997). In Christensen's analysis, a disruptive change is one that begins as an innovation with high cost and no obvious market. Established firms conclude that the innovation is neither useful to their customers nor a threat to their business and ignore it. However, the new technology experiences more rapid improvement than the mainstream technology and eventually displaces older products. The new technology is developed by new companies for specialized markets outside of the mainstream, but as it matures those companies become dominant because the established firms are not able to quickly master the new technology.

Early packet-switching was an expensive way to move data long distances. When computer power was expensive, the cost of creating separately addressed packets, transmitting them through the network, and reassembling the message at the destination was far higher than setting up a circuit and transmitting the data through that circuit. The Arpanet failed in its specific purpose of saving money by sharing computer resources among geographically separated ARPA researchers. AT&T's corporate private line networks (using modems over analog lines or synchronous digital transmission lines) were a much cheaper way to move data long distances in the early 1970s than the Arpanet structure.

AT&T correctly viewed the early Arpanet as a project for academic research with potential military applications, not as a serious alternative approach to business and consumer communications. While AT&T vigorously opposed efforts to insert competition into its monopoly on voice long distance service, it did not oppose the early packet-switching networks or attempt to take control of them. The Arpanet had very limited capacity, and even with a zero price to users, that capacity was not fully occupied. The low demand at zero price suggested that little if any of AT&T's revenue was at risk from the new technology. The military and academic control of early packet-switching networks also made it politically awkward to oppose them. Similarly, IBM did not consider the efforts of 1970s hobbyists to create computers out of the early microprocessors relevant to its business.

IBM and AT&T argued over the boundary lines between their respective domains of data processing and monopoly communications service during the 1970s, and many observers predicted a stronger clash between the two giants in the future as computer and communications technology became more closely connected. Instead, both were partially displaced from their controlling positions by the rapid advances in microprocessors and packet-switching controlled by Intel, Microsoft, 3M, Cisco, and many other new companies. Powerful cheap microprocessors allowed networked small computers to provide the services of a mainframe and also allowed the inexpensive production of routers and other network equipment as a substitute for expensive telephone company switches. However, that competition took considerable time to develop. After twenty years of packet-switching networks, the Internet still carried only a tiny fraction of the nation's communications, and it did not become an important method of nonacademic communication until the 1990s.

9

From Mainframes to Microprocessors

The extraordinary success of IBM's System/360 line of computers thoroughly established IBM as the dominant computer company in the world. IBM's rapid growth and steady high profit rate made it the favorite stock of securities analysts and gave IBM the highest stock market value of any company in the world. While investors sought to participate in the benefits of IBM's worldwide dominance, governments sought to limit a dominance that had created worries in many countries about American control of high technology and worries in the United States about IBM's monopoly power. The latter worries inspired antitrust litigation.

In the United States antitrust suits may be filed by the Department of Justice or by private parties who are entitled to receive three times their damages if they are successful in proving antitrust violations and resulting loss. IBM's antitrust experience extended back to an important 1936 Supreme Court decision that found IBM's practice of tying the lease of its tabulating machines to the purchase of its cards illegal. It also included a 1956 consent decree settling DOJ charges that it monopolized the tabulating machine market. IBM's first significant computer antitrust problems arose from its efforts to maintain its position in supercomputers against Control Data's innovations. When Control Data Corporation announced its 6600 in 1963, it was the fastest computer available and was quickly ordered by prestigious customers such as the atomic weapons laboratories, the National Security Agency, and aerospace firms. IBM's System/360 plans did not include a machine competitive with the CDC 6600.

Following CDC's announcement, IBM's Thomas Watson, Jr., castigated his top executives:

Last week Control Data had a press conference during which they officially announced their 6600 system. I understand that in the laboratory developing this system there are only 34 people, including the janitor . . . Contrasting this modest effort with our own vast development activities, I fail to understand why we have lost our industry leadership position by letting someone else offer the world's most powerful computer. (Watson and Petre, 1990, p. 383)

IBM added a high-end machine to its planned set of System/360 computers. The announced machine succeeded in delaying CDC orders for the 6600, but IBM was not able to deliver the promised performance and eventually abandoned the supercomputer market. IBM settled CDC's private antitrust suit by paying CDC $100 million and selling IBM's Service Bureau Corporation to CDC for less than its market value.

While Control Data's private suit was pending, the DOJ filed antitrust charges in January 1969 alleging that IBM monopolized the computer industry in violation of Section 2 of the Sherman Act. The DOJ sought to divide IBM into several separate companies in order to increase competition in the computer industry. The DOJ included IBM's actions against Control Data as part of its evidence that IBM sought to monopolize the computer industry. The DOJ also complained that IBM's long-standing practice of bundling software and service with its computers was an illegal tying of its products and that IBM's educational discounts were attempts to control the education market and influence the future computer choices of people trained on IBM machines.

Under IBM's standard contract, a customer paid for the hardware and received the operating system, access to a wide range of IBM-supplied application programs, and extensive technical support without separate fee. That full-service approach was attractive to many companies with limited computer expertise but also limited the development of separate markets for the products bundled with IBM hardware. While IBM denied all of the antitrust charges, it also decided to begin charging separate prices for its services and to reduce its educational discounts. Thomas Watson, Jr., described the decision to unbundle prices as a controversial one taken in order to reduce antitrust liability:

Burke Marshall [IBM general counsel] . . . stood up at an executive conference and told us that things had to change. We were going to have to undo the bundle and price each of our goods and services separately. "But why?" people kept asking. "Why change now?" He went through his explanation again and again until finally he lost his temper. "Because you've got a tie, [expletive], you've got a tie! It's illegal! If you try to defend it in court, you'll lose!" He was shouting in a voice an octave above normal. I went back to my room with [Vincent] Learson [IBM president] and a couple of others. "The guy really means this," somebody said, and I decided that we ought to follow Burke's advice rather than risk a showdown in court. (Watson and Petre, 1990, p. 381)

IBM's private settlement with Control Data and its modification of specific practices challenged by the DOJ did not end the DOJ suit. The DOJ's proposal to divide IBM into multiple companies and IBM's contention that it neither possessed monopoly power nor had done anything wrong left the parties far apart and limited the opportunities to negotiate a settlement. A contentious and prolonged pretrial discovery period extended for six years, including two appeals to the Supreme Court over document demands and sanctions for failing to provide documents. In 1975, the actual trial began in federal district court in New York before Judge David Edelstein, the same judge who had presided over the earlier IBM case that had ended with the 1956 consent decree. The trial continued for six years of interminable wrangling over major issues and legal minutia.

After pursuing the case through portions of five presidential administrations, the DOJ dismissed the case in January 1982 at the same time as the AT&T divestiture agreement. By that time the case had become an embarrassment to the DOJ. It made many people doubt the DOJ's ability to prosecute a major antitrust case against a large company willing to spend heavily on legal fees. The DOJ's failure to bring the IBM case to a conclusion was similar to the FCC's failure to bring the Telpak case to a conclusion, which had created doubts about that agency's competence to regulate AT&T. By the time the IBM case was dismissed in 1982, the computer industry was very different from the industry of the late 1960s, making continued argument over old issues seem increasingly anachronistic. For some time before the dismissal, the DOJ had been seeking a convenient way to end the suit. The DOJ's success in the AT&T case provided an opportunity to drop the IBM case without creating political repercussions.

The standardized interface between the System/360 central processing units and storage devices such as disk drives and tape drives created an opportunity for competitors to replace individual components of the computer system. Computers of the 1960s were generally sold or leased as complete systems including combinations of central processing units (CPUs), tape drives, disk drives, programs, and other components necessary to supply the customer's needs. Although separate prices were charged for individual system components, the competition among computer producers was on a systems basis because of the impossibility of mixing components from computer systems produced by different companies. In the late 1960s several companies developed tape and disk drives compatible with those produced by IBM. This allowed the companies to sell a tape drive or disk drive in direct competition with the corresponding IBM tape or disk drive rather than only as part of a complete competitive system.

The new competitors were known as plug-compatible manufacturers (PCMs) because they claimed that their products allowed the customer to unplug the IBM drive, plug in the competitive drive, and continue all operations as if the IBM drive were still in place. The plug-compatible manufacturers for components of IBM systems were comparable to the CPE manufacturers in the telephone market (see Chapter 10). In both cases the competitor attempted to produce a piece of equipment separate from that supplied by the dominant company and to interconnect it with other components provided by the dominant company. However, while AT&T simply prohibited attachments to the network before 1968, IBM could not do so because it would have been an illegal tying arrangement under the antitrust laws.

Before the PCM competition began, IBM charged relatively high prices for its peripheral equipment in relationship to the cost of producing it, making replacement drives an attractive opportunity. By the beginning of 1970, its competitors had captured 6 percent of IBM's installed base of tape drives and 4 percent of its base of small disk drives, and they were just announcing products to replace IBM's large disk drive, the 2314. In 1970, the 2314 disk drive system produced $293 million in revenue for IBM, more than any other single product (Computer Industry Census, 1971). At that time, a customer rented a 2314 system (controller plus eight disk spindles) for $5,300 per month. The system provided access to 232 megabytes of data, 1 percent of the capacity of a 20-gigabyte personal computer hard drive that could be purchased for less than $200 in 2002. IBM studied the economics of its competitors and initiated a series of actions designed to eliminate them from the market: price cuts, long-term leasing plans, improved products, and bundling of previously separate units. IBM's defensive actions eliminated the competitive threat: fifteen out of the seventeen PCMs left the market after suffering large losses (Brock, 1975, pp. 109–136; 1989).

Several PCM companies filed antitrust suits against IBM, complaining that IBM's aggressive tactics were an illegal use of its monopoly power. In 1973, in the first case tried (*Telex v. IBM*), a federal district court in Oklahoma found in favor of Telex and awarded actual damages of $118 million (tripled by law to a payment of $353 million) plus costs and attorney's fees. At that time, it was the largest antitrust damage award ever granted. However, the *Telex* decision was overturned on appeal, and IBM also won the other three peripherals cases that came to trial. The courts upheld IBM's right to cut its prices and redesign its products even if those actions were damaging to its competitors so long as there was some rationale for the actions other than destroying competitors. In reviewing the *California Computer Products v. IBM* case in 1979, the Ninth Circuit Court of Appeals stated:

> IBM, assuming it was a monopolist, had the right to redesign its products to make them more attractive to buyers—whether by reason of lower manufacturing cost and price or improved performance. It was under no duty to help CalComp or other peripheral equipment manufacturers survive or expand. IBM need not have provided its rivals with disk products to examine and copy . . . nor have constricted its product development so as to facilitate sales of rival products. (Court of Appeals, 9th Cir., 1979, p. 744)

While IBM won its antitrust battles (other than the privately settled Control Data case), its efforts to defend itself against antitrust charges limited its flexibility. According to Thomas Watson, Jr., "Our annual legal bill went up into the tens of millions of dollars . . . The antitrust case began to color everything we did. For years every executive decision, even ones that were fairly routine, had to be made with one eye on how it might affect the lawsuit" (Watson and Petre, 1990, p. 386). IBM was less aggressive in exploiting new technological opportunities during the 1970s than in the 1960s, but how much of the change was caused by the lawsuits and defensive mentality within IBM is uncertain.

While IBM successfully defended its peripheral equipment against the PCM companies in the early 1970s, the PCM companies reduced IBM's market power and pricing freedom. Furthermore, they facilitated entry of companies producing compatible CPUs by providing a source of peripheral equipment to attach to those CPUs. Competition to IBM through compatible CPUs had been attempted earlier by RCA (the Spectra series), but RCA had been unprofitable and left the market.

Gene Amdahl was one of the key designers of the System/360. In 1970, he left IBM to create his own company and planned to build advanced "plug-compatible CPUs" that could be used as replacements for the 360/370 CPUs. In 1971, Fujitsu and Hitachi began an effort to build computers compatible with the 360/370, but had difficulty obtaining adequate information to ensure compatibility. When Amdahl Corporation encountered financial difficulties in 1972, Fujitsu purchased an interest in the company. The joint venture thus gained access to Amdahl's detailed knowledge of IBM's architecture and technology, to Amdahl's own innovations, and to advanced Japanese semiconductor technology developed by a consortium of Japanese companies under MITI sponsorship (Flamm, 1988, pp. 194–196). The Amdahl-Fujitsu-Hitachi partnership announced a line of IBM-compatible computers in 1974 and later split into separate Amdahl-Fujitsu and Hitachi efforts.

The critical importance of Japanese semiconductor technology in making the Amdahl-Fujitsu partnership a constraint on IBM indicated the increasingly close connection between advances in computers and advances in semiconductors. There had always been a close relationship between improvements in electronics and improvements in computers, but in the 1960s IBM's market power and systems approach to selling computers had maintained some separation between the semiconductor and the computer industry. The minicomputer companies (especially DEC and Data General) had relied on advances in semiconductors for their competitive edge and had introduced new semiconductor technology more rapidly than IBM. With the Amdahl-Fujitsu partnership, that approach spread to mainframe processors as well, though many customers still preferred the IBM brand name and IBM service. An even closer connection between computers and semiconductors developed in personal computers where the CPU was a single chip. IBM's competition in the 1970s from compatible peripheral equipment companies and from compatible CPU producers allowed customers to create a clone of an

IBM mainframe system. Despite that development, IBM was able to maintain its control of the mainframe market, growing from $8.7 billion in 1973 data processing revenue to $49.6 billion in 1986 (13.4 percent annual growth rate in revenue), while Amdahl received $1 billion in 1986 (2 percent of IBM's revenue) (Flamm, 1988, p. 102). The Amdahl-Fujitsu mainframe cloning effort of the 1970s was repeated with more success and more detriment to IBM's market position in the personal computer market of the 1980s.

The success of the System/360 made it difficult for IBM to introduce radical changes. Although it was under no legal compulsion to maintain compatibility, it risked loss of its growing and profitable customer base if it did not preserve their investment in software and training by compatible improvements. IBM announced the System/370 in 1970, a family of computers that maintained the standards of the System/360 but added dynamic address translation for time-sharing along with other improvements. In the early 1970s IBM began planning a Future System for announcement in 1975. The Future System was planned to be a substantial departure from the 360/370 mainframes and was designed to support distributed processing and data communications. IBM encountered difficulties in completing plans for the Future System as well as concerns about compatibility with earlier computers. IBM abandoned its planned Future System and substituted further upgrades of the 360/370 architecture (the 4300 and 3030 series) in the late 1970s (Ceruzzi, 1998, pp. 161, 252). IBM's technological choices in the 1970s allowed it to continue dominating the mainframe market, but not to extend its dominance into the developing market for distributed processing. As the newer approaches to computing grew more rapidly than the mainframe market, IBM's overall position in the computer industry declined.

Intel and the Microprocessor

In 1968, Robert Noyce and Gordon Moore left Fairchild and established Intel (short for Integrated Electronics) with the assistance of venture capitalist Arthur Rock. Intel hired Fairchild research engineer and part-time Berkeley lecturer Andy Grove as its director of research (and later as CEO). Intel instituted the personnel practice of offering relatively low salaries (often an actual pay cut from the person's previous job) along with generous stock options, giving all employees a strong financial interest in the success of the firm. The Intel compensation model was widely adopted by later innovative technical companies, but was a substantial departure from the previous approaches to compensating technical experts. The academic institutions, the nonprofit research corporations, and Bell Labs all provided steady salaries with occasional bonuses or prizes for exceptional accomplishments, but made no direct connection between personal income and the success of the organization. The Intel model was more market-oriented and shifted some of the risk and reward from the corporation to the individual employee.

Intel's initial business was developing a semiconductor memory chip to replace computer core memories. By 1968 integrated circuits were commonly used for computer logic, but magnetic cores remained the standard form of memory. Core memories had been greatly improved with much lower cost than at their beginning with the Whirlwind and SAGE computers, but the opportunities for further cost reduction in magnetic cores strung with tiny wires were much more limited than for integrated circuits. Many technology specialists recognized that the rapidly improving integrated circuits would eventually be cheap enough to replace core memory, but semiconductor memory products had not yet replaced core at the time Intel was founded. Building on research begun while the group was still at Fairchild, Intel developed a manufacturing process that could produce integrated circuits at a low enough cost to replace magnetic core memories.

Intel introduced its 1,024-bit (1K bit) memory chip (called the 1103) in October 1970, at a price lower than competing core memories (Jackson, 1997, p. 55). The 1103 and later improvements by Intel and other semiconductor companies quickly ended the market for core memory, and most computers produced after 1970 used semiconductor memory. While magnetic core and semiconductor memories were based on very different technologies, they were close enough substitutes in computer memories that there was very little transition time. As soon as Intel and others began producing semiconductor memories at a lower price than core memories, the market for core memories disappeared. The switch from core to semiconductor computer memory provided demand for very large numbers of integrated circuits of a single type and induced manufacturing innovations designed to reduce the cost of mass-produced chips. The semiconductor memory market was characterized by large-scale production of a standardized product with the choice of producer determined by price, in contrast to the specialized price-insensitive production of the earlier military and space markets for integrated circuits.

The development of a consumer electronic calculator market during the early 1970s created a similar mass market for integrated circuit logic modules. Electronic calculators had been produced on a small scale for many years but only in the late 1960s did semiconductor chips become cheap enough for electronic calculators to replace mechanical calculators on jobs that either could perform. While electronic calculators of the late 1960s from Wang Laboratories, Hewlett-Packard, and others were able to take the market away from expensive mechanical calculators, they cost several thousand dollars each and did not generate a consumer market. In the early 1970s a number of producers used integrated circuits to produce inexpensive calculators. By 1972 one could purchase a basic electronic calculator for $150, while Hewlett-Packard introduced the HP-35 at $400, which could also compute logarithmic and trigonometric functions. Two years later Hewlett-Packard introduced the programmable HP-65 for $795 and designated it a "personal computer" (Ceruzzi, 1998, p. 213). The mass market for electronic calculators in the 1970s induced a mass market for the semiconductor logic chips required to produce them. The advent of complex programmable calculators such as the HP-65 also sparked the development of user groups and newsletters to help sophisticated users overcome obstacles to the utilization of their "personal computers."

The microprocessor developed directly out of the market for complex calculators. Japan's Nippon Calculating Machine Corporation was developing an electronic calculator called Busicom and had requested that Intel design and manufacture a set of logic chips for the calculator. Intel engineer Marcian E. Hoff proposed simplifying the chip design by building a miniature general purpose computer with a subroutine capability. Hoff based his idea on the success of the Digital Equipment PDP-8, which had a very simple central processor but which was used to run a wide variety of programs. In Hoff's design, the particular details of the Busicom calculator would consist of programs in a read-only memory chip, while the remaining components would include a general purpose processor, general purpose memory chip, and input-output capability (Jackson, 1997, p. 71; Ceruzzi, 1998, p. 218). The Hoff approach reduced the number of logic chips required for the calculator by substituting software contained in memory chips.

Stan Mazor and Federico Faggin of Intel performed the detailed design work necessary to turn Hoff's idea into a working silicon chip, and all three names were on the patent granted in 1974. Intel leader Robert Noyce negotiated a reduced price to Busicom in exchange for Intel retaining rights to sell the chip to other customers for anything other than calculators. Intel announced the new design as the 4-bit 4004 microprocessor in 1971, which along with three supporting chips for memory and input-output could operate as a tiny general purpose computer. The 4004 had extremely limited capabilities and was difficult to program, creating considerable uncertainty over its commercial potential. However, Intel's announcement of the 4004 initiated a race to develop improved microprocessors between Intel, Motorola, and a number of other companies. In 1972, Intel offered an improved 8-bit chip as the 8008 microprocessor. The 8008 project had begun as a custom design project for Computer Terminal Corporation that required processing a byte (8 bits) at a time rather than the 4 bits that were adequate for a calculator's decimal digit. After other companies announced competing microprocessors, Intel announced an improved 8-bit chip, the 8080 in 1974. The 8080 was compatible with the 8008 but had substantially greater capability (Ceruzzi, 1998, p. 221).

Intel believed that its microprocessors would be most useful as components of larger systems. While programming the early microprocessors was difficult, it was simpler than designing custom circuits. Just as its first two microprocessors had emerged from efforts to simplify the circuit designs of a calculator and a computer terminal, Intel believed that the effort to program one of its microprocessors would be rewarded by turning it into a special purpose controller that could be produced in large quantities without reprogramming. The company did not believe that there would be a substantial market for personal computers built around its microprocessors because of the lack of complementary products that were needed to make a stand-alone computer useful and did not attempt to develop its own personal computer.

Personal Computers and Workstations

The first widely influential personal computer was the Altair, designed by H. Edward Roberts, owner of the hobby shop MITS in Albuquerque, New Mexico. The Altair used Intel's 8080 microprocessor and was publicized in a January 1975 cover story in *Popular Electronics*. MITS purchased 8080 chips at $75 each from Intel and added other components necessary for a working computer. The Altair was sold as a $400 kit for self-assembly and advertised as equivalent to a small minicomputer. Although the microprocessor at the heart of the Altair had substantial capabilities, the original Altair had extremely limited capability. With no programming languages or commercial programs available and no input-output devices, it could be laboriously programmed by flipping toggle switches and provided output through blinking lights. It had 256 bytes of semiconductor memory and no data storage to hold the programs for later use after the power had been turned off. Despite its limitations, the Altair found a strong market among hobbyists who were willing to pay the modest price in order to get the parts to build themselves a personal computer, and MITS was overwhelmed with orders. The Altair's open design easily accommodated improvements devised by others, and the Altair kits became the basis for much better computers than the originals.

The most significant legacy of the Altair was the founding of Microsoft. Bill Gates and Paul Allen had been friends and business partners in high school, and had worked together as programmers at TRW while Gates was still in high school. They had become experts at using the PDP-10 and had utilized Intel's 8008 chip in a traffic-counting machine. At the time of the *Popular Electronics* article on the Altair, Gates was an undergraduate at Harvard and Allen was working at Honeywell. Allen proposed that they write an interpreter to allow Basic programming language to be used on the Altair. They utilized the PDP-10 in the Harvard computer center and programmed it to simulate the 8080 chip. After several weeks of intense work, Gates and Allen (with help from Harvard student Monte Davidoff) created a working version of Basic that Allen could demonstrate to Roberts, using an improved Altair with more memory and a paper-tape reader for input and output. In the spring of 1975 Allen went to work for MITS and soon afterward Gates, Davidoff, and others joined him to establish Microsoft, with a licensing agreement that gave MITS exclusive rights to sell their program with certain limitations. The exact relationship between the Microsoft programmers and MITS was the subject of substantial dispute when Microsoft's Basic became popular but Microsoft eventually prevailed with full rights, and the Basic versions developed at Harvard and Albuquerque became the foundation product for the new company.

Alternatives to both the Intel microprocessor and the MITS personal computer quickly became available. Intel designer Federico Faggin left Intel in 1974 after a dispute over credit for his innovations and founded Zilog with funding from Exxon Enterprises. In early 1976, Zilog released the Z80, a substantial improvement over the Intel 8080 that retained full compatibility with the earlier chip. The Z80 was used in Radio Shack's 1977 model TRS-80, one of the earliest fully assembled and widely distributed personal computers. MOS Technologies produced the 6502, a microprocessor used in the Commodore PET and the Apple II, both introduced in 1977. Motorola began a substantial microprocessor development program soon after the Intel 4004 was available and began selling the 6800 soon after the Intel 8080 appeared, followed by the more powerful 68000 in 1979. The Motorola 68000 was used in early workstations and the later Apple Macintosh computer, providing an alternative architecture to Intel long after other early companies dropped out of the microprocessor business.

Personal computers began to move from the realm of hobbyists to business users in 1979 when Daniel Bricklin and Robert Frankston offered the spreadsheet program VisiCalc for the Apple II computer. Steve Jobs and Steve Wozniak had introduced the Apple II in 1977 using the MOS Technologies 6502 microprocessor, and Apple's color graphics and inexpensive disk drive distinguished it from other contemporary personal computers. VisiCalc simplified laborious hand calculations routinely used in many businesses and created a practical reason to buy the Apple II in addition to its widely recognized suitability for games. Total sales reached 100,000 by mid-1981 (Ceruzzi, 1998, p. 268), far higher than popular early computers such as the IBM 1401 that had 10,000 installations.

The major computer makers largely ignored the hobby and game-oriented microprocessor-based computers of the 1970s, but in July 1980 IBM's Corporate Management Committee accepted a recommendation from its Entry Level Systems unit in Florida that IBM should build a personal computer. In order to reduce development time, IBM decided on an open architecture with components procured from other companies. The IBM proprietary part of the computer was a read-only memory chip holding the basic input-output system (BIOS). Even though most of the components were available to anyone, so long as IBM controlled the BIOS no one could build an IBM clone. IBM chose the Intel 8088 chip as its microprocessor. The 8088 had a 16-bit internal structure and an 8-bit bus, allowing the machine to work with 8-bit enhancement products available from other companies but giving it better performance than the first generation of 8-bit microprocessors. IBM procured its Basic interpreter from Microsoft and also chose Microsoft to write a disk operating system (DOS) for the new computer. At that time Microsoft had forty employees and had not written an operating system, but it licensed an existing operating system from Seattle Computer Products and modified it into DOS for the IBM machine. Microsoft made extraordinary efforts to succeed with its most critical project but often felt overwhelmed by the detailed interaction required by the much larger IBM organization where "IBM had more people writing requirements for the computer than Microsoft had writing code" (Wallace and Erickson, 1992, p. 197).

In August 1981 (one year after the decision to begin the project), IBM announced its Personal Computer with 64 kilobytes of memory and a 160-kilobyte floppy disk drive for $2,880 (Miller, 1997, p. 110). Basic, VisiCalc, and the EasyWriter word processing program were available from the beginning while additional programs and hardware improvements followed quickly. IBM's monochrome monitor could display an eighty-character line while earlier models displayed only forty characters, making word processing on the PC easier than on earlier models. The availability of word processing and spreadsheet programs, together with the IBM name, made the new computer an immediate choice among businesses. While the PC was not at all competitive with "real computers" managed by corporate computing staff, it was useful on many tasks previously done with typewriters and calculators. IBM sold 35,000 PCs by the end of 1981, and sales accelerated in 1982. When Mitch Kapor wrote the spreadsheet program Lotus 1-2-3 to take direct advantage of the PC characteristics, Lotus replaced VisiCalc as the spreadsheet of choice, and the IBM PC's position as a business computer was enhanced. The IBM PC running Lotus 1-2-3 and the WordPerfect word processing program became standard in many companies and some homes.

In 1982, three former Texas Instruments employees formed Compaq Computer Corporation with the goal of creating a clone of the IBM PC. They hired programmers to replicate IBM's BIOS functions without looking at IBM's BIOS code. In 1983, Compaq delivered an IBM PC clone that was able to run Lotus 1-2-3 and Microsoft Flight Simulator, the two programs that relied on the details of the IBM machine and were considered the best test of compatibility. Phoenix Technologies also created a compatible substitute for IBM's BIOS and offered it for sale, allowing any company to build an IBM clone. IBM's open architecture and the ability of other companies to build a substitute for the IBM BIOS eliminated IBM's control of its creation, and far more IBM-compatible computers were sold by companies other than IBM than by IBM itself.

IBM attempted to take control of the personal computer market in 1987 with a new series of machines designated the PS/2. The PS/2 series was reminiscent of IBM's earlier System/360. PS/2 was a compatible set of four computers of different sizes without full compatibility to IBM's earlier PC and AT models. The PS/2 models ranged from an 8-MHz 8086 processor to a 20-MHz 386 processor. The new models used 3.5-inch floppy disk drives instead of the earlier 5.25-inch drives, used an improved 640-by-480 monitor display resolution, and a new bus called Micro Channel Architecture that was not compatible with earlier machines and expansion cards (Miller, 1997, p. 124). IBM also announced a new operating system, OS/2, that would be jointly developed by IBM and Microsoft and would replace Microsoft's DOS. IBM attempted to create a proprietary client-server architecture by combining its PS/2 systems connected by LANs using IBM's Token Ring protocol with IBM mainframes connected by IBM's System Network Architecture (Bresnahan and Greenstein, 1999, pp. 29–31). The IBM plan correctly forecast the movement toward the client-server model and presented a complete package of products to establish IBM dominance in the emerging model comparable to its dominance of the earlier mainframe market.

The IBM plan failed. There was no dominating source of IBM monopoly power in the combination of elements, and IBM did not provide adequate technological or price advantages to make customers choose its combination over open-market combinations. By the 1987 announcement of the PS/2, the clone makers together already sold more personal computers than IBM. The clone makers created an alternative to IBM's Micro Channel Architecture. Microsoft continued working on its Windows graphical overlay for DOS, initially described as a transition to the joint IBM/Microsoft OS/2. Microsoft's announcement of Windows 3.0 in 1990 effectively ended the IBM/Microsoft partnership and the OS/2 development effort. Many users adopted Ethernet LANs instead of IBM's Token Ring protocol and adopted TCP/IP for networks instead of IBM's

SNA. The descendants of the IBM PC dominated the personal computer industry and were tied together in networks as IBM had expected, but IBM played only a minor role. All the components were procured from specialists in that component and tied together by open standards. Programs from Microsoft and processors from Intel determined the evolution of the personal computer, and the designation of "IBM-compatible" personal computer was replaced by the more accurate "Wintel" personal computer.

In 1981, Apollo delivered the first microprocessor "workstation," based on a Motorola microprocessor and Apollo's operating system, with a price beginning at $40,000. The workstation was an expensive sophisticated version of the personal computer. At a time when personal computers were just emerging from the hobbyist stage, the far more expensive workstations provided individual support for computing-intensive engineers. In 1982, Vinod Khosla founded SUN Microsystems to commercialize a research project known as the Stanford University Networked workstation. SUN acquired both hardware and software expertise by hiring Andy Bechtolsheim of Stanford and Unix expert Bill Joy of Berkeley (Ceruzzi, 1998, pp. 281, 282). SUN adopted an "open systems" strategy and built its initial workstations around the Motorola 68000 microprocessor, the Unix operating system, Ethernet networking, and a nonproprietary internal bus. SUN adopted the advertising slogan "the network is the computer" and played an important role in developing networks of small computers as a substitute for mainframes. Early networked workstations were so expensive that only those with very high demand for computing (as well as the technological sophistication to utilize Unix) could justify the cost. However, the model of linked workstations gradually expanded its range of applicability as prices declined and the distinction between workstations and personal computers disappeared. The development of inexpensive Ethernet cards, together with simplifications in the Ethernet structure that allowed it to work on twisted copper wires instead of coaxial cable and to be combined into hubs in order to set up complex local networks, led to routine networking of personal computers in office environments. When those networks of personal computers were linked to data servers, they provided an alternative to the mainframe business computers.

10

The Computer-Communications Boundary

In the 1950s and 1960s, telephone companies were a closed world. The telephone company took full responsibility for end-to-end service and controlled all parts of the equipment utilized in making a telephone call. Telephone company personnel typically spent full careers with the company, with little mobility between telephone companies and other companies. AT&T's public relations efforts emphasized the differences between telephone service and other kinds of service in an effort to clearly distinguish itself from other electrical technology companies. That emphasis developed in part by its efforts to defend itself against the 1949 antitrust suit that sought to separate Western Electric from the remainder of the Bell System. If Western Electric simply produced ordinary electrical equipment that could be procured on a competitive market from any company, then the separation would increase competition in that market and simplify regulation of telephone service. On the other hand, if Western Electric produced highly specialized equipment developed to meet Bell System specifications, then it could be an efficient "supply arm" of the regulated monopoly. Similarly, the emphasis on hardwired telephones installed only by a telephone company technician maintained the appearance of full integration and telephone company control, while a voluntary effort to develop plug-in telephones would have allowed greater separation between the telephone instrument and the telephone network.

The advancing computer industry interrupted this self-contained world. Early projects required joint use of computers and communications, but they were handled on a special case basis. As discussed in Chapter 4, AT&T pioneered what later became known as modems in order to carry radar data over telephone lines to the SAGE computers.

However, that project was done under military contract, and it required specially engineered private lines to carry the data. AT&T developed a commercial version of data communication through private line networks for early computer-communications systems such as the SABRE airline reservation system. The special cases evolved into a more general problem of how to manage computer and communications interaction with the development of time-sharing computers in the late 1960s and early 1970s. Time-sharing computers could be utilized locally (with terminals attached directly to the computer) but were most useful if they could be accessed remotely over ordinary telephone lines.

The increased use of computer technology in the telephone system and the increased use of telephone lines in computer systems brought the two industries into close interaction. That interaction created potential competition between computer companies and communications companies and created opportunities to develop innovative new products utilizing combinations of computers and communications. The competitive interaction was complicated by the existence of regulation for the communications companies but not for the computer companies and the restriction of AT&T to regulated activities through the 1956 consent decree. If the regulatory boundary could be extended around new services that incorporated both communications and computers, AT&T would have an opportunity to control that market through its effective monopoly of the communications lines. If the regulatory line was contracted to exclude combinations of communications and computers, AT&T could be prohibited by the consent decree from offering the combined services.

By 1970 there was widespread agreement on several general principles:

1. Telephone service should remain a regulated monopoly.
2. The computer industry and data processing services should remain unregulated.
3. Computers and telephone service should be combined to allow remote computing.

The combination of the three principles meant that it was necessary to draw a dividing line between the unregulated computer industry and the regulated telephone industry, and to find ways to facilitate the integration of telephone lines into computer communication. Alternatively, it would have been possible to construct a separate digital data network to interconnect computers, but early demand was inadequate to support a separate network of efficient size. AT&T had an incentive to accommodate computer traffic in order to maintain the universal nature of its network. AT&T's position since the days of Theodore Vail had been that "one system" was the socially desirable way to provide communication services.

Drawing a line between computers and communications was not a simple process. The boundary line affected the balance of power and profits between AT&T and IBM as well as other telephone and computer companies. The boundary line also helped determine the range of consumer freedom to adopt new technology. The line-drawing exercise centered around two separate questions:

1. What distinguished a computer terminal from a communications terminal?
2. In what ways could the telephone network be combined with nontelephone company computers to create new kinds of services?

The process of deciding the two questions required examination of the social justification for many of AT&T's practices and eventually led to a substantial narrowing of the scope of AT&T's monopoly. The process was controversial and lengthy, but resulted in a reasonable adjustment of the 1960s institutions to the new technologies of the computer industry. The substantive policy adjustment was completed with the FCC's 1980 Computer Inquiry II decision, but the process of interpreting that decision and phasing in the changes mandated by it extended for several years later.

Computer-Assisted Messages: Communications or Data Processing?

In the early 1960s, Bunker Ramo provided a stock quotation service to brokerage offices using its own computers and leased AT&T lines. The service was treated as an unregulated data processing service. When Bunker Ramo added a message-switching capability to its service in 1965 to allow brokers who used the stock quotation system to transmit buy and sell orders, AT&T refused to continue leasing the necessary communications lines to Bunker Ramo. According to AT&T, the addition of message switching made the service communications rather than data processing. At that time AT&T did not allow resale of its services. If Bunker Ramo was providing a data processing service, then AT&T was leasing the lines to Bunker Ramo for its own use, but if Bunker Ramo was providing a communications service, then it was reselling AT&T's communications lines to other companies in violation of the AT&T tariff provisions.

Bunker Ramo filed a complaint with the FCC, causing the FCC to begin consideration of the dividing line between communications and data processing. After five years of consideration, the FCC promulgated its first computer boundary rules in 1971. The Computer I rules attempted to apply the previously clear distinctions of regulated communications and unregulated data processing to the new hybrid services according to relative use. If the primary use of a service was communications, it was regulated hybrid communications. If the primary use was data processing, it was unregulated data processing.

In the Bunker Ramo case at issue, the 1971 rules meant that if the service primarily transmitted stock quotations (data processing) with occasional broker orders, then it was an unregulated service entitled to access to AT&T's lines, but if broker orders increased to a large portion of the system, then it would become an unauthorized communications service improperly reselling AT&T's services. The 1971 rules provided a guideline for settling specific disputes but did not provide a framework for the development of hybrid services. Services that would naturally have been offered as a unified service in a free market were either not offered at all or were split into two distinct services, one part regulated as a communications service and the other unregulated as a data processing service. At the time of the 1971 rules, remote users of a single time-sharing computer already exchanged messages. Two years later, 75 percent of the Arpanet traffic was e-mail despite its design as a computer resource-sharing tool (Hafner and Lyon, 1996, p. 194). The new computer networks of the 1970s routinely combined elements of traditional data processing and elements of traditional communications in a wide variety of ways, leaving the FCC's 1971 attempt to extend the 1960s boundary line increasingly inconsistent with technological opportunities.

Smart Terminals: Teletypewriters or Computers?

AT&T provided teletypewriters for sending and receiving written messages as part of its regulated communications services. When time-shar-

ing began, AT&T's regulated teletypewriters and associated communication lines were routinely used to provide remote access to the shared
computer. IBM, DEC, and many other companies produced a wide variety of computer terminals. Those terminals were normally used to access time-sharing computers through direct wiring in a local configuration or by attaching to an AT&T-supplied "data set" (modem) to access a
remote computer using the telephone network. AT&T's Dataspeed 40/4
was a "smart terminal" designed to communicate with a computer and
also to perform some processing functions on its own. It was an intermediate step between the original "dumb terminals," which merely originated and terminated communications, and the later system of networked small computers. AT&T filed a tariff for the Dataspeed 40/4 as a
component of its Dataphone Digital Service, just as it had for a long time
tariffed teletypewriter terminals as part of a communication service. IBM
objected that the Dataspeed 40/4 was really a small computer designed
to work with larger computers, just as IBM's unregulated smart terminals were designed to do. From IBM's perspective, AT&T was extending
its regulated communications service into the data processing industry.

The FCC's Common Carrier Bureau initially supported IBM and rejected AT&T's tariff. On review in 1976, the commission allowed the
tariff to go into effect but noted that smart terminals did not fit clearly
into the existing rules and initiated a proceeding (Computer II) to develop new boundary rules between computers and communications.
The smart terminal was an indication that computer technology was
moving toward networks with intelligence widely distributed, rather
than the initial time-sharing configuration of simple terminals communicating with a central computer. As that trend continued, any regulatory distinction between "computer-like" and "communications-like"
terminals became increasingly artificial.

The FCC's Notice of Proposed Rule Making in the new proceeding
suggested that terminals performing a "basic media conversion" (similar
to a traditional telephone set or teletypewriter terminal) would be classified as communications equipment (regulated), while terminals performing more than "basic media conversion" would be classified as data
processing equipment (unregulated). The commission's proposed distinction was opposed by a wide variety of commentators. While AT&T
and GTE claimed that the proposed line provided too strict limits on
what they could provide under regulation, IBM and other computer

equipment companies challenged the proposed line for leaving too much flexibility to the regulated carriers, expanding the scope of regulation, and increasing the opportunities for cross-subsidy.

Interconnection of Customer-Owned Equipment with the Telephone Network

While the FCC was attempting to refine its definition of the boundary between regulated communications and unregulated data processing in the late 1970s, it was continuing to deal with a long series of controversies over the rights of telephone users to attach their own equipment to the telephone network. From the early days of telephones, AT&T had prohibited customer-owned attachments to its network. Restrictions were included in customer contracts prior to regulation and were incorporated in tariff language in 1913. Tariffs constitute the contract between the regulated company and its customers. They are filed with regulatory authorities and generally go into effect automatically unless specifically disapproved. The tariffs contain the rates to be paid as well as "terms and conditions" that constitute a detailed contract between the carrier and anyone who chooses to take service from the carrier.

AT&T enforced its "foreign attachments" ban vigorously though unsystematically. In one case, the telephone company prohibited customers from putting a cover on the telephone directory because a cover was an attachment to the telephone book, which was telephone company property. However, AT&T allowed many unauthorized recording devices to be attached to the network through haphazard procedures in enforcing its restrictions. Although there were several controversies over AT&T's strict prohibition of attachments to the network (including the important Hush-A-Phone federal appeals court decision in 1956 that placed some limits on AT&T's freedom to exclude harmless attachments), the issue did not become important until the advent of time-sharing computers in the late 1960s. A strict application of the original restrictive AT&T approach either would have prohibited communication with computers over telephone lines or would have required AT&T to supply the computer. In practice, AT&T supplied teletypewriter terminals and modems as the terminating equipment for data lines and allowed the interconnection of an AT&T-supplied modem with customer-owned computers. AT&T offered data lines as well as voice lines and considered its end-to-end responsibility for data lines to include the terminal device and the modem but not the computer itself. However, as time-sharing computers proliferated during the late 1960s, both AT&T and the FCC recognized a need to provide greater freedom for specialized data communication devices developed outside of AT&T.

In 1968, the FCC used a dispute over a device known as a Carterfone to reduce AT&T's control over equipment attached to the telephone network. The Carterfone contained a cradle into which an ordinary telephone handset could be placed. The Carterfone transmitted voice signals from a mobile radio transmitter to the telephone handset and converted the voice signals received from the handset into radio signals for broadcast to the mobile radio telephone without the need for a direct electrical connection between the two. AT&T prohibited the Carterfone and threatened to suspend telephone service to customers who used it to connect early mobile radio systems to the land-line telephone network. The commission found that although the Carterfone violated AT&T's tariff, the tariff itself was illegal and violated the requirements specified in the earlier Hush-a-Phone case. The commission ordered AT&T to file new tariffs to allow the connection of all devices that did not cause actual harm.

Both AT&T and the FCC understood that the Carterfone case would be important in developing the demarcation line between the regulated communications industry and the unregulated computer industry. AT&T chairman H. I. Romnes chose not to fight the Carterfone concept and saw advantages for AT&T in allowing a wider variety of terminals to be connected to the system. AT&T could not supply all of the specialized equipment that might be required by computer users and had no interest in forcing computer users off the public network. However, Romnes and other AT&T executives believed that centralized control of the telephone network and of the signals used to control that network was necessary.

An AT&T executive committee compiled a long list of potential harms that could result from freely interconnecting customer-supplied equipment. Most of the potential harms were related to network signaling. Telephone terminal equipment provides signals to the network that set up and discontinue the call and that provide for billing. Improper signaling from customer terminal equipment could cause the central office to fail to respond, to prematurely terminate a call, or to cause errors in billing. Consequently, AT&T sought to retain control of network signaling. Rather than promulgating standards required for attachments, AT&T offered a Protective Connecting Arrangement (PCA) that would isolate the customer equipment from the network. According to AT&T's post-Carterfone tariffs, any customer who wished to attach terminal equipment to the network was required to order a tariffed PCA from AT&T and attach the customer terminal equipment through the PCA. The PCA provided all network signaling (Temin with Galambos, 1987, pp. 44, 45).

Although AT&T's offer of liberal connection of customer-provided terminal equipment through PCAs was accepted as a cooperative action going beyond the minimum legal requirements at the time, it did not constitute a stable position. AT&T viewed the PCA tariffs as a dramatic opening up of the network beyond what many of its executives thought desirable. The FCC viewed the PCA tariffs as an appropriate interim measure while the desirable long-term arrangements were being developed. The FCC allowed the tariffs to go into effect without formally approving them, thus reserving its right to find them unlawful at a later time.

Throughout the 1970s controversies over interconnection of terminal equipment to the telephone network continued. John deButts replaced Romnes as AT&T CEO in 1972 and began active opposition to the early competitive policies. According to Peter Temin, deButts responded to the FCC's actions "by drawing on the traditional conception of the Bell System rather than by articulating a new one . . . by inspiring the System's many employees to believe again that the corporation's familiar goals—the objectives Vail had given it—were laudable and achievable" (Temin with Galambos, 1987, p. 70). DeButts established a high-profile program of intensive opposition to the FCC's efforts to further liberalize interconnection. AT&T asserted that attaching customer-owned equipment to the telephone network would harm the network and that consequently the telephone companies must have complete control over all equipment attached to the network in order to manage the system for the benefit of all users. AT&T also contended that attaching customer-owned equipment to the telephone network would upset the established system of revenue and cost sharing across the country and would cause increases in basic telephone rates and consumer dissatisfaction.

During 1973 deButts publicly expressed his opposition to terminal competition and sought the assistance of state regulators in blocking the FCC's policies. The FCC was responsible for regulating interstate communication and the state regulators were responsible for intrastate communication. However, most terminal equipment was used to originate and terminate both intrastate and interstate calls. The established process for dividing authority over equipment used for both interstate and intrastate communication was a complex cost allocation system to determine the division of costs that should be assigned to interstate and intrastate jurisdictions, but that system did not clarify which body had responsibility to authorize changes such as interconnection standards. Several states led by North Carolina challenged the FCC's authority to require AT&T to allow customer equipment to be connected to the telephone network. In 1976, the Fourth Circuit Court of Appeals ruled that the state regulators did not have the authority to issue regulations overturning the FCC liberalization program within their states (Court of Appeals, 4th Cir., 1976, p. 787). This ruling allowed the development of competition in terminal equipment on a nationwide basis rather than according to separate state regulations, but the question of boundary lines between state and federal authority has continued as a frequent subject of controversy and litigation to the present.

In 1975, the FCC established a system of technical standards for the connection of customer-provided equipment without using AT&T's PCA, contrary to the recommendations of AT&T and the state regulatory commissions. Those standards were implemented in 1977 after extensive litigation. The standards were defined in great detail and adopted as formal rules for equipment to be connected to the telephone network, including types of allowable plugs, voltages, and many other specific requirements (47 C.F.R. §68). The standards essentially froze then-existing Bell System practice (with the addition of more flexible plugs to replace previous hardwired connections) into a rigid interface between the customer-supplied equipment and the public telephone network. The Bell System had previously chosen not to implement coordinated changes in central office equipment and subscriber equipment and had treated the existing subscriber equipment as a constraint on the kind of central office equipment that could be installed. The FCC-mandated standards formalized that Bell System policy. They provided great freedom for either customers or the telephone companies to introduce new equipment so long as the new equipment followed the same standards for connecting and passing signals at the boundary. The standards slowed the introduction of new services such as ISDN that required co-ordinated changes in customer and central office equipment, but the FCC later modified the rules or granted waivers to facilitate the intro-duction of new technology.

After the codification of standards, the telephone companies contin-ued to supply terminal equipment under tariff as part of their regulated communication service. The telephone company-supplied terminal equipment was recorded on the regulatory books, allocated between state and federal jurisdictions, and used as a component of the regulated rate-making process in accordance with long-established procedures. Suppliers other than telephone companies were unregulated and sold their products through retail stores for simple items such as ordinary telephones and through direct sales for complex items such as private branch exchanges (PBXs). Although the competitive equipment mar-ket developed rapidly after interconnection rights were established, the mixture of regulated and unregulated products provided either directly to customers by competitors or bundled with telephone services created confusion and complaints.

The Deregulation of Terminal Equipment

In 1980, the FCC concluded its Computer II inquiry with a crucial de-cision. As part of that decision, the commission abandoned its long-standing attempt to distinguish between telephone and data processing terminal equipment. Instead, it deregulated all terminal equipment. In its Computer II decision, the commission sought to separate equipment that could be supplied on a competitive market from regulated monop-oly services, and therefore to shrink the boundaries of regulation. The commission concluded:

> We find the continuation of tariff-type regulation of carrier provided CPE neither recognizes the role of carriers as competitive providers of CPE nor is it conducive to the competitive evolution of various termi-nal equipment markets. We find that CPE is a severable commodity from the provision of transmission services. The current regulatory scheme which allows for the provision of CPE in conjunction with reg-ulated communication services does not reflect its severability from transmission services or the competitive realities of the market place

. . . Deregulation of carrier provided CPE would separate the costs associated with the provision, marketing, and servicing and maintenance of CPE from the rates charged for interstate common carrier services. Thus, the deregulation of CPE fosters a regulatory scheme which separates the provision of regulated common carrier services from competitive activities that are independent of, but related to, the underlying utility service. In addition, the separation of CPE from common carrier offerings and its resulting deregulation will provide carriers the flexibility to compete in the marketplace on the same basis as any other equipment vendor. (FCC, 1980, pp. 446, 447)

Under the Computer II rules, AT&T was allowed to provide customer premises equipment (CPE) only through a "fully separate subsidiary" with strict limitations on the permissible interactions between the unregulated subsidiary and the regulated company. The changes ordered in the Computer II decision provoked great controversy in the industry and resulted in numerous petitions for reconsideration as well as requests that the federal appeals court overturn the decision. After two reconsideration orders and affirmation by the appeals court, the basic structure of the Computer II decision was implemented. The commission was particularly concerned about the valuation of the huge amount of CPE ($14 billion in AT&T book value) that would be transferred to the unregulated affiliate. Transfer of assets from the regulated company to the unregulated affiliate at too low a price, for example, would result in a competitive advantage for the affiliate compared to independent companies, and would create higher regulated rates than would occur under proper valuation. In order to allow time to conduct valuation studies and in order to minimize the effect on rates, a long phase-in schedule was developed. All new equipment installed after January 1, 1983, was to be provided on an unregulated basis, while "embedded" equipment (equipment already installed as of January 1, 1983) would remain on the regulated books of the telephone companies through a long phase-in, which was later modified by the divestiture agreement.

The Computer II decision completed the CPE policy story by shrinking the boundary of the regulated telephone network to exclude CPE. With that decision, the long-standing question of what attachments to the telephone network must be considered part of the regulated industry was definitively answered. The regulated industry was redefined to stop at the end of a wire to the customer's premises, and any equipment attached to the customer side of that wire was excluded from the regulated industry. The boundary was defined with public interface standards. All equipment on the customer's side of the boundary was for the use of that customer only and was excluded from the complex revenue sharing and subsidy mechanisms of the regulated telephone industry.

From the current perspective, the deregulation of CPE was an obvious and beneficial action. The question is why it took so long and required many years of litigation and gradual adjustments in order to decide and implement that policy. However, during the 1970s that approach was not at all obvious. No telephone company at that time allowed customers to routinely connect their own equipment to the network. There was little alternative information available to judge AT&T's claim that such interconnection would be harmful. Consequently, the FCC moved very slowly and gradually to establish limited competition and then increase the rights of customers to interconnect their own equipment as the limited competition appeared to be working without harm to the network.

The 1980 CPE decision was a crucial step in the development of data communications and the Internet. Prior to the decision, the telephone companies distinguished data communication service from voice service by the kind of terminal equipment attached. If a customer needed data communications, the telephone company provided a modem as the terminal equipment, while if a customer needed voice, the telephone company provided an ordinary telephone handset. Different levels of data communication service provided over a voice-grade channel were charged at different rates according to the speed of the modem supplied. There was no necessary relationship between the variation in the data communications prices and the underlying cost of differing levels of modems. Those decisions were made by telephone company management together with state regulators for a variety of corporate and political purposes. After customers gained the right to connect their own equipment, an independent market in modems developed and eclipsed AT&T-provided modems. Customers could order ordinary telephone service and connect any kind of modem to it with no additional charges from the telephone company. The decision reduced AT&T's ability to practice price discrimination between customers with different valuations on data speed and increased the incentive to develop and purchase high-speed modems. After the decision, differences in the cost of various services provided over voice-grade lines were determined entirely by differences in the cost of terminal equipment that customers chose to attach to the lines.

The FCC's 1980 Computer II decision allowed complex combinations of equipment to be attached to the telephone network so long as it conformed to the specified standards. Consequently, it was possible to develop a substantial private network, either voice or data, and to interconnect that private network with the public telephone network. From a regulatory perspective the private network was simply customer premises equipment and therefore entitled to interconnection with the public telephone network.

The Deregulation of Enhanced Services

The Computer II decision also created the legal category of "enhanced services" and defined an enhanced service as one that "combines basic service with computer processing applications that act on the format, content, code, protocol or similar aspects of the subscriber's transmitted information, or provide the subscriber additional, different, or restructured information, or involve subscriber interaction with stored information." Enhanced services were distinguished from basic regulated service that was "limited to the common carrier offering of transmission capacity for the movement of information" (FCC, 1980, p. 387). The concept behind the legal definitions was that basic communication service consisted of communication that was delivered in the same form in which it was received while services in which the form of the message was modified by computer were enhanced.

Under the 1980 Computer II decision, enhanced services were deregulated and excluded from either state or federal regulation. The decision assumed that enhanced service providers would obtain basic service from the regulated carriers and then add their own computer processing to develop new kinds of services. The definition removed the uncertainty of previous categories in which a large number of messages transmitted (such as current e-mail systems) could transform a data processing service into a regulated communication service. The most significant enhanced service is the Internet, which did not yet exist at the time the definition was created.

The Computer II decision created a favorable legal structure for the development of enhanced services. Enhanced service providers had a guaranteed right to utilize the underlying communication infrastructure, but freedom from regulations imposed on that infrastructure. At the time, enhanced services were a very small and uncertain category but as data communications became important, the Computer II structure prevented AT&T from taking actions to protect its own monopoly.

Several factors helped create a successful transition from a monopoly network that included terminal equipment to one that allowed customer-owned terminal equipment to be freely attached. First, the old structure clearly did not work in the context of computer communication. There was an external impetus to changing the policy that eliminated the status quo as a viable option. The stability of policy and the difficulty of implementing change generally mean that policies are designed for the old technology and considerable effort is required to change them to conform to a new technology.

Second, the changes required to accommodate the new technology only made minimal changes in the previous distribution of property rights. The new enhanced service category was very important for the future development of the Internet, but neither the Internet nor any other substantial enhanced services existed at the time it was created. The legal category of enhanced services was an effort to accommodate a potential future development. Although the creation of that legal category limited AT&T's potential property rights in that set of services, it did not eliminate existing services from the monopoly umbrella. The CPE deregulation had a more substantial effect on existing property rights, but it was the result of an incremental process. By the time the Computer II decision was reached, customer-owned CPE could already be attached to the network as a result of the standards program. The deregulation was important, but AT&T's battle to treat the CPE as an intrinsic part of the telephone network had already been lost. The deregulation of CPE reduced the opportunities to rearrange the regulated prices to the disadvantage of competitive CPE providers and allowed CPE to rapidly develop into a competitive market.

Third, the CPE deregulation and the development of enhanced services fit into an easily explained and widely accepted rationale. CPE was used entirely by a single customer, and it made sense to allow that customer freedom to choose its equipment so long as that equipment did not cause harm to the public network. Enhanced services were another form of consumer freedom to use the telephone network. While the enhanced service concept violated previous strict rules on resale, those rules were tolerated by the regulators without strong support, and were eventually overturned.

Enhanced services were closely related to the freedom granted by CPE deregulation. In the era of strict noninterconnection, it was impossible to provide enhanced services because nothing could be added to the network except what the telephone company chose to add to it. With CPE deregulation, customers gained much more freedom to utilize the network as they chose by selecting appropriate CPE. An ordinary telephone call, data communication, or a sophisticated private communication system could all be utilized with the same telephone company service simply by choosing different CPE. Similarly, enhanced services could be created by attaching computers to the telephone network. That could have been done after CPE deregulation without any specific new category if only used privately.

The enhanced services category guaranteed the right to offer services that combined computer and communications functions to the public without becoming a regulated common carrier. The Computer II decision provided the institutional foundation for the Internet as an unregulated communications system. The original services that were the basis for the enhanced category ("value-added" carriers such as Telenet) never developed into important communications services, but the category provided a protected space for the later Internet to develop.

The computer boundary-drawing efforts maintained the monopoly telephone system while restricting its scope and power. It was possible to narrow the boundaries of the monopoly without a major rearrangement of prices or a major change in the regulatory and corporate processes that had developed for the telephone industry. By drawing the regulated boundary around the public network of basic telephone service, the decisions allowed privately provided equipment to be attached to the network and protected the new services from monopoly control. The decision essentially declared part of the traditional telephone industry to be unregulated data processing.

The computer decisions gained political feasibility by protecting most of the existing property rights, while reserving future developments to the competitive market. By placing the regulated boundary line close to the public network of basic services, the decision allowed considerable freedom to innovate without facing the opposition of the monopoly telephone company. By maintaining the existing price structure and revenue flows, the decisions reduced political opposition to the change. While AT&T and the other telephone companies (along with the state regulators) opposed the liberalizing movement, it was hard to generate political support for their preferred policy of limiting consumer freedom to utilize alternative suppliers for equipment that conformed to AT&T-developed standards.

11

Fringe Competition in Long Distance Telephone Service

Early long distance voice transmission was extremely expensive, leaving most of the market to telegraph even when voice transmission was available. A crucial component of the long distance expense was electronics. Transcontinental service was unavailable until vacuum-tube technology was sufficiently developed to build an electronic amplifier. Electronics was required in order to carry multiple conversations over a single wire or to construct high-capacity transmission facilities. In the era of expensive electronics, long distance toll service was a labor-intensive process as multiple operators set up calls and created the necessary records for billing.

The Bell System recognized the crucial role of electronics in reducing the cost and improving the quality of long distance telephone service. The research program that led to the transistor was motivated by the goal of replacing long distance operators with electronic equipment that allowed toll calls to be directly dialed by customers. In the postwar period the rapidly declining cost of electronic components created continuous reductions in the cost of providing long distance service. Microwave radio, coaxial cable repeaters, toll switches, and customer billing systems all benefited from electronic component improvements. In a competitive market the reduced cost of providing long distance voice service would have induced a comparable reduction in the prices charged. However, the regulated monopoly market transferred some of the cost reductions to the local market and created an increasing gap between the cost and price of providing long distance service.

A process known as "separations" was used to transform the cost reductions in long distance service into price reductions for local service. The Communications Act of 1934 had assigned jurisdiction over intrastate calls to the various state regulatory commissions and had assigned authority over interstate calls to the FCC. At the time the Act was passed only about 2 percent of telephone traffic crossed state boundary lines and therefore Congress accepted the arguments of state regulators that they ought to be allowed to continue managing the rate structures according to local political concerns just as they had prior to the Act's passage. However, most telephone equipment was used jointly for local and interstate calls. The Communications Act prescribed that issues related to the separation of costs among jurisdictions should first be analyzed by a joint board of federal and state commissioners, who would present a recommendation to the FCC for final action. The first formal separations manual approved by a joint board went into effect in 1947. It split telephone equipment into a number of categories and generally allocated them between federal and state jurisdictions on the basis of relative use.

In the years following the initial separations manual, inflation and a relatively constant technology caused local telephone companies to seek authorization from state regulatory commissions to increase local telephone rates while the cost of providing long distance service was declining. When the FCC initiated an investigation of AT&T's interstate rates in 1951 as a step toward requiring rate reductions, the states protested that the high earnings indicated a need for a change in the separations formula rather than for a reduction in interstate rates. The state regulators generally attempted to keep local rates as low as possible by increasing the cost allocated to the interstate jurisdiction and consequently increasing the share of interstate revenue paid back to local operating companies. If a greater share of costs was allocated to the interstate jurisdiction, then AT&T's recorded interstate earnings would fall and its recorded intrastate earnings would rise without any change in the rates. Such a move would eliminate the painful necessity for state commissioners to grant local rate increases to make up the earnings deficit while also eliminating the need for AT&T to reduce long distance rates.

Under pressure from congressional leaders and state regulators, the FCC agreed to changes in the separations formula in 1951 that shifted costs from the intrastate to the interstate jurisdiction and consequently increased the local company's share of interstate toll revenue. The pattern was repeated several times, resulting in a number of technical changes to the separations formulas that had the cumulative effect of shifting a substantial share of the cost of providing local service from the intrastate to the interstate jurisdiction.

The local exchange companies were allowed to recover the portion of their costs allocated to the interstate jurisdiction from the interstate toll revenue, whether they were affiliated with the Bell System or not. For affiliated companies, this was a process of intracorporate accounting (known as "division of revenues") while for unaffiliated companies it represented real payments from AT&T to the independent telephone companies (known as "settlements"). AT&T described the arrangement as a "partnership" among AT&T long lines (the interstate carrier), the Bell-affiliated local operating companies, and the independent telephone companies. The effective price per minute of access service provided was far higher for smaller high-cost independent telephone companies than for low-cost urban companies, but such price disparities did not affect the interstate long distance rate structure that was set on a geographically averaged basis. The separations and settlements arrangements caused interstate switched long distance prices to be far above the cost of providing transmission between the local central offices. The interstate revenue sharing system was a particularly important source of support for the small rural companies. They often had a high ratio of long distance to local calls and could recover a large share of their costs (in some cases as much as 85 percent of their non-traffic-sensitive costs) from the pool of interstate toll revenue (Brock, 1994, pp. 66–70).

The increasing differential between the cost of providing long distance service and the price charged for it created strong incentives for entry into the market. Potential entrants had to overcome regulatory barriers to entry, establish interconnection arrangements for local origination and termination of long distance calls, and secure rights-of-way or FCC licenses for microwave radio transmission, in addition to the ordinary business requirements of building and operating the necessary network and successfully marketing their service. The separations system greatly complicated the policy question of whether to allow entrants to provide long distance service. AT&T claimed that long distance service (along with the entire telephone network) was a natural monopoly and could be most efficiently provided by a single company. It supported this natural monopoly claim with evidence on the low marginal cost of adding capacity to existing long distance routes and the low cost per circuit for high-density coaxial cable routes compared to low-density routes.

If AT&T priced its services according to cost, then the natural monopoly claim would be self-enforcing if true. That is, there would be no need for regulatory protection for the natural monopoly because companies desiring to serve a portion of the market would have higher costs than AT&T and no incentives to enter. However, AT&T's price structure provided incentives for new companies to enter the long distance market. AT&T reconciled the entry incentives with its natural monopoly claim by asserting that its prices were determined by social objectives rather than the underlying cost of service. Rates were geographically averaged (a call from New York to Chicago was priced at the same rate as a call between two small towns the same distance apart) even though the cost of service on dense routes between major cities was much less than the cost of service on sparse routes. Furthermore, long distance rates were set above the cost of service in order to subsidize all local rates to some extent and to subsidize local rates in rural areas extensively.

There was argument over both the facts of AT&T's case for monopoly and the social policy associated with it. Potential competitors viewed the social pricing arguments as AT&T's way of protecting its inefficient method of operating. They viewed the excess of price over their projected cost as an indication of the superiority of their proposed networks and operating methods over those of AT&T. They observed that many of AT&T's pricing policies were determined by the company, not ordered by regulators, and that a large portion of the claimed subsidy payments were simply accounting transactions among various components of AT&T. State regulators generally supported AT&T's arguments and were concerned about any changes that could require them to raise local telephone rates as well as the complaints and political controversy those hikes would invite. The FCC believed that the subsidies existed and complicated AT&T's pricing policy but was skeptical of AT&T's natural monopoly argument. The FCC's initial preferred solution was competition in "specialized" services that did not play a major role in the subsidy system, while leaving the switched services as an AT&T monopoly in order to preserve the subsidy system. Later the FCC became a vigorous proponent of competition and sought to reduce the level of the subsidies as well.

As will be discussed in Chapter 12, the Department of Justice generally supported the views of AT&T's potential competitors. It was skeptical of both the natural monopoly argument and the subsidy argument. It viewed AT&T and the regulatory system jointly as an impediment to competition and sought to create conditions conducive to long distance competition. As AT&T, its competitors, and multiple government bodies each attempted to settle the controversy in their own way, the political interaction eventually resulted in a policy of competition in long distance services, the divestiture of AT&T's long distance services from its local services, and continued subsidies through high access charges that created ongoing controversies and a catalyst for further changes in industry structure.

Competition in Specialized Services

As discussed in Chapter 7, AT&T maintained its long distance monopoly against the threat of entry based on microwave radio transmission technologies, first by advocating an FCC policy against licensing new entrants and later by its Telpak tariff with extensive volume discounts for large customers that were the most likely to build private microwave systems. The Telpak tariff was controversial from the beginning, but the FCC's inability to decide the questions it raised allowed the tariff to remain in effect for twenty years (1961–1981). Both private microwave systems and AT&T's Telpak tariff made it far cheaper per circuit to procure a large bundle of private line circuits than to procure a small number. Many companies could have benefited from sharing a set of Telpak lines, but AT&T prohibited either resale or sharing. Similarly, the FCC policy that allowed private microwave systems did not allow companies that built those systems to sell capacity to others. AT&T's private-line price structure and the availability of microwave transmission technology created an opportunity to profitably supply the market for small numbers of private lines if an entrant could get an FCC microwave license as a common carrier rather than as a private user.

Four years after the FCC's Above 890 decision that authorized private microwave systems, Microwave Communications Incorporated (MCI) filed an application in 1963 for a public microwave system between St. Louis and Chicago. MCI was a new company founded by Jack Goeken, who proposed a limited microwave system costing about a half-million dollars that would have less capacity than many private systems. Rather than supplying the capacity for a single company's intracorporate communication, Goeken's proposed system would provide low-cost and low-quality service for many different companies.

Because Goeken's proposal was for providing service to others, it could not be routinely granted under the private microwave policy. AT&T and Western Union together with the local carriers along the proposed route opposed MCI's application. They complained that the service would meet no demonstrated need, that it would result in wasteful duplication of facilities, and that it would cause radio interference to existing and future facilities of the established common carriers. After protracted proceedings before the FCC, the hearing examiner accepted the recommendation of Common Carrier Bureau Chief Bernard Strassberg to approve the MCI application. The hearing examiner wrote:

> MCI sites are small; the architecture of the huts is late Sears Roebuck tool shed, and they are without the amenities which Bell employees, for instance, are accustomed, and servicing and maintenance are almost improvisational; but there is no reason to believe that the system will not work, unless one is bemused by the unlikely occurrence of the catastrophes to which the carrier witnesses gloomily testified. (Henck and Strassburg, 1988, p. 104)

The hearing examiner's decision was appealed to the full commission where it was approved in 1969 by a 4–3 vote. The three dissenting commissioners viewed the case as a challenge to the established system of regulated monopoly communications services and nationwide rate averaging. They saw the case as prejudging major policy issues of interconnection and rate structure under the guise of a limited hearing for a small-scale construction application. Their opposition was based on a correct forecast that the MCI case provided an important precedent and was much more significant than the actual construction applications would suggest. The majority emphasized the actual facts of the MCI applications rather than the significance of the decision for future policy. The expected initial service was seventy-five voice circuits, and thus the proposed capacity of the new competitor was no more than what would have been expected from a single company operating under the private user authorization. The majority was unwilling to deny what in effect was a shared private system that provided small users with the benefits of private system costs. The commission's focus on the specific applications rather than the broader policy issues raised by new competition allowed it to experiment without determining an explicitly pro-competition policy.

It is unlikely that MCI's application would have been approved if MCI had proposed providing services identical to those provided by AT&T. Although there was no explicit grant of monopoly to AT&T, the commission had established a policy that duplication of facilities and services was generally unwise. Near the time of the initial MCI decision, the FCC denied a request from GTE to build its own microwave system to carry toll traffic among its telephone companies because the proposed system would duplicate AT&T facilities. However, MCI proposed "specialized" services that would differ from the services provided by AT&T and would be customized to meet special needs. The differences between MCI's and AT&T's services were an important component in both the substantive reasoning and the legal justification of the decision. Strassberg was seeking ways to accommodate data transmission and "fill in the voids" of the AT&T services rather than providing direct price competition (Henck and Strassburg, 1988, p. 102). Complaints from computer service companies and others about AT&T's inability to meet their specialized needs provided encouragement to the commission to allow MCI's proposed new services, just as it had allowed terminal competition at about the same time in order to meet specialized computer needs for terminal equipment. Thus the initial MCI decision was part of the effort to accommodate the technological change of time-sharing computers rather than an explicit policy in favor of competition.

Following the 1969 approval of MCI's initial application, a large number of additional applications for similar service were filed. Many of the applications came from MCI under the ambitious and aggressive leadership of William McGowan, who had replaced Goeken as MCI's head. Rather than evaluating each application through a formal hearing, the FCC established a general policy regarding specialized services. In 1971, the commission concluded:

> We find that: there is a public need and demand for the proposed facilities and services and for new and diverse sources of supply, competition in the specialized communications field is reasonably feasible, there are grounds for a reasonable expectation that new entry will have some beneficial effects, and there is no reason to anticipate that new entry would have any adverse effect on service to the public by existing carriers such as to outweigh the consideration supporting new entry. We further find and conclude that a general policy in favor of the entry of new carriers in the specialized communications field would serve the public interest, convenience, and necessity. (FCC, 1971, p. 920)

The proposed systems were trunk private line systems that did not extend to individual customer locations. Individual customers needed short private line circuits from the local telephone companies to connect their premises with the proposed new systems. The FCC ordered that established common carriers would be required to interconnect with the new carriers to provide local distribution facilities. The decision did not define precisely what "specialized" services included or what the exact interconnection requirements were; it left those terms vague, to be settled by later decisions. However, the decision was understood by its authors to open up the existing private line market to competition as well as to allow new services by the new carriers.

At the time of the Specialized Common Carrier decision in 1971, the FCC did not intend to open the switched market to competition so as to avoid upsetting the price structure created by the separations and settlements process. In that year the Bell System (including both AT&T and the operating companies) received $9 billion dollars in local telephone revenue, $7.9 billion in switched long distance revenue, $0.3 billion in telephone toll private line revenue, and $0.4 billion in Telpak revenue. Because the Telpak rates were much lower than single-line rates and the switched market was not open to competition, the $0.3 billion in telephone toll private line revenue was the primary competitive target. The telephone private line revenue constituted about 3 percent of the Bell System total toll revenue and 1.6 percent of the Bell System total operating revenue (FCC, 1974, p. 28).

Competition in Switched Services

The simple private line services of both AT&T and MCI were designed to connect two points without going through a switch. In MCI's version, MCI provided the circuits between MCI offices and connected to the customer's final destination with a local telephone company-provided private line between the customer's location and the MCI office. The effect was to create a permanent circuit between two points. However, both companies offered more complex arrangements of private lines in order to serve large corporate customers. For example, a private line could be connected into a company's private branch exchange (PBX) and therefore allow the utilization of that line by all extension phones connected to the PBX. Lines could also be connected to a terminating central office, allowing a person in one city to use the corporate private line system to call a person in another city who was not at the corporate offices. Furthermore, a local call could be placed to the corporate PBX and connected into the private line system in order to allow an employee to make a call from his or her home to a location on the corporate private network. The many possible arrangements blurred the line between private line and switched service, but the restriction to a single company's internal network limited the extent to which private line service could be substituted for switched service.

In 1975, MCI introduced a new service that it described as shared private line service. It was equivalent to the corporate employee calling the company PBX and being connected into the corporate system, except that it was offered to the public instead of only the employees of a single company. Under the new Execunet service, an MCI customer could call from any phone within the local calling area to the MCI office as an ordinary local call. Upon receipt in the MCI office, the call would then be connected into the MCI private line system and delivered to the terminating city over MCI facilities. In the terminating city, the call would be delivered to the final destination over local telephone company facilities.

The MCI Execunet service was an extension of the practice of sharing private lines among employees of a single company to the practice of sharing private lines among customers of MCI. In an ordinary competitive market, it would simply have been a response to pricing anomalies and would have eroded away the price discrimination implicit in the prior limitation on the sharing of private lines to employees of a company. Because of the regulatory boundary that had been drawn between private line and switched service, with a far greater subsidy component built into the switched service, the Execunet service was a challenge to the existing revenue flows. The Execunet service was of lower quality than the AT&T switched service but otherwise was equivalent to switched service from the customer's point of view.

MCI's Execunet tariff was described as a "building block" tariff from which individuals could select the components they wanted rather than taking only the particular components bundled together by the company to make a complete service. Neither the FCC staff nor AT&T recognized the implications of the new tariff at first, and it went into effect without opposition. However, once AT&T understood what the tariff allowed, it protested informally to the FCC and then filed a formal complaint. The FCC quickly (in July 1975) found the MCI tariff improper and ordered it discontinued. After MCI succeeded in obtaining a stay of the FCC order from the D.C. Circuit Court of Appeals, the FCC held more extensive proceedings on the issue and reaffirmed its finding that Execunet was beyond the scope of the MCI service authorizations.

MCI's appeal of the FCC order resulted in one of the most significant policy changes in the history of the telecommunication industry. The appeals court found in favor of MCI on procedural grounds. The court looked for formal findings that AT&T's monopoly of switched service was in the public interest or that MCI's facility authorizations restricted it to a particular service. Because there were no such findings, the court ruled that the FCC could not retroactively limit MCI's service authorization over the existing facilities (Court of Appeals, D.C. Cir., 1977). The FCC appealed the decision to the Supreme Court, but the Court refused to hear the case.

After the D.C. Circuit Court of Appeals found that the FCC failure to explicitly limit MCI's authorization allowed it to proceed with Execunet over existing facilities, AT&T announced that it would not provide interconnection arrangements for MCI's Execunet service. The FCC supported AT&T's decision, leaving MCI's victory temporarily hollow. MCI returned to the court and again won a resounding victory with a ruling that AT&T was obligated to provide interconnection for the service.

In MCI's original Execunet service, MCI ordered ordinary business lines from the state-regulated local tariff to connect its offices with the local telephone company central office. MCI expected to receive the same service and pay the same rate for local connections between its switch and the local telephone office as any other business would obtain for local telephone service. AT&T observed that minutes flowing between a local central office and an AT&T toll office effectively paid a very high rate for local service because of the way those minutes were used to allocate the cost of the local exchange to create a claim on long distance revenues. AT&T did not pay for access service by the minute but could compute an implied cost per minute by dividing the total revenue distributed to the local companies through the separations and settlements process by the total number of long distance access minutes used. After the appeals court ruled in 1978 that AT&T was required to provide interconnection for MCI's Execunet service, AT&T filed a new interstate tariff with the FCC known as ENFIA (Exchange Network Facilities for Interstate Access) in which it proposed to charge the new competitors the full amount of AT&T's estimated contribution to local exchange through the settlements and division of revenues process. AT&T claimed that MCI could not obtain interconnection facilities under the state-regulated local business rates but must obtain them from the far higher, federally regulated ENFIA tariff.

MCI stridently opposed AT&T's proposed ENFIA tariff. It denied that there was any subsidy flow from long distance to local service and claimed to be simply providing a shared version of established private line service. It did not receive AT&T's "trunk side" connections that transmitted information for signaling and billing through the local switch. Consequently, MCI's service was lower in technical quality and required a long dialing sequence to convey the necessary signaling information to the MCI switch. MCI required ordinary local business lines for customers to call its office in order to initiate an Execunet call and claimed that it should pay the established local business rate. Furthermore, MCI supplied financial information to the FCC that indicated the ENFIA rates would convert its profits on Execunet into losses and asserted that AT&T was attempting to drive it out of business.

Because of the court-imposed necessity of established connection and the difficulty of fully resolving the controversy, the FCC supervised negotiations between the parties to develop an interim solution while an access charge proceeding was conducted. After extensive negotiations a settlement was developed that both sides were willing to accept as an interim solution until the development of access charge rules. The settlement agreement provided a compromise rate that was far higher than local business rates but lower than AT&T's calculation of the average cost per minute from the existing cost allocation process. The 1978 settlement remained the basic structure for payments between the competitors and AT&T until the access charge rules were implemented following the divestiture in 1984.

Although it was established as an interim compromise settlement, the initial ENFIA agreement incorporated a major policy decision that has continued to influence the development of the telecommunication industry. Earlier competition in CPE and private line services had resulted in a movement of prices toward cost, as is the normal expected result of competition. Because the competitive potential was so circumscribed, the price changes had relatively little effect on the total system of revenue flows from toll charges to defray the cost of local telephone companies. With Execunet, the burden of the charges could no longer be easily shifted. Allowing MCI to provide Execunet by ordering connecting service from existing local tariffs would have pushed the price of long distance service toward the cost of providing service and eventually eroded away the revenue flows to local telephone companies.

The ENFIA tariffs created a legal distinction between two physically identical services. If a person made a call to any local business not providing long distance service, the call was charged at the existing local tariff rate. If a person made a call to the local MCI office that was then relayed over the MCI network, the call was charged at the much higher ENFIA rate. The legal and price distinction between technically identical calls for local communication and for connecting the long distance carrier has been maintained to the present in order to allow the local companies to share in the long distance revenue. However, as will be seen in Chapter 12, enhanced service providers (including Internet service providers) were allowed to provide service equivalent to the original MCI Execunet plan. Customers could reach them with an ordinary local call and then relay their information out onto the enhanced services network, and such carriers were not required to pay the early ENFIA charges or the later access charge replacements. Consequently, an economic and regulatory distinction was created between ordinary long distance providers and enhanced service providers, developing an important regulatory boundary line and contributing to the separate evolution of voice services and data communications services.

The Transition to Optical Fiber

The early long distance competition was enabled in part by the ability to build microwave networks without a continuous right-of-way. In the early 1980s rapid progress in reducing the cost of optical fiber systems made them cheaper than microwave for transmission of high-density communications. While the potential benefits of optical fiber communication systems were understood in the 1970s, the Bell System considered them too expensive for deployment. For long-haul communication on the densest routes, it continued improving its coaxial cable systems, which could carry up to 10,800 simultaneous voice conversations per coaxial cable pair with repeaters spaced every mile on the L5 system introduced in 1974. In the late 1970s the Bell System envisioned the next major innovation in high-capacity long-haul transmission to be a waveguide system that was being designed with a capacity of 230,000 simultaneous conversations (Bell Laboratories, 1977, pp. 328, 340). However, the waveguide system was never built, and optical fiber transmission systems replaced both coaxial cable and microwave on dense long-haul routes.

In an optical fiber transmission system, the electrical signal carrying information is translated into an infrared optical signal with a light-emitting diode or a semiconductor laser (also called a laser diode). The signal travels through an optical fiber with very low attenuation and is detected by a photodiode and translated back into an electrical signal. The low attenuation of the optical signal allows much longer transmission distances between repeaters than coaxial cable. The fiber itself is relatively inexpensive, and multiple fibers can be incorporated into a single cable for the later addition of electronics when additional capacity is needed (Freeman, 1999, pp. 240–253). A substantial portion of the cost of an optical fiber transmission system is the electronics required to translate between electrical and optical signals and to create and detect the optical signals. Consequently, the cost of transmission over optical fiber systems has declined continuously, and optical fiber transmission systems have gradually replaced other technologies even when their full capacity was not needed for the particular application. As of 2002, the optical fiber systems are limited to transmission and the optical signals must be converted to electrical signals for switching, but technology specialists expect all-optical systems including optical switching to be deployed in the future.

The improving optical fiber technology created a potential problem for AT&T's long distance competitors because AT&T possessed the necessary continuous rights-of-way and they did not. However, they were able to arrange the necessary rights-of-way along railroads and public highways and successfully made the transition from microwave to optical fiber networks. MCI was the first company to deploy substantial optical fiber transmission systems. MCI's growth accelerated after the Execunet litigation freed it to enter the switched long distance market, but it was difficult to find routes for new microwave systems that did not interfere with existing ones in the crowded Northeast corridor. In 1982 and 1983, MCI leased railroad rights-of-way from Amtrak and CSX and placed orders for 152,000 miles of optical fiber with Northern Telecom and Siecor Corporation (a joint venture of Corning Glass and Siemans).

After arranging rights-of-way with other railroads, MCI began building a nationwide optical fiber backbone transmission system. It continued to expand its microwave and satellite capacity to serve routes off the backbone. As optical fiber costs continued to decline, the fiber network was greatly expanded while microwave and satellite were largely abandoned (Cantelon, 1993, pp. 336–343). By the mid-1980s AT&T, Sprint, and MCI had all constructed nationwide optical fiber backbones. Continued rapid improvement in optical fiber transmission systems encouraged additional companies to build new optical fiber systems in hopes of profiting from the continuing gap between the cost of transmitting information and the prices charged by the existing companies for that transmission.

12

Divestiture and Access Charges

In the United States, regulation does not exempt a company from the antitrust laws. The role of the Department of Justice (DOJ) in enforcing the antitrust laws and that of the Federal Communications Commission in interpreting and administering the Communications Act of 1934 create the possibility for divergent public policies toward the communications industry. Neither agency has jurisdiction over the actions of the other, and each agency has considerable freedom (within the confines created by a generally worded law and applicable court decisions) to exercise its judgment in determining the most appropriate policy.

AT&T's aggressive actions to block MCI's initial competitive activity revived long-standing antitrust concerns about AT&T in the DOJ. Public opposition by John deButts, AT&T's CEO, to the FCC's initial competitive actions increased the concerns. In 1974 during the Ford administration, the DOJ filed an antitrust suit against AT&T, alleging that AT&T participated in three separate markets: local telephone service, long distance telephone service, and the provision of customer premises equipment (CPE). The local telephone service market was a natural monopoly subject to state regulation. The long distance and CPE markets were potentially competitive but were dependent on interconnection with the local market. According to the DOJ, AT&T used its market power in local service to limit competition in the long distance and CPE markets. The AT&T opposition to terminal attachments was not motivated by a concern for protecting network integrity but by a desire to monopolize the CPE market. Although CPE was rapidly becoming a competitive market by the trial date, the CPE stories were used as an indication of general corporate policy against competition. AT&T's refusal to provide the private line interconnection requested by specialized car-

200

riers, and AT&T's provision of inferior "line side" connection instead of "trunk side" connection for switched competition, were interpreted as efforts to extend monopoly power into the long distance market.

Some of the charges were developed after the initial filing of the suit as continued controversies during the 1970s refined the DOJ perspective. The DOJ asserted that not only had regulation failed to prevent AT&T's competitive abuses but that regulation was a key component in AT&T's ability to commit those abuses. The FCC was not intentionally serving AT&T's interest, but the commission was hamstrung by AT&T's abusive process. The DOJ claimed that AT&T's regulatory interventions and court appeals went beyond the legitimate exercise of its right to plead its case and constituted a pattern of engaging in litigation it knew it would lose in order to raise the costs of rivals and prevent them from becoming active competitors of the Bell System (Noll and Owen, 1989, p. 307).

AT&T's defense painted a very different picture of the industry. According to AT&T, the entire telephone business was a natural monopoly with economies of scale, scope, and vertical integration that would be lost if service was provided by multiple companies. The Bell System had operated the telephone business as a regulated monopoly for many years with the approval of state and federal regulators. AT&T was subject to pervasive state and federal regulation that controlled prices and entry and limited AT&T's total profits. Although AT&T had a high market share, it did not possess monopoly power in the legal sense (the power to control prices and exclude competitors) because regulators rather than AT&T controlled entry and prices. Particular problems cited by the DOJ were isolated incidents that occurred as a large corporation sought to accommodate confusing and contradictory policy changes by state and federal regulators. AT&T's pricing policies, rather than being designed to eliminate competition, sought to maintain revenue flows that had long been approved by regulatory authority. AT&T's regulatory and legal activities were the legitimate exercise of its right to petition the government.

AT&T and the DOJ largely agreed on the record of particular incidents, market shares, and other facts that are often controversial in antitrust cases. The essential dispute concerned the nature of the industry and the opportunities to participate within it. Both sides agreed that at least some portion of the telephone industry was a natural monopoly that could be better provided by a single company than by fully competitive companies. According to the DOJ, the natural monopoly services included only the local exchange while CPE, long distance, and other services could be provided by competitive companies with no loss in efficiency if only AT&T would agree to appropriate interconnection arrangements between its natural monopoly services and the competitive services. According to AT&T, the natural monopoly extended to all aspects of the telephone business, and any competitive activity would only prosper if provided with artificial regulatory advantages.

Both sides agreed that regulation was important but disagreed on how it was affecting actions in the industry. According to the DOJ, regulation was contributing to AT&T's monopoly power in creating incentives for AT&T to exclude competitors. According to AT&T, regulation prevented it from adjusting prices to the ordinary competitive levels in order to maintain specified revenue flows and subsidies for particular services and therefore created pockets of opportunity (referred to as "cream skimming") for a company supplying particular services to benefit from the regulatory policies applied to AT&T.

For the first four years after it was filed in the U.S. District Court in the District of Columbia, the suit moved slowly as AT&T unsuccessfully sought dismissal on the grounds that regulation precluded application of antitrust standards. Documents were exchanged, and positions were refined. In 1978, the case was reassigned to Judge Harold Greene after the original judge withdrew because of serious illness. Greene established a strict timetable for trial, requiring the parties to develop stipulations and detailed pretrial contentions in order to begin the trial in September 1980 (later postponed slightly to the beginning of 1981). AT&T's aggressive challenges to pro-competitive regulatory policy began to disappear after Charles Brown replaced John deButts as CEO. As the trial date approached, the parties began intensive negotiations toward reaching a settlement. However, at the end of 1980 the top DOJ officials were Carter administration officials likely to be replaced when the newly elected Ronald Reagan was inaugurated in January 1981. They were unable to complete the settlement prior to leaving office or to secure support of the new administration for the proposed settlement, and the trial began in early 1981 while the Reagan administration was still formulating its policy toward the case.

The case was controversial within the early Reagan administration. Assistant Attorney General for Antitrust William Baxter shared the general perspective of DOJ economists that the problems in the industry came from the combination of regulation and competition. He wanted to draw a clean line between the regulated monopoly parts of the industry and the potentially competitive parts of the industry and had no confidence in regulation or injunctive relief. His goal was to remove the structural problems of the industry through divestiture and then allow the competitive market to work without further government intervention.

Secretary of Defense Casper Weinberger adopted the long-standing Department of Defense position that an integrated AT&T was desirable for national security. Believing that the case should never have been brought and should be abandoned, Weinberger espoused the AT&T position that there were economies of scope in the industry and asserted that defense communications required a unified company that could meet all requirements. Secretary of Commerce Malcolm Baldrige also opposed the case. Baldrige was particularly concerned about the advantages that foreign firms would gain from Baxter's divestiture plan. Baxter's effort to break the tie between Western Electric and the Bell operating companies and increase the diversity of telephone equipment sources meant that opportunities would be created for foreign firms to sell in the U.S. market while most foreign telecommunication equipment markets would remain largely closed to U.S. sales. President Reagan himself did not take an active role in deciding the outcome of the case, so far as can be determined from available records (Temin with Galambos, 1987, pp. 223–229).

Baxter's inability to convince other senior officials of the wisdom of his plan and the inability of other Cabinet members to convince Baxter of the wisdom of their plans caused the administration to proceed in two different directions simultaneously. The DOJ continued with the trial and the goal of divestiture as a "narrow antitrust" approach. The other agencies united on a new congressional effort to pass legislation that would solve the broad policy concerns of the industry. The Republicans had gained control of the Senate in the 1980 election, and Senator Robert Packwood became chairman of the Senate Commerce Committee. With Reagan administration (excluding the DOJ) support, Senator Packwood introduced a bill to provide a legislative solution to the telecommunication policy problems. The Packwood bill followed the FCC's Computer II lead in imposing strongly separated subsidiaries between

AT&T's regulated basic service and its more competitive services. The bill required the FCC to prescribe accounting systems for the carriers and to prescribe cost allocation rules for the division of costs of jointly used activities between regulated and unregulated services, but it did not require a divestiture.

After extensive consideration while the AT&T trial was in progress during 1981, the Packwood bill was approved by the Senate in a 90-4 vote in October of that year. AT&T supported the bill while MCI opposed it. The FCC along with the Departments of Defense and Commerce supported the bill, while the Justice Department remained concerned that it did not provide strong enough controls on AT&T's market power (Temin with Galambos, 1987, pp. 217–276). Despite the overwhelming support of the Senate for the bill, the House version failed to pass and the bill never became law. The failure to pass the Packwood bill left the Commerce and Defense Departments without a method to implement their views on telecommunication policy and increased Baxter's freedom to pursue the divestiture solution.

When the DOJ finished presenting its evidence in the antitrust court, AT&T requested a directed verdict. Rather than simply denying AT&T's motion, Judge Greene wrote an extensive opinion reviewing the evidence in detail. Judge Greene's September 1981 opinion showed that he was convinced by the DOJ's presentation of the case against AT&T and that AT&T would have a difficult if not impossible job of rebutting the case. Greene's opinion indicated that he was likely to rule against AT&T if the trial continued to a conclusion and intensified AT&T's incentive to settle the case.

The Divestiture

All through the pretrial and trial period, AT&T had adamantly opposed divestiture because it would cause "the destruction of the most advanced, efficient and successful communication system in the world," "would seriously inhibit, and perhaps even prevent, the planning and implementation of a host of networking principles such as the sharing of facilities and the efficient aggregation or alternate routing of traffic," and would cause the "reckless destruction of the world's most successful research institution and industrial laboratory" (AT&T, 1980, pp. 199–203). However, as the chances for a legislative solution and the chances of winning the trial both diminished, AT&T began to think a simple divestiture decree might be more satisfactory than continuing the fight against divestiture. Baxter had earlier asserted that he could settle the case with a two-page divestiture decree. After approval by top AT&T management and the board of directors, AT&T asked Baxter to draft a divestiture decree as the basis for negotiations. The DOJ prepared the first draft on December 21, 1981, and after a short period of negotiations, the parties reached a settlement that became known as the Modified Final Judgment (MFJ) because its legal structure was a modification of the 1956 consent decree between the Department of Justice and AT&T.

The theory of the decree was to leave the competitive or potentially competitive businesses with AT&T, and to separate those businesses from the monopoly local exchange companies. The DOJ believed that such a division would remove both the incentive and the ability of the Bell Companies to discriminate against competitors because there would no longer be a single company providing integrated services. The MFJ divided AT&T into eight new companies, seven regional Bell Operating Companies (BOCs) that were expected to provide monopoly local telephone service in their geographical areas, and a much smaller AT&T that included long distance service, Western Electric (now Lucent Technologies), and other potentially competitive products and services. In order to partially meet the DOD concerns that the divestiture would result in fragmented responsibility for responding to emergency communications needs, the MFJ required that "the BOCs shall provide, through a centralized organization, a single point of contact for coordination of BOCs to meet the requirements of national security and emergency preparedness" (U.S. District Court (D.C.), 1982, section I(B)).

The new AT&T became dependent on the local exchange companies for access to its long distance and enhanced services, and for connection of its customer premises equipment, just as AT&T's competitors were dependent on those local exchange companies. Because the local exchange companies were prohibited from participating in the competitive businesses, they would have no incentive to restrict their access services to their own operations. Although the divestiture was designed to remove the ability and incentives of the local operating companies to discriminate among suppliers of long distance service, the DOJ was still concerned that the former Bell operating companies would favor AT&T.

It consequently demanded strict equal-access provisions in the Modified Final Judgment. The DOJ had no authority over the actual charges for local exchange access (charges were under the jurisdiction of the FCC), but it could impose general requirements on AT&T as part of the settlement agreement. The DOJ wanted to assist the viability of long distance competition by ensuring that the competitive carriers paid no higher rates per unit of traffic for access to the local exchange than AT&T did. Thus, even if a local exchange carrier found it cheaper per unit of traffic to serve AT&T because of AT&T's higher traffic density, it was required to charge all carriers the same rate per unit until 1991.

A related provision was designed to eliminate the potential price advantage to AT&T because its switches were sometimes collocated with those of the local operating companies. According to this provision, competitive switches located within five miles of an AT&T switch should be considered in the same tariff zone as the AT&T switch. Thus a BOC could not charge AT&T a lower price than nearby competitors because the AT&T switch was located in the same building as the BOC switch (U.S. District Court (D.C.), 1982, appendix B). The BOCs were also required to develop a presubscription system that allowed them to automatically route communications to the interexchange carrier chosen by the subscriber without using access codes. The presubscription system equalized the dialing requirements for using AT&T and competitive interexchange providers.

The MFJ requirements not only prohibited favoritism to AT&T, but also sought to minimize the competitive advantages AT&T had gained from its historical position. The equal charge per unit of traffic and the non-distance-sensitive nature of access charges for closely located offices reduced the advantages AT&T gained from its established market position, its volume of local exchange traffic, and its switches collocated with those of the BOCs. AT&T retained the advantages of brand recognition and loyalty, the most extensive long distance network, and 96 percent of the toll revenue in the year of the divestiture agreement, but obtained access at the same prices as its competitors.

AT&T initiated a vast planning and implementation process to accomplish the divestiture. By the end of 1982 AT&T had transformed the general principles of the MFJ into a 471-page plan of reorganization. With over one million employees and nearly $150 billion in assets, AT&T's operations were complex and interrelated. Many difficult problems, ranging from assignment of personnel, to division of jointly used assets, to reprogramming operational systems to work independently, had to be solved. The divestiture process was completed over a two-year period of intensive work and became effective on January 1, 1984.

Access Charges

William Baxter and h████████ at the antitrust division of the Department of Justice th████████ had settled the major telecommunication policy problem████████vestiture agreement of January 1982. They had often contr██████ ████mplex and confusing regulatory approach to policy with the simple and clean solution created by structural separation of the monopoly ██ d competitive aspects of the industry. Although Baxter's initial boast that he could produce a two-page divestiture decree missed the final length by twelve pages, the Modified Final Judgment was still far simpler than the hundreds of pages of detailed regulations developed by the FCC or proposed in the earlier nondivestiture attempts to develop a complex consent decree. However, the apparent simplicity came from setting out general principles that left many critical issues for later resolution.

The most critical policy issue during the divestiture implementation period was the development of a method of sharing revenue between long distance and local companies that would fit the new industry structure and meet other policy goals. The development of an appropriate sharing mechanism had been an FCC goal ever since the Execunet court decision opened the long distance market to competition, but the proposed divestiture brought new urgency and new constraints. Key to the new price structure was the concept of "access charges." The MFJ specified that a system of access charges paid by long distance carriers to local exchange carriers for the service of originating and terminating long distance calls must replace the existing AT&T-administered system of sharing long distance toll revenue with the local companies.

In the earlier case of CPE, the financial separation of CPE from the regulated revenue flows among companies was based on the principle of free interconnection. A customer could order any service from the telephone company and attach any CPE that conformed to publicly available technical standards for that service without any payment to the telephone company that was dependent on the customer-provided CPE.

The focus of state regulators' opposition to CPE competition was the free interconnection arrangement that reduced some financial flows to the local companies. The theory of the DOJ case considered long distance service analogous to CPE. Both were potentially competitive markets dependent on interconnection with the monopoly local companies. Both should be severed from the local companies and provided on a competitive market. The divestiture and the associated equal-access requirements were designed to provide ███████ terconnection rights for long distance companies as had been ███████ lier for customer-owned CPE.

The MFJ did not specify how the fir████ arrangements between local companies and long distance companies should be disentangled, other than that the pre-divestiture settlement system should be replaced by a system of access charges applied uniformly to all long distance companies. The simplest approach would have been to follow the CPE model and allow any long distance company to connect to any local service company with no payment other than the established local service charge. That was the approach originally sought by MCI with its Execunet service, in which it expected to consider the local connection to an MCI switch equivalent to the local connection to any PBX and pay the established local business rate for service received. However, applying the CPE approach to long distance financial arrangements would have eliminated the complex set of payments among telephone companies (established with extensive political guidance) under the separations and settlements procedures. It would have caused a substantial increase in local telephone rates as well as possibly threatening the availability of telephone service in high-cost rural areas.

State regulators and many congressional leaders were determined to maintain at least some of the established revenue flows from long distance to local service. They vigorously opposed any effort to impose the CPE model. Yet maintaining those revenue flows required creating a legal and pricing distinction between local services used to originate long distance calls and other local services. It also required vigilant regulatory oversight to maintain the resulting price discrimination.

While the overall level of access charges affected the distribution of the cost burdens between local and long distance customers and between urban and rural customers, the precise structure of the access charges was critical to the competitive battle among long distance companies. For example, a volume discount on the connections between a local company and a long distance company would provide the divested AT&T with great advantages over its much smaller long distance competitors. The central importance of the size and structure of access charges to telecommunication policy and to the competitive health of many companies caused vast efforts to be devoted to constructing, arguing over, and implementing an access charge plan.

Following the Execunet decision, the FCC had attempted to develop a comprehensive access charge plan and had issued a tentative plan in 1980. However, extensive opposition to this proposal prevented its final adoption until after the divestiture agreement was reached. The AT&T-DOJ agreement of January 1982 dramatically changed the context of the industry for which the 1980 access charge plan was designed. It also gave new urgency to developing such a plan. Despite the complaints of both AT&T and MCI that it was unfair, the ENFIA compromise agreement had provided a satisfactory method of compensating local carriers so long as the competitors were niche players in an industry dominated by AT&T. However, the proposed MFJ required an end to the existing separations and settlements system at the January 1, 1984, divestiture date. After that time compensation of local companies from long distance could come only from access charges.

The Department of Justice asserted that the divestiture did not imply any requirement for change in the existing local service rates. A critical point of contention in the litigation was how settlements payments affected the interpretation of the historical record. AT&T, supported by many state regulators, interpreted its actions as an attempt to preserve the set of social prices determined and approved through the political process that led to geographic averaging, large payments to rural companies, overpriced long distance service, and underpriced local service. From that perspective, entrants were simply parasites profiting from socially desirable differences between price and cost, and providing no useful economic function. MCI and the DOJ developed a theory that no subsidies had been proved and that all revenue flows were under AT&T's control and determined by AT&T in its own interest. Many small-company representatives and state regulators, who had no doubt about the existence and the beneficiaries of the revenue flows, feared that the MFJ would eliminate all subsidy flows and dramatically increase local rates while reducing the profitability of small telephone companies.

The FCC needed to create an access charge plan that would work under the industry structure created by the divestiture (based on an assumption of maximum reliance on competition and cost-based prices) and would also survive the political review of many interested parties who were primarily concerned to maintain the benefits to them of the status quo. Thus the task of the FCC was to radically change past arrangements in order to transform a politically determined monopoly pricing structure into a price structure compatible with competitive market forces while also maintaining the income distribution effects of past arrangements in order to avoid creating a political backlash. The impossibility of reaching the two incompatible goals engendered extensive controversy over how to construct a reasonable plan with an appropriate balance of the two objectives.

The FCC adopted its basic access charge plan for the post-divestiture period at the end of 1982 and then revised it several times later to meet various political concerns. The essential idea was to initially maintain prices close to their pre-divestiture levels by imposing a substantial charge per minute on long distance carriers for the origination or termination of telephone calls. Prices would gradually be brought closer to competitive levels by increases in a charge to consumers known as the subscriber line charge (SLC) while simultaneously reducing the charges paid by long distance carriers. The FCC's initial plan called for a relatively rapid phase-in of the SLC but, with political objectives greatly slowing that process, the fundamental goal of replacing high access charges with a subscriber line charge was accomplished over a long period of time extending until the end of the century.

The initial interstate access charge assessed on long distance providers was slightly over sixteen cents per conversation minute. Access charge payments were by far the largest single expense of long distance carriers (requiring approximately half of total switched toll revenue) and thus modest variations in the level or structure of charges could substantially affect the competitive conditions among carriers. There was extensive controversy over many details of the access charge plan and its implementation and vast amounts of regulatory and political effort expended in adjusting to the many constraints raised by both government and private parties.

The charges to the carriers were imposed for traffic flowing between a local telephone company office and the long distance carrier's office known as a point of presence (POP). When those rates were high, they created an incentive for users to find alternate ways of connecting their premises with the long distance carrier POP without going through the local company central office. This process was known as "bypass" and it represented the earliest form of competition within the local exchange. The divestiture theory assumed that local exchange was a natural monopoly, and in many cases the state regulatory commissions prohibited competition with the local exchange company, making it a legal monopoly as well. However, access was considered subject to federal rather than to state jurisdiction because it was a part of an interstate call. Consequently, the state commissions had no authority to prohibit connections between customers and interexchange carriers that bypassed the monopoly local exchange company.

During the development of the access charge plan and its initial implementation, the opportunities for bypass and the desirability of bypass were vigorously contested. The FCC asserted that high access charges would create bypass and therefore allow high-volume customers to escape access charges while increasing the charges for low-volume customers to meet the fixed revenue requirement. The FCC concluded that bypass put a limit on how high access charges could be and provided a reason for rationalizing the price structure to bring it closer to cost. The FCC's essential argument was that the monopoly power of local exchange companies was limited and an attempt to impose an excessive price for the service of originating and terminating long distance calls would induce alternatives to local telephone company-provided access services. Critics of the FCC plan, who generally desired to maintain the relatively high long distance prices and the subsidy structure supported by those prices, disputed both the opportunities for bypass and the policy relevance if they existed. They argued that bypass was more difficult than the FCC had estimated and therefore unlikely to be a problem. However, they also argued that if it was a problem it should be prohibited by law rather than by reducing the incentives to bypass.

In July 1983, Republican Senator Packwood and Democratic Congressmen John Dingell and Timothy Wirth (the respective committee chairmen with telecommunication responsibility) introduced compatible bills to overturn the FCC's access charge plan. Both bills explicitly prohibited the FCC's SLC, sought to maintain the status quo revenue flows in the industry after the divestiture, and mandated extensive subsidies to high-cost areas. Both bills dealt with bypass by prohibiting it and imposing penalties on any company that used alternative means of connecting to the interexchange company in order to avoid paying access charges to the local exchange company. The House version passed but the Senate version did not. Had such a bill become law, it would have frozen the price structure of the early 1980s in place and raised heavy legal barriers to any local competition. The FCC was able to preserve its authority to implement the access charge plan and flexibility for future changes by working out a compromise with prominent senators in which the FCC modified its plan in ways recommended by the senators and the Senate abandoned its effort to pass legislation to overturn the FCC plan.

The initial access charge arrangements were developed under tight time pressure. The divestiture made it necessary to institute a new plan because the old system of sharing revenue would not work after the divestiture. The access charge filings in October 1983 for implementation with the January 1984 divestiture included 43,000 pages of tariffs and 160,000 pages of support material (Brock, 1994, pp. 173–214). All of that material had to be examined by FCC staff and evaluated amid strong objections from those who would pay the access charges. A number of shortcuts were taken in order to simplify the process.

The Enhanced Service Provider Exemption

The most significant shortcut taken during that chaotic time was the treatment of enhanced service providers (ESPs). Prior to the implementation of access charges, ESPs had not participated in the separations and settlements system administered by AT&T. Instead, users made a local call to the ESP office, often by computer, and then the ESP transmitted the information to its final destination. The ESP arrangement was identical to the original MCI Execunet arrangement (prior to the imposition of ENFIA charges), except that the ESPs were not carrying ordinary voice traffic. ESPs were an infinitesimal piece of the market and there was no concern about them siphoning off revenue used to subsidize other services as there was with MCI's initial long distance competition.

During the access charge proceeding, the FCC reasoned that ESPs and interexchange carriers (IXCs) were essentially identical in the services they needed from local exchange carriers. In both cases, a call would go from an end user through the local exchange carrier to the office of the ESP or IXC and then out over that company's network to its final destination. Consequently, the FCC planned to impose access charges on ESPs identical to those imposed on IXCs that carried voice traffic. However, there were a number of technical difficulties in defining precisely how the access charges should be computed and collected from ESPs. In the voice case, there was a clear originating user who paid the IXC for the call and that IXC in turn paid both the originating local exchange company and the terminating local exchange company access charges. In the ESP case, the patterns of interaction were more varied (transmitting e-mail, interrogating a computer, and so on), and therefore care was required to specify comparable access charges for ESPs as for IXCs. The commission consequently announced its intention to equalize the charges but gave a temporary access charge exemption to ESPs while it further considered their special needs. The exemption allowed ESPs to continue receiving access through ordinary local calls as they had in the past. A number of other temporary measures were taken in order to allow access charge implementation for the primary services while deferring the resolution of controversies over less significant services.

After the divestiture, the access charge plan was gradually refined and the various temporary arrangements replaced by permanent rules. In 1987, the commission proposed its rules for bringing ESPs under the access charge arrangements and ending the exemption they were given in 1983. However, by that time the Internet was beginning to grow rapidly. Internet service providers (ISPs) were classified by the FCC as enhanced service providers because they processed the user's data at their location before transferring it out over the Internet. The online community at that time was large enough to stir up extensive political opposition to the FCC's proposal but still small enough that imposing access charges on ESPs would have produced only a tiny percentage of the total access revenue. Equalizing the payment obligations of voice and enhanced services would have increased the cost for users of ESPs and decreased the cost for users of voice services because the total access revenue requirement was fixed, but voice services were so much larger than ESP services that the resulting decrease in voice long distance prices would hardly be noticed by consumers. Consequently, the political argument for preserving the ESP exemption became dominating and the FCC dropped its proposal. The commission did not formally announce a long-term policy but essentially made the original temporary exemption permanent.

As the Internet exploded during the 1990s, the ESP exemption became very significant. Even with the reduced access charge levels of the 1990s, it would have been impossible to offer cheap flat-rate access if access charges were imposed on ESPs equivalent to those on IXCs. Under the system designed for voice communications, a rigid regulated set of access charges controlled the prices paid by long distance carriers to the local exchange companies. Under the 1983 "temporary" ESP exemption, dial-in Internet users and ISPs are free to use ordinary local services to connect customer computers with the Internet equivalent of long distance company POPs.

The 1984 divestiture continued a long series of efforts to manage the regulated monopoly by setting structural boundaries on its scope and controlling the interaction across those boundaries. That effort began with the 1956 consent decree in which AT&T was allowed to keep its integrated structure in return for giving up its right to provide nonregulated products and services. That decree made AT&T's corporate boundary consistent with the regulatory boundary and allowed the regulated monopoly to include the entire network and all equipment attached to the network. AT&T's influence on companies and products outside of the boundary was limited by the requirement to license all patents.

The FCC's 1980 Computer II decision shrunk the regulated monopoly boundary by excluding CPE and enhanced services. Although no divestiture was required, AT&T was required to provide any products or services outside of the regulated boundary through a "fully separate subsidiary" with strict rules that made the subsidiary almost a separate company. The boundary rules required AT&T to provide circuits to companies that wished to create enhanced services by combining basic communications and computer processing and to interconnect its network with customer-provided CPE according to a public set of standards incorporated into the FCC rules.

The DOJ-imposed 1984 divestiture was a more radical form of the FCC's Computer II separate subsidiary requirement. The divestiture further reduced the boundaries of regulated monopoly to include only local exchange service and created separate companies rather than separate subsidiaries of a single company. The boundary between local and long distance service (or more formally, between intra-LATA and inter-LATA service where LATAs were the legal definition of local service for the divestiture) was controlled by requiring separate companies on each side of the boundary and by prescribing the payments required for services comprised of components from both sides of the boundary. The divested Bell Operating Companies were prohibited from providing long distance service by the divestiture decree and the long distance companies were prohibited from providing local service by the state regulatory commissions.

Boundary regulation was successful in providing greater scope for alternatives to the regulated monopoly services, but it also imposed a rigid and potentially inefficient structure on the telecommunication industry. The divestiture theory required that the local exchange monopolies be prohibited from providing long distance service lest they recreate the competitive problems that led to the antitrust suit. The case for divestiture assumed that there are no economies of scope in producing services on both sides of the boundary and that there is a clear distinction between natural monopoly local exchange service and potentially competitive long distance service. The combination of BOC objections to limitations on the scope of their business and continued technological change created dissatisfaction with the lines drawn by the divestiture and led to the repudiation of boundary regulation in the Telecommunications Act of 1996.

III

Interconnected Competition
and Integrated Services,
1985–2002

13

Mobile Telephones and Spectrum Reform

The Computer II and divestiture solutions to the institutional problems of the communications industry were based on rigid boundaries. Both solutions attempted to preserve the benefits of the regulated monopoly (stability, low prices for basic service) while providing more opportunities for technological progress by creating a sharply defined boundary between the regulated monopoly portions of the industry and the competitive portions of the industry. Alternatively stated, both policy interventions sought to make portions of the communications industry more like the computer industry and to regulate interaction across the boundary between competitive and monopoly services. The many dimensions of regulation and technology did not fit neatly into the legal categories created in either decision even at the time it was made, and the fit became more awkward as technological change continued.

The categories were useful even though they were not exactly correct. Flexible interpretations reduced the problems created by the disparity between the legal categories and industry conditions. For example, the divestiture identification of opportunities for competition with long distance service only applied on dense routes. Long, sparsely utilized routes continued to have natural monopoly characteristics. That problem was mitigated by defining local service very broadly (sometimes encompassing an entire state) in sparsely populated areas and more narrowly in densely populated areas. That interpretation created more consistency between "long distance" and "dense routes" than would have occurred by simply identifying long distance with number of miles.

Similarly, the Computer II definition of "enhanced service" was based on distinguishing 1970s analog voice circuits from sophisticated versions of communication that included computer processing. A strict in-

219

terpretation of the 1980 definition would have either prevented the telephone companies from upgrading their technology or required them to continually redefine the line between their competitive unregulated enhanced services and their monopoly regulated basic services as they added computer processing power, combinations of analog and digital transmission, and access to databases to supply improved communication services. Instead, the FCC adopted a series of refinements that allowed the telephone companies to use improved technology without reclassifying their services from basic to enhanced. However, even with creative administration, the early 1980s boundaries could not be smoothly adjusted to the new technologies of the post-divestiture period.

After the Computer II and divestiture decisions, there were two distinct but interacting pressures for further policy change:

1. The decisions themselves created an inconsistent structure with differing assumptions used by the FCC and the DOJ. Furthermore, the BOCs disagreed with the role assigned to them in the divestiture and sought greater freedom to participate in a wider range of business.
2. Technology continued to change, allowing new forms of communication that were not fully expected in the divestiture solution.

Parties that were dissatisfied with the post-divestiture institutional structure (especially the divested Bell Operating Companies) were able to use the changing technology and the problems of fitting together the FCC policies, the DOJ policies, and the new technological opportunities as a catalyst for legislative action.

The earlier rapid progress in basic electronic components continued at approximately the same rate. As integrated circuits became cheaper and cheaper, many new products and methods of using them became economically feasible. Three different technologies, all based in part on electronics, created pressure for revising the divestiture solution: wireless communication, optical fiber communication, and packet-switched communication. All three had been used in the earlier time frame, but declining prices expanded their role in the post-divestiture period. The first two changes were in physical communication media that provided the first serious alternative to the century-old practice of connecting individual telephones to a switch with copper wires. The third change was a protocol change rather than a change in physical communication medium. Packets could carry any kind of information, creating potential changes in the telephone system and raising questions about the past identification of regulatory boundaries with physical transmission media (broadcasting over the air, telephone by copper wire, cable TV by coaxial cable). This chapter focuses on wireless telephones while the following two chapters examine local competition (begun with optical fiber improvements) and packet-switched communications.

The monopoly structure of the telephone industry was built around technology that required a copper wire pair to connect each telephone instrument with the central office switch. That technology led to political support for the Bell System perspective that competition was undesirable in telephone service and the associated institutional structure of regulation, politically determined price structures, and limits on entry. It also tethered telephone customers to their fixed phones, prohibiting them from conversing while in automobiles. Radio technology offered the promise of much more flexible communication, and extensive efforts were made to develop effective wireless communication systems. Early efforts were hampered by two distinct problems: (1) the high-cost and high-power requirements of electronic components made radio communication systems bulky and expensive; (2) radio communication systems required the use of electromagnetic spectrum under licenses from the FCC while the FCC's spectrum management techniques designed for broadcast controversies were unsuitable for mobile telephone spectrum.

The technical limitations on radio-based communication were solved through the continuous electronics progress of the second half of the twentieth century. Inexpensive integrated circuits that could operate on low power made low-cost lightweight radio sets feasible. Mobile radio systems advanced from specialized uses where the benefits of mobile communication outweighed high cost and heavy equipment (police, fire, and military communication) to an expensive adjunct to the copper wire telephone system for individuals who placed a high value on the ability to talk from their automobiles (real estate agents and other early cellular telephone users) to a general substitute for the copper wire telephone. Ubiquitous low-cost mobile telephones called into question the divestiture assumption that local telephone service was a natural monopoly. So long as local service was provided by copper wires connected to a central switch, it was hard to envision efficient competition. If service could be economically provided by radio, then there was no reason not to have competition in the local exchange. The institutional structure for spectrum allocation and licensing also improved because of the pressure created by technological opportunities and consumer demand for mobile communication. The process of spectrum reform was slow and politically controversial. While substantial progress has been made, spectrum allocation and licensing policies continue to limit the full utilization of technological opportunities in mobile communication.

Early Land Mobile Telephones

The earliest commercial radio-telephone service began in 1929 aboard ships where heavy equipment with high power requirements could be accommodated and where wealthy passengers with no other options for communication were willing to pay high enough fees to support the expensive service. The initial demand for land mobile service came from police departments with the first one-way system (receive-only radios without transmitters) begun by the Detroit police department in 1928 and two-way systems begun in the early 1930s. Edwin Armstrong's introduction of frequency modulation (FM) in 1935 as an alternative to the then-standard amplitude modulation (AM) greatly improved the prospects for mobile radio. FM signals required less power than AM signals and were much more resistant to propagation problems created by moving vehicles.

World War II accelerated the refinement of FM mobile radio as vast numbers of two-way FM radios were produced for ships, airplanes, tanks, and infantry units. By the end of the war the FM mobile radio technology had been greatly improved, and there was an extensive knowledge base on the production and operation of FM mobile radio. After the war, commercial mobile radio systems were introduced for taxi dispatch and other uses in addition to the prewar demand from police, fire, and other public services. The systems were generally not interconnected to the telephone network. They performed a self-contained communications function in which, for example, a taxi dispatcher could communicate with a moving taxi over a radio link, but a telephone user could not communicate with a moving taxi.

AT&T introduced mobile telephone service (with interconnection to the phone network) in 1946. The systems featured a mobile two-way FM radio in a vehicle that could communicate with a single transmitter within a metropolitan area. Initial manual connection of the base station with the telephone network was later replaced by automatic switching. The original mobile telephone channels utilized 120 kHz of spectrum to transmit a voice telephone bandwidth of 3 kHz, and the limited spectrum allocated to mobile telephony meant that there were only a few channels available in each city. Furthermore, those channels were not trunked in the early years. That is, each set of subscribers was assigned a single channel to share sequentially, as in party-line telephone service. If the assigned channel was busy, but another channel was available, the subscriber could not switch to the available channel. While trunking (allowing any user to utilize any available channel) greatly increases the efficiency of calling, it would also have created high costs in the early radios while electronics was expensive. Excess demand for the limited channels available led to extensive waiting lists and poor service for those who obtained it. With a large number of customers assigned to each channel, the probability of obtaining an open channel when desired was low.

After extensive technological progress in radio and electronics during the two decades after the war, an enhanced version of the service was introduced in the mid-1960s. It was known as Improved Mobile Telephone Service (IMTS) and greatly increased efficiency with automatic trunking and a reduction in channel bandwidth to 30 kHz. IMTS also increased customer convenience by allowing two-way conversations (instead of earlier push-to-talk directional switching) and direct dialing. However, no new spectrum was allocated for IMTS, and the service remained very limited.

Although AT&T introduced mobile telephone service, it did not maintain the tight monopoly on mobile service that it did on wired telephone service. The FCC licensed a group of independent operators (known as the radio common carriers or RCCs) along with AT&T. In addition, under the terms of the 1956 consent decree, AT&T agreed not to produce mobile radios, and Motorola became the primary supplier (Calhoun, 1988, p. 35).

AT&T sought additional spectrum for mobile telephone service in 1949 while the FCC was considering the allocation of the UHF band for television (470 MHz to 890 MHz). AT&T's proposal revived an earlier plan for 150 channels with 100 kHz spacing. However, the FCC allocated the entire band to UHF broadcast television, creating seventy new broadcast channels of 6 MHz each. The UHF decision was a critical roadblock to the development of mobile telephone systems and left the entire mobile telephone industry dependent on a block of spectrum that was only equivalent to a fraction of a single broadcast channel. Even though UHF television was not nearly so successful as originally projected, the FCC continued with efforts to promote UHF stations (such as supporting a 1962 law requiring that all televisions be able to receive UHF as well as VHF stations). Despite the support of the FCC and Congress, UHF broadcasting remained a limited alternative to the VHF stations and much of the spectrum allocated to UHF television was not fully utilized while mobile telephone continued as a minor service with long waiting lists. Mobile suppliers and potential mobile users continued efforts to secure additional spectrum without success.

Cellular Spectrum Allocation

The breakthrough for spectrum and for mobile telephony in general came from the elaboration of an AT&T plan to create a cellular mobile telephone service. The essential concept of a cellular plan was to substitute a large number of low-power transmitters for the single high-power metropolitan transmitter of the earlier system. The low-power transmitters would provide adequate reception within a limited distance but would neither provide service nor create interference across a large area. Consequently, the same frequency could be used for more than one conversation within a single city at the same time. The number of times a frequency could be reused depended on the size of the cell, but in principle a large number of conversations could occur simultaneously on a single channel in different sections of a metropolitan area.

Each cell required a radio transmitter, some control functions, and communication with the other cells. Each time a moving vehicle crossed a cell boundary, it required a hand-off to the new cell, including automatically changing frequencies (because the same frequency could not be used in adjacent cells without creating interference) without creating a break in the conversation. With very large cells, a cellular system looked much like the original structure (which could be considered a cellular system with a single cell per city), but as the cells were subdivided to create greater spectrum efficiency the cost rose rapidly.

The cellular concept was originally described in the late 1940s, but the technology was not available at that time to implement it at a reasonable cost. Cellular telephony required mobile radios that could receive and transmit on many different frequencies and control systems that were far more complex than automatic trunking systems. However, an idealized representation of cellular service was critical for the eventual success of reallocating spectrum from UHF television to mobile telephone service. So long as only one conversation per channel could occur in any one city, it was clear that mobile telephones would remain a niche market under any foreseeable allocation of spectrum. The political and rhetorical argument for retaining spectrum in the mass-market "free television" service rather than allocating it to an elite service that would remain closed to most consumers was strong.

The cellular concept changed the political argument by creating the possibility that mobile telephones would become a mass-market service if a "reasonable" amount of spectrum was allocated to the service. Providers could start with relatively large cells in order to conserve on equipment and then subdivide those cells as demand grew in order to serve many more customers without requiring additional spectrum. Potential benefits of a widely available mobile telephone service could be contrasted with the limited benefits observed from the underutilized UHF television channels.

The FCC appointed an Advisory Committee for Land Mobile Radio Services that concluded that new spectrum was required and could best be found by either reallocating some UHF broadcast spectrum to land mobile or developing a sharing plan. A House of Representatives committee observed that 87 percent of the spectrum available below 960 MHz was allocated to broadcasting, with less than 0.5 percent allocated to mobile telephones, and called for additional spectrum for mobile telephones. In 1968, the FCC proposed reallocating UHF channels 70 through 83 for cellular telephone service (Calhoun, 1988, p. 48). After a contentious proceeding in which AT&T and other mobile interests argued for a reallocation while the broadcasters defended the existing allocation to UHF television, the FCC decided in 1970 to create cellular spectrum out of the underutilized top end of the original UHF television allocation. After reconsideration, the commission allocated 40 MHz for initial cellular service (the equivalent of just under seven television broadcast channels) and that was increased to 50 MHz at a later time.

The 1970 decision in the cellular reallocation proceeding treated the new service as an extension of monopoly telephone service and limited use of the spectrum to telephone companies. At that time, AT&T served about half of the existing base of roughly 70,000 mobile telephone customers nationwide, while the many independent radio common carriers served the remainder (Calhoun, 1988, p. 49). Cellular was treated as a new service rather than an upgrade of existing mobile telephone service and was considered too complex for the small business RCCs. AT&T developed the cellular concept into a specific architecture known as Advanced Mobile Phone Service (AMPS) in 1971. The AMPS design was based on an assumption of monopoly service, and it created a standardized plan with centralized control consistent with the wireline telephone network of the time. It used the mature FM analog technology for radio links and centralized switches that controlled the cell sites.

After appeals from the RCCs, supported by the Department of Justice, the FCC reconsidered its telephone company exclusivity policy and opened the allocation to "any qualified common carrier" while retaining its original plan to license only one carrier per geographical region. Most observers, including the RCCs, considered the policy change insignificant because they were unlikely to win a contest against AT&T for a monopoly license. The RCCs filed a court appeal of the FCC decision. After AT&T announced plans for a 1975 test system in Chicago with mobile units not manufactured by Motorola, Motorola became a major force opposing the expected AT&T monopoly in cellular, supporting the RCCs in their appeal of the FCC decision and filing a joint application with an RCC for developing a cellular test system. After an adverse court decision and further extensive controversies and proceedings, the FCC decided in 1982 to split the 40 MHz of spectrum into two licenses for each area, with one license reserved for the telephone company (wireline license) and one reserved for a party other than the telephone company. The dual licensing approach was adopted over AT&T's objections and despite technical studies that indicated splitting the spectrum would create higher costs and lower efficiency.

The 1982 decision determined the framework for awarding licenses and allowed the implementation of cellular service. The first system began operating in Chicago in October 1983, and twenty-five cities had cellular service available by the end of 1984. The extended regulatory controversies over licensing procedures delayed the U.S. implementation of commercial cellular telephone service to four years after Japan's

1979 inauguration of cellular and two years after Europe's implementation of cellular (Bekkers and Smits, 1999, pp. 29–31). Initial cellular service was an expensive niche product. It required professional installation of a $3,000 phone and associated equipment in the customer's automobile plus service fees near $50 per month and forty cents per daytime minute of use, but was eagerly sought by those who needed to make business calls from their automobiles and by wealthy personal users who appreciated the convenience and status of mobile telephones (Murray, 2001, p. 83).

The long delay between the initial allocation decision (1970) and the final licensing rules (1982) meant that the AMPS architecture was obsolete in two different senses before it was implemented:

1. Technologically, the progress in computer technology during the 1970s made digital coding of voice signals economically feasible and provided opportunities for economical distributed control that were not available in the 1970 time frame when AMPS was developed. In the wireline network, digital central office switches began service in 1975 and digital carrier systems for interoffice trunks became common. Although cellular service was dependent on computers for control processing, the AMPS system was frozen in a rigid framework and did not utilize the technology that became available between its design and its implementation.
2. Conceptually, the AMPS system was designed for a centralized monopoly market structure at a time when both AT&T and policymakers generally agreed that monopoly provision of telephone service was desirable. Those assumptions changed substantially before it was implemented. The cellular spectrum was divided into two pieces but the system design was not changed. The FCC issued its cellular licensing rules just after AT&T and the DOJ reached the agreement that led to the divestiture. In the divestiture, the regional Bell Operating Companies inherited the cellular licenses and the right to participate in the wireline category for licenses not yet awarded, while the new AT&T lost its cellular business.

While the delay led to obsolescence of the AMPS framework, it also helped develop cellular mobile telephone service as an alternative to the wireline networks. If licenses had been awarded in the early 1970s, they almost certainly would have gone exclusively to AT&T and to the independent telephone companies in their serving areas. Cellular service would have begun earlier, but only as an adjunct to wireline telephone service rather than as an alternative. Once cellular was established as a monopoly service, it would have been difficult to implement competition.

Cellular Licensing Problems

The cellular spectrum allocation decision and associated technical rules determined the structure of a duopoly cellular service, but the FCC still had to choose specific cellular operators and award them licenses. The cellular licensing process was chaotic, and its problems created political interest in new procedures for future licensing. When initial applications were accepted in 1982 (limited to the thirty largest markets), the FCC used comparative hearings to decide between mutually exclusive applications, much as it did in broadcast controversies.

In the broadcast context, a rigid channel and geographic allotment process allowed specific channels in specific cities. Because only one licensee could broadcast on that channel-city combination, multiple applications were mutually exclusive. When there was more than one applicant for a broadcast license, the FCC held a formal hearing before an administrative law judge (with opportunity for review of the judge's decision by the commissioners) in which the various applicants extolled the virtues of their proposals and criticized the vices of their opponents' proposals and the judge decided which proposal best fit the "public interest." In contrast to the broadcast license applications, many non-broadcast spectrum controversies could be resolved by technical adjustments to prevent the applications from being mutually exclusive. For example, in private microwave services for long distance communication within an organization, two applications for the same route and frequency could not both be granted as requested but could generally be "coordinated" with adjustments in the plans that would allow both to operate in a satisfactory manner.

The cellular plan was designed analogous to broadcasting, with two licensees allowed in each geographical area. The country was divided into over 300 Metropolitan Statistical Areas (MSAs) and over 400 Rural Service Areas (RSAs). The license for Block B (wireline) was generally awarded without contest, either because there was only one relevant telephone company in the area or because the relevant telephone companies worked out a private settlement to avoid competing for the license. However, many parties perceived a significant market opportunity in the cellular business and filed applications for the nonrestricted Block A frequencies, with the number of applications increasing rapidly over time. The FCC received 200 applications in the June 1982 filing window for the top thirty markets, 500 applications in the November 1982 filing for the next thirty markets, and 700 applications in the March 1983 filing for markets 61 through 90 (Calhoun, 1988, pp. 122–124).

The comparative hearing process was incapable of distinguishing among the applications in a meaningful way. The FCC had already specified the primary technical parameters of the systems and therefore no applicant could gain an edge by proposing innovative technology or improvements in spectrum efficiency. The purpose of the comparative hearings in the broadcast context was to provide political control over content, but the cellular service was an extension of telephone service with no content provided by the cellular carriers. Consequently, all serious applications were effectively identical, providing a reasonable engineering plan to implement the technical specifications contained in the FCC rules.

The FCC concluded that after extensive time and resources devoted to analyzing applications and conducting comparative hearings, it was making decisions on such fine points of detail that the results were largely random. The FCC decided that a lottery would be quicker and fairer than an extensive proceeding that chose one applicant over another according to minor details of the application. In April 1984, the FCC adopted lottery rules that applied to the already filed applications for MSA markets 31–90 and to future rounds of cellular applications. The lottery rules induced an extensive effort to settle conflicting applications in markets 31–90 where no new applications could be filed. The applicants traded and purchased applications from each other, largely ignoring the FCC's antitrafficking rules that prohibited selling applications, and settled fifty-eight of the sixty markets among themselves, leaving only two markets for lottery.

The lottery inspired far more applications as individuals and promoters sought to benefit from the cellular licenses. Although the FCC rules required that all applicants be qualified to operate a cellular system and certify that they intended to operate it if awarded a license, promoters offered to provide applications to anyone who wished to speculate in the cellular lottery. Valid cellular applications required detailed engineering specifications, but it was possible to develop one application and then duplicate it any number of times with different names for the applicant. The 700 applications for the comparative hearing process in markets 61–90 increased to 5,000 in the first lottery window (markets 91–120) and 15,000 for markets 121–150.

The FCC was incapable of reviewing all of the applications or enforcing its rules that required only serious applicants to apply and limited the kinds of trades that could be made. In part, that limitation was due to an administrative structure that imposed fees for each license application but did not allow the FCC to use the fees to hire more staff. The FCC was dependent at that time entirely on congressional appropriations and was working under a hiring freeze during much of the cellular application period. Thus applicants paid fees explicitly designed to recover the cost of processing the application, but the FCC could not use the fees to hire staff. As the number of applications increased, the staff reduced scrutiny of applications. More significantly, it would have been impossible to fully enforce the rules regardless of the number of staff available because the large number of players and the incentive to break the rules created too much opportunity. It was analogous to requiring a bank to leave large amounts of money unguarded on the sidewalk and expecting the police to apprehend anyone who stole it.

The law required the FCC to choose the licensees that would best serve the public interest and to award the license without charge. Yet a cellular license was a valuable commodity with the identity of the licensee largely irrelevant to the public so long as a competent entity built and operated the system. In an economic sense, the comparative hearings and later lotteries awarded a valuable property right in a particular slice of spectrum, but legally the licensee had no property rights in the spectrum. The spectrum institutional theory required the FCC to choose the best one of the mutually exclusive applications, but the FCC was incapable of doing that because all fully qualified applicants were essentially identical. Given the similarity of the applications in the top ninety markets, the lotteries made sense as a quick and fair way to choose among the look-alike applicants. However, the lottery also

changed the incentive scheme and created incentives for purely speculative applications.

The FCC's rules provided that cellular licenses "will be granted only
in cases where it is shown that the applicant is legally, financially, technically and otherwise qualified to render the proposed service . . . and the
public interest, convenience and necessity would be served by a grant
thereof" (47 C.F.R. §22.901(a)). After evidence of speculation in the applications subject to lottery, the commission added the following certi-
fication requirement for later rounds of applications:

> I also certify the applicant is the real party in interest in this application
> and there are no agreements or understandings, other than those speci-
> fied in this application, which provide that someone other than the ap-
> plicant shall have an indirect or direct ownership interest. It is also
> certified that the application intends to construct and operate the sta-
> tion as proposed and that there are no agreements or understandings
> that are inconsistent with that intent. (47 C.F.R. §22.923(b)(7))

Although it is unlikely that a person who lives distant from the site
of the application and has no experience with telecommunication will
build and operate a cellular service if awarded a license, it is difficult to
make a legal case for disqualification. People move to start new businesses; they can obtain financing for businesses with good prospects
such as cellular; qualified people can be hired to construct and operate
the system. The applications contained proper technical documentation
for building a system. Thus there was no way to quickly and easily separate serious applicants from pure speculators.

While it is fairly certain from the vast numbers of applications received and the ways in which applications were promoted that many of
the applicants committed perjury in certifying that they intended to
construct and operate the system, attempting to disqualify people for
misrepresenting their intentions risked delaying the licensing process
through extensive litigation. Furthermore, the speculative applicants
and organized sponsors of speculative groups were creative in finding
ways to comply with the letter of the FCC rules while violating the intent. Consequently, the FCC adopted a "hands off" policy on the applications until after the lottery. When an application won the lottery, it
was then subject to scrutiny by the FCC staff as well as the public, and
the license was sometimes denied for various defects in the application.

Many controversies ensued from the lottery process and most were decided on delegated authority by the FCC staff, but some went to the entire commission and to the courts for resolution with consequent extensive delays in establishing cellular service by the eventual license winner.

There was widespread dissatisfaction with the cellular licensing process. Those who believed that licenses should be awarded by traditional public interest criteria (especially Democratic congressional critics of the then-Republican-led FCC) criticized the FCC for failing to be more diligent in weeding out speculative applications and enforcing its antitrafficking rules. Those who believed the licenses should be awarded on more market-oriented criteria (including many on the FCC staff and leadership and most economists who considered the subject) believed that extensive resources were being wasted on inefficient procedures and rules that failed to get the licenses to the best party, and that the antitrafficking rules only accentuated the problems by limiting the ability of successful speculators to sell their windfall from the government to the party that valued it the most.

As is characteristic of markets with high demand but poor institutions, substantial wealth was earned by those who were able to create an effective market, either by finding legal ways around the antimarket rules or by violating the rules without being penalized. Although the licenses were initially awarded to a person who was not really interested in or capable of operating a cellular system, and were awarded in much smaller geographic areas than were efficient for developing a cellular system, entrepreneurs pieced together extensive systems through innovative agreements with initial applicants and purchases from the lottery winners. Cellular systems were built throughout the country, first by the telephone companies who received their licenses without controversy and then by the nonwireline company that was often delayed by license controversies and a transfer from the lottery winner to a serious operating company. As duopoly cellular service became widely available and the cost and size of phones declined, cellular service expanded from 92,000 customers at the end of 1984 to 3.5 million at the end of 1989. Cellular revenue in 1989 reached $3.3 billion, 4.1 percent of the $81.2 billion in revenue reported by local telephone companies in that year (FCC, 2001, tables 12.2 and 12.3; FCC, 1989, p. 7).

After only one year of operation, systems in New York, Chicago, and

Los Angeles began experiencing capacity problems, and all three operators petitioned the FCC for more spectrum. The cellular theory was that operators would initially build relatively large cells to conserve on capital costs, and would then subdivide the cells as demand increased. An attractive feature of cellular that helped sway the debate toward reallocating spectrum from broadcast was that with a "reasonable" allocation to cellular, capacity could be increased indefinitely by splitting the cells as many times as necessary. That was a correct argument with regard to spectrum but it glossed over the fact that the cost of service rises rapidly with decreases in cell size. It was cheaper for a cellular operator to seek additional spectrum than to split cells in order to increase capacity because there was no specific price for spectrum other than the political and legal costs of pursuing the request. The cellular operators hoped to use their initial license to gain a dominating position in an expanded wireless communication service by convincing the FCC to add spectrum to initial licensees as demand expanded. The FCC added 5 MHz to each license (from 20 to 25 MHz), but declined to grant the large blocks of additional spectrum to initial cellular licensees that would have been necessary to provide economical wireless service to a large portion of the population.

Spectrum Institutional Reform

The institutions of spectrum regulation were developed for radio broadcasting in the 1920s and 1930s and were adapted for television broadcasting in the 1940s and 1950s. Nonbroadcasting uses of the spectrum were a minor factor during the crucial institutional development period. As nonbroadcasting uses became much more significant, they were forced into the structure designed for broadcasting. While the incumbent broadcasters, the FCC, and the members of Congress were generally satisfied with the institutional structure, many outside observers considered it rigid and inefficient.

The process of allocating specific portions of the spectrum for specific uses, along with detailed technical rules on how the services should be implemented, prevented entrepreneurs from introducing new services or new ways of providing old services even when there would be no interference with existing users. The use of comparative hearings to determine the licensee when there were "mutually exclusive applicants" for a particular license was slow and cumbersome and subject to political manipulation. The critics generally proposed more use of market processes in the spectrum allocation and licensing procedures, including various combinations of more ownership rights for incumbents, more flexibility in choosing technology and services within a particular frequency band, and auctions rather than comparative hearings to decide among mutually exclusive applicants. Proposals for reform met extreme skepticism at first but gradually gained support, especially after problems in the cellular telephone licensing process emphasized the deficiencies of the old structure.

Ronald Coase proposed use of a market system for spectrum in 1959 testimony before the FCC:

> In presenting my case, I suffer from the disadvantage that, at the outset, I must attack a position which, although I am convinced it is erroneous, is nonetheless firmly held by many of those most knowledgeable about the broadcasting industry. Most authorities argue that the administrative assignment of radio and television frequencies by the Commission is called for by the technology of the industry. The number of frequencies, we are told, is limited, and people want to use more of them than are available.
>
> But the situation so described is in no sense peculiar to the broadcasting industry. All the resources used in the economic system are limited in amount and are scarce in that people want to use more of them than exists . . . But the usual way of handling this problem in the American economic system is to employ the pricing mechanism, and this allocates resources to users without the need for government regulation . . . There is no reason why the same system could not be adopted for radio and television frequencies . . . Such a system would require a delimitation of the property rights acquired, and there would almost certainly also have to be some general regulation of a technical character. But such regulation would not preclude the existence of private rights in frequencies, just as zoning and other regulations do not preclude the existence of private property in houses . . .
>
> I am told that it is necessary to choose those who should operate radio and television stations to make sure that the public interest is served and that programs of the right kind are transmitted. But, put this way, the case for governmental selection of broadcast station operators represents a significant shift of position from that which justifies it on technological grounds . . . For over 30 years, the federal gov-

ernment has been selecting broadcast station operators on the basis, among other things, of their good character and their devotion to the public interest. By now one would expect the broadcasting industry to be a beacon of virtue, shining out in a wicked world. Such, I am afraid, is not the case. (Benjamin, Lichtman, and Shelanski, 2001, pp. 37, 38)

The first question directed to Coase at the end of his testimony was "Are you spoofing us? Is this all a big joke?" While Coase's analysis was sound and his proposal received considerable attention in the academic community, it had no political support. He focused on broadcasting where there was strong support for the existing system, rather than on nonbroadcast uses of the spectrum where the failures of the system were more evident. While the broadcasting industry was not "a beacon of virtue," it was politically responsive as had been sought in the original 1927 legislation prohibiting private ownership of spectrum.

Greater flexibility was added to the spectrum allocation and licensing process in many small steps with emphasis on "flexibility" and "deregulation" rather than on market processes. The crucial political requirement was to distinguish flexibility in nonbroadcast services from a challenge to the broadcast structure. In 1980, the FCC's Office of Plans and Policy (OPP) issued a working paper by Douglas Webbink advocating increased property rights for incumbents, elimination of antitrafficking rules that limited the transfer of licenses, and elimination of detailed rules that limited licensees to narrowly defined activities (Webbink, 1980). OPP working papers were frequently used to signal possible changes in FCC policies. They had no legal effect and were issued under the author's name with a disclaimer that they represented only the author's views, but were generally approved by the FCC chairman before being released.

While Ronald Coase and other academics had advocated auctions much earlier, the FCC staff and commissioners were unconvinced until the combination of economic arguments, Reagan administration free market ideology, and observed problems in the cellular licensing process caused a careful examination of how auctions could be used. The criticism that spectrum auctions were simply a theoretical concept advocated by economists who did not understand the engineering problems of managing spectrum was blunted when senior FCC staff engineer Alex Felker joined senior staff economists Kenneth Gordon and Evan Kwerel in developing detailed proposals (Felker and Gordon, 1983; Kwerel and

Felker, 1985). According to Kwerel and Felker: "Since the assignment method has little effect on who holds a license in the long run, we conclude that ownership distributions would not be significantly changed if initial authorizations were awarded by auction. . . . [A]uctions would reduce the delays and transactions costs involved in initial assignments and avoid the need for resale" (1985, p. 10). The next year FCC chairman Mark Fowler endorsed auctions in congressional testimony, but encountered strong opposition from Democratic leaders and failed to win auction authority.

While the congressional Democrats blocked FCC auctions and criticized the FCC for allowing speculation in cellular licenses, Mark Warner, then a Democratic fund-raiser (and later elected Governor of Virginia in 2001), made a personal fortune by conducting private auctions of cellular licenses. Beginning in 1986, he convinced large numbers of lottery speculators to hire him as their agent and then he auctioned their interests to companies attempting to build complete cellular systems, earning substantial commissions in the process (Murray, 2001, pp. 148–151). Warner's success supported the Kwerel and Felker argument that licenses would eventually go to the party that valued them the highest regardless of the initial method of distribution, but did not convince Congress to allow the FCC to conduct auctions.

Debate continued for several years with Republicans generally supporting auctions (and the first Bush administration including auction revenues in its proposed budgets) and Democrats generally opposing auctions. In 1993, newly inaugurated President Bill Clinton, a Democrat, announced support for spectrum auctions in order to increase revenue without new taxes at a time of large budget deficits. Congress provided auction authority to the FCC in the Omnibus Budget Reconciliation Act of 1993, and the FCC began planning auctions for future licenses.

PCS and Auctions

The FCC expanded wireless opportunities by creating a "new" service called Personal Communications Service (PCS) and setting up a spectrum allocation and licensing procedure separate from cellular service. In the original description, PCS was envisioned as a service that would simplify communication and economize on telephone numbers by providing each person a single telephone number. Small portable phones could be plugged into a home or office wireline telephone system that would allow the person to be reached at the single number, or could be used in a wireless mode while walking around. The system was planned for higher frequencies than cellular, smaller cells, digital rather than analog operation, and was closely tied to "intelligent network" computer technology to allow the person to be reached anywhere at the same number. As proponents of the concept described it to the FCC in the late 1980s, the new service would gain much greater spectrum efficiency than cellular through microcells and digital technology, but the very small cells would make service to automobiles difficult. Considerable effort was made to distinguish PCS from cellular in order to justify allowing new companies into the market with a different set of rules instead of adding to the spectrum of the existing cellular licensees.

The FCC began formal consideration of PCS in 1990 and developed three major improvements over the cellular allocation and licensing process:

1. Use of a market-oriented "overlay" process to facilitate the reallocation of spectrum for PCS.
2. Use of auctions rather than comparative hearings or lotteries to select the initial licensees of the new service.
3. Flexibility in the definition of the service and in the technology to be utilized instead of a restrictive definition and specified technical standards.

While the time lag between the beginning of the cellular rulemaking and first licenses was fifteen years (1968–1983), the comparable time lag in PCS was only five years (1990–1995). Contrary to initial promotional efforts, PCS has become indistinguishable from an upgraded cellular service with digital transmission. The FCC also relaxed the rigid technical rules for the original cellular service, allowing the 1980s cellular licensees to convert to digital transmission.

The FCC reallocated 140 MHz (from 1,850 MHz to 1,990 MHz) of spectrum from point-to-point microwave service to the new PCS service, almost three times the 50 MHz allocated to cellular telephone service. The band was lightly used but did contain "4,500 point-to-point microwave links for railroads, oil drilling rigs, utilities, and local governments" (Hazlett, 2001, p. 513). Existing users opposed the reallocation and emphasized the critical services that they provided and the expense (estimated at $1 billion) of relocating to higher frequencies that were available and feasible for point-to-point microwave but not for cellular service. The FCC solved this version of the standard incumbent's objection to spectrum reallocation by creating PCS "overlay" rights to the spectrum. A new PCS licensee could use the spectrum so long as it did not interfere with existing microwave systems. New spectrum was made available for the microwave users and they were required to convert to the new frequencies within five years, with the cost of conversion paid by the PCS licensees. PCS licensees could make private agreements to get microwave users to convert earlier.

The 1,850–1,990 MHz spectrum was much more valuable for cellular/PCS use than for microwave. The extensive speculation in 800-MHz cellular licenses had provided market values for cellular spectrum and allowed the argument over reallocation to be converted into dollar terms. Earlier spectrum disputes were qualitative controversies over which service was more important to the public with the decision made on political grounds. In this case, the FCC acknowledged that both services were important to the public and avoided choosing between them by providing spectrum for both with compensation for moving expenses. Rather than defending a finding that PCS was more "in the public interest" than point-to-point microwave systems, the FCC merely found that the spectrum users could provide services at a higher frequency and that PCS providers would be willing to pay them to relocate in order to obtain access to their original frequencies. The FCC's PCS process was a partial market solution that allowed the spectrum to be used more efficiently, but did not allow the microwave users to collect the economic rents that they would have received if given full ownership rights to the spectrum.

The FCC developed a careful auction methodology with the assistance of staff and academic economists with expertise in game theory and auction design. The PCS spectrum was split into six license blocks of differing sizes plus a section for unlicensed uses. Auctions for the A and B blocks, each of which contained 30 MHz of spectrum with unrestricted eligibility, finished in early 1995. The auctions went smoothly and raised over $7 billion for the U.S. Treasury to the great delight of FCC chairman Reed Hundt, who presented a huge check to President Clinton and Vice President Al Gore in a widely publicized event. However, the auction success in the A and B blocks was followed by a failure in the C block. The auction legislation provided that the FCC's auction procedures should ensure "disseminating licenses among a wide variety of applicants, including small businesses, rural telephone companies, and businesses owned by members of minority groups and women" (47 U.S.C. §309(j)(3)(B)). That provision was inconsistent with the theoretical benefits of auctions—that is, moving licenses quickly to the parties that value them most. Even with comparative hearings and preference arrangements for members of particular groups, it was impossible to ensure that licenses remained with those groups unless transfer of licenses was prohibited and careful attention was given to the details of ownership and control.

The FCC reserved the C block of 30 MHz for "small businesses" and divided it into 493 geographical sections so that smaller companies across the country could operate a local PCS business. Instead of paying the entire auction amount upon winning, C block winners were only required to pay a 10 percent deposit and allowed to pay the balance over ten years. The FCC did not limit the number of markets that a "small business" could bid for in the auction. The ability to control a license with only 10 percent of the auction price created an incentive for companies to seek multiple C block licenses. NextWave and two other companies won large numbers of licenses in the C block auction and then defaulted on their obligations and declared bankruptcy. The absence of clear precedent on exactly what property rights the various parties possessed led to extensive litigation and prevented anyone from using the spectrum. Although the C block fiasco emphasized problems in the particular rules used, it did not stop the further use of auctions. Auctions were used for the remaining PCS spectrum and expanded to other services as well.

A further innovation in the PCS market was flexibility in the definition of the service and in the technology used to implement it. Earlier services were tightly defined with strict limits on how the service could be used, creating regulatory distinctions among similar services. For example, cellular spectrum could not be used to provide fixed wireless telephone service even if no interference resulted from that use. The technology and maximum power and antenna heights were specified. PCS provided a much more general definition of the service, allowing PCS providers to use their spectrum for a wide variety of specific services according to market demand.

The FCC declined to specify a technical standard, allowing different companies to choose the technology they thought best. While that decision has often been criticized for allowing incompatible systems, it avoided locking in an old technology as the FCC had done with the earlier AMPS standard for analog cellular service. At the time the PCS rules were written, digital time division multiple access (TDMA) technologies were thoroughly understood, but code division multiple access (CDMA) appeared to have possibilities for superior performance. Experience with CDMA was limited at that point, and if a standard had been adopted it almost certainly would have been a TDMA standard, prohibiting companies from implementing the CDMA technology. With freedom to make their own choices, some companies chose TDMA (in two different versions) and some chose CDMA, but it appears likely that CDMA, will eventually become the dominant standard by market choices.

The first PCS system (Sprint Spectrum in Washington, D.C.) began operation in late 1995, and other systems soon followed. The digital services provided improved quality and much higher spectrum efficiency with at least three digital channels created out of the spectrum used for one analog channel. The A and B blocks alone provided more spectrum than the entire cellular allocation. With greatly increased capacity, more competitors, and cheaper and lighter phones, mobile telephone prices declined and usage accelerated.

In eleven years of cellular deployment (1984–1995), wireless telephones reached 34 million subscribers by the end of 1995. In six years of PCS combined with cellular service, wireless telephones added another 84 million subscribers for a total of 118 million by the middle of 2001, 61 percent of the 192 million wired telephone lines at that time (FCC, 2002, tables 9.1 and 12.2). After seventeen years of development there were as many wireless telephones as there were wired telephone lines in 1970 after ninety-four years of development (U.S. Census, 1975, p. 783). While wireless communication remained more expensive than wired communication for most customers, the additional convenience of mobile communication had already made wireless phones competitive with wired for some customers, and expected technological improvements made wireless a major source of potential future competition for wired telephones.

In the 1960s, expensive computers were carefully scheduled to maximize their ability to satisfy the combined requirements of many different users. Today, inexpensive small computers with similar capabilities to those of the 1960s are devoted to the occasional requests of one person. Similarly, in the 1960s, expensive microwave communication systems were carefully scheduled to maximize their ability to carry the combined communications requirements of many different users. Today, inexpensive small microwave communication systems (PCS telephones) are devoted to the use of one person. Just as the reduction in computer prices has induced a dramatic increase in the number of computers used, so the reduction in wireless communication prices has induced a dramatic increase in the number of wireless telephone users. However, the analogy does not hold with regard to spectrum requirements. There is no component of computers that is in fixed supply, and the number produced can be increased indefinitely. Wireless communication systems require access to spectrum and spectrum cannot be multiplied indefinitely. The same electronics advances that have reduced the cost of wireless communication systems have also allowed more intensive use of the spectrum through smaller cells and more sophisticated coding techniques, but spectrum availability remains a constraint on the exploitation of wireless communication opportunities.

While considerable progress has been made in improving the spectrum management process, there is still no straightforward way to move spectrum from low-value applications to high-value applications as the market routinely does for other resources. Two different kinds of reforms have been proposed to make the spectrum process more efficient:

1. Establish complete property rights in spectrum (defined by frequency range, geographic area, and maximum allowed spillover into other frequencies and geographic areas) and allow the owners of spectrum complete flexibility to supply any service with their spectrum so long as it does not interfere with other spectrum owners, and to sell, subdivide, or lease their spectrum as they choose.
2. Remove current exclusive licenses for particular frequency ranges and geographic areas and replace them with large blocks of spectrum for unlicensed use, subject to rules on power and noise levels, in order to encourage full development of spread spectrum, ultra wideband, software-defined radio, and other innovative methods of wireless communication.

The two ideas provide inconsistent guidance for policy reform. The current spectrum system is analogous to publicly owned land that can only be used when a specific permit is granted for utilization of a specific piece of ground for a specific purpose. The first idea is to convert the publicly owned land to privately owned land by granting formal property rights in the land. The second idea is to continue public ownership and manage the spectrum in a way analogous to national parks: freely available to all who would like to use it with rules to limit adverse impact on other users, but no exclusive permits for occupying particular sections.

The property rights perspective is well grounded in economics. It has been frequently proposed and has many good theoretical properties. Generally, the market works best with well-defined property rights and free transferability. The traditional uses of spectrum and allocation procedures seem amenable to transfer into a property rights regime. Most of the spectrum reforms of the last fifteen years and academic reform proposals for the last forty years have been attempts to create the economic equivalent of spectrum property rights (while a statutory prohibition on spectrum ownership remains in effect) and to utilize market processes for managing spectrum: presumption of license renewal, flexibility in technical and service characteristics, auctions to choose licensees. Further development of property rights would facilitate the transfer of spectrum from low-value uses to high-value uses and increase efficiency. The standard methods of utilizing spectrum have required a high signal-to-noise ratio for effective communication and have made spectrum utilization appear analogous to land use with one party holding exclusive primary rights to a particular frequency and geographic area combination and some spillover effects (externalities) to neighboring property.

More recent technologies such as CDMA and ultra wideband have raised questions about the analogy between spectrum and privately owned land. Those and other spread-spectrum techniques carry information on a low power signal spread across a wide frequency range and can recover the signal in the presence of high noise levels. Additional users add to the noise and increase the cost of recovering the desired signal, but there is no need for exclusive rights. The "price" of spectrum is the cost of using more complex electronics to convey information in the presence of high noise or to automatically shift to a less congested portion of the spectrum with software-defined radio. Proponents of the "national park" perspective on spectrum assert that unlicensed spectrum would already be more efficient than licensing and that the benefits of unlicensed spectrum will increase with future technology.

Both reform ideas are motivated by a search for improved technical and economic efficiency in the spectrum process. Neither idea retains support for the political control of spectrum that was at the heart of the 1927 and 1934 laws establishing the current framework. Those who support the current structure would reject both concepts. The political and technical uncertainty regarding how best to manage spectrum, together with the critical importance of spectrum management for the telecommunication sector and the overall economy, guarantees that spectrum will be an ongoing policy controversy.

14

Local Competition and the
Telecommunications Act of 1996

The 1984 divestiture of AT&T, together with the high access charges and rigid regulatory boundaries associated with it, created dissatisfaction and efforts to modify the structure. The Bell Operating Companies (BOCs) complained that the limitations imposed on their services by the Modified Final Judgment (MFJ) curbed their efficiency and technological progress. The long distance companies complained about the high access charges imposed by the BOCs with regulatory approval. The high access charges created incentives to provide an alternative form of communication between large customers and the interexchange carriers' points of presence (POPs), developing a limited form of competition inside the "natural monopoly" local exchange boundary.

Competition in the local exchange followed the same steps as competition in long distance, but the sequence was completed over a decade in the local market while it occupied a quarter-century in the long distance market. The first step was high-volume private line service in limited locations with no interconnection between the entrant and the incumbent (in long distance, private microwave competition after the FCC's Above 890 decision; in local service, competitive access providers (CAPs) using optical fiber technology to provide alternative local connections between large businesses and interexchange companies in the center of large cities). The second step was more general private line competition, with interconnection between the entrant and the incumbent so that the entrant could offer private line service to locations away from its physical facilities (in long distance, "specialized" carriers after the FCC's MCI and Specialized Common Carrier decisions; in local service, interconnected private line services of CAPs and local exchange carriers). The third step was competition in switched services by extending intercon-

244

nection arrangements from the incumbent's private line services to the incumbent's switched services (in long distance, limited switched-service competition after the federal appeals court's Execunet decisions; in local service, limited local switched-service competition after state public utility commission authorization). The fourth step was a major policy intervention designed to create a structure to facilitate competition (in long distance, the DOJ-imposed divestiture and FCC access charge plan; in local service, the Telecommunications Act of 1996).

In both the long distance and local competition stories, technological change that reduced the cost of information transmission provided incentives for institutional change. In long distance, improvements in microwave radio created opportunities for entrants to offer services at prices below those offered by the regulated monopoly. Optical fiber rings created similar opportunities in local service. Rapidly developing cellular radio services and data communications services contributed to skepticism about the natural monopoly characteristics of local exchange service while providing less direct competition to the local exchange carriers than the companies using optical fiber rings.

At the time of the 1982 divestiture agreement, there was no reason to believe that local exchange service could be an efficient competitive market even if policies that favored competition were adopted. There was no alternative technology to the telephone company network of copper wires connecting user locations and central office switches, and that technology seemed to have natural monopoly characteristics. Consequently, it was difficult to see either social benefits or competitive viability from encouraging new carriers to install alternative copper wire networks. Although wireless technologies were available, they were too expensive to be competitive with wired telephone service except in cases where mobility was particularly valued. Because of the technological limitations of the time, the divestiture theory assumed that local exchange would remain a monopoly and focused on preventing the extension of monopoly power to competitive services through structural separation and strict boundary limitations.

By the mid-1990s there were more technological alternatives to the copper wire telephone network. The cost of transmission over optical fiber systems had declined rapidly, making it feasible to connect a wider range of customers directly onto fiber networks. Rapidly increasing demand for data communications provided an incentive to build high-capacity fiber networks that could be used for both voice and data. Cable television systems provided an alternative route to most residences and a source of potential competition after the technology was upgraded. Cost and size reductions in wireless telephones along with increased spectrum and more efficient transmission techniques made cellular wireless telephones a potential alternative to the wireline network. If competition for local telephone service was feasible, the strict divestiture boundaries to separate competitive and monopoly services were unnecessary. The Telecommunications Act of 1996 voided the MFJ and replaced it with a policy designed to promote interconnected competition without strict boundaries on the services particular companies could offer.

Competitive Access Providers

As the long distance optical fiber networks became operational during the mid-1980s, local telephone companies also began using the new technology to provide dense local communications. Telephone companies utilized fiber to replace earlier trunk lines connecting metropolitan switching offices, especially the common T-1 trunks, which carried twenty-four conversations multiplexed onto a copper wire. By the end of 1985 the long distance carriers had installed 20,000 route miles of optical fiber containing 456,000 fiber miles. At that time, the local companies had installed a comparable amount of fiber containing 497,000 actual fiber miles. Long distance and local carriers continued to install fiber rapidly during the later 1980s, increasing their total route and fiber miles by over 400 percent between 1985 and 1990 (FCC, 1998, tables 1–5).

Fiber technology was relatively expensive per mile installed but carried such a high capacity that it was the least expensive way to transfer high-density streams of data between two points. The fiber technology created a divergence between the cost of providing service and the price structure. The divergence was similar to that seen in long distance private line rates in the 1950s at the time of the original private microwave decision. In the 1980s, telephone companies charged high rates compared to their cost of providing service for high-capacity local private lines. A company was entitled to order a private line from a local exchange company to connect its premises to an interexchange POP and use that line instead of switched access. Lower private line rates would cause more customers to choose that option and reduce switched-access revenue, providing an incentive for the telephone companies to keep private line rates high.

Many states prohibited competition within the local exchange. However, interstate access was not subject to state jurisdiction because it was considered a part of an interstate service. Several companies recognized that they could take advantage of the high switched-access rates charged by the local exchange carriers, as well as the above-cost private line rates, if they could develop alternative facilities to connect large users with the interexchange carriers. Insofar as the facilities were designed for interstate access, they would be free from state regulation or state prohibitions on competition to the local exchange carrier. The FCC wanted to discourage bypass of switched-access rates by rate reform, but had no objection to individual customers or alternative access providers putting pressure on the rates through competition. The incentives created by the access charge structure together with the technological opportunities created by the availability of optical fiber technology generated the first form of local competition subsequent to the elimination of turn-of-the-century competition decades earlier. The two leading companies in the new competition were Metropolitan Fiber Systems (later acquired by WorldCom) and Teleport Communications Group (later acquired by AT&T).

Teleport Communications was created by the Port Authority of New York and New Jersey, and then taken over by Merrill Lynch and Western Union. The original idea was to create a better "data port" to the rest of the world with a collection of seventeen shielded satellite earth stations on Staten Island and a fiber link to the World Trade Center in Manhattan and other major locations. Teleport's association with Western Union gave it the significant benefit of utilizing Western Union's rights-of-way and legal privileges granted during the nineteenth century. With the AT&T divestiture, a market was created for access services that connected customers to the POPs of long distance companies.

Teleport's first service, introduced in 1985, was high-speed private line "DS-3" (45 megabits per second) digital service interconnecting long distance company POPs and major customers. At that time, New York Telephone did not offer DS-3 service and instead offered the lower-speed DS-1 service (1.544 megabits per second). Teleport offered a substantial price advantage over multiple DS-1 circuits for very high-volume customers, but could not economically serve lower-volume customers because of construction costs of $100,000 per mile and up to $100,000 for each link to a new building. By the end of 1987 Teleport was serving the equivalent of 60,000 voice circuits with 70 percent of the circuits devoted to interexchange POP-to-POP traffic (Tomlinson, 2000, pp. 21, 36). The company abandoned its initial purpose of serving as a satellite gateway to New York and developed a broader emphasis on providing high-speed digital private line service in major cities using optical fiber technology.

The second major local access company began in Chicago about the same time as Teleport and after some early name changes became Metropolitan Fiber Systems (MFS). In 1984, the predecessor to MFS leased rights-of-way in abandoned tunnels beneath the Chicago Loop that had once housed a narrow-gauge railway for hauling coal, but construction of an optical fiber communications system was delayed because of financing difficulties. MFS began service to its first customer at the end of 1987 and had less than $1 million in revenue in 1988 (Tomlinson, 2000, p. 61). Illinois Bell responded to the potential competition more quickly than New York Telephone and created a fiber hub in 1987 to interconnect long distance carriers (Teleport's initial market niche).

MFS and other fledgling local competitors gained credibility after a May 1988 fire destroyed Illinois Bell's Hinsdale central office located near O'Hare International Airport, disrupting communications to O'Hare, emergency services, ordinary subscribers, and large numbers of long distance circuits that were routed through that office. In some cases, both the primary and emergency back-up circuits were routed through the Hinsdale office and both were destroyed. After an extraordinary effort, a complete new central office switch was installed and service fully restored in three weeks. While Illinois Bell was proud of its accomplishment in compressing a normally multimonth central office switch installation into three weeks, customers who had lost business because of the outage were much more open to ordering part of their service from alternative carriers in order to guard against a repeat disaster. The Hinsdale fire helped both potential customers and regulators view alternative carriers as a valuable source of physical diversity for critical communications (Tomlinson, 2000, p. 83).

The competitive optical fiber companies expanded from a combined total of 133 route miles in 1987 to 782 route miles in 1989 to 2,071 route miles by the end of 1991 while remaining a tiny fraction of the 150,000 route miles of optical fiber in the combined local exchange telephone networks in that year. The interstate services provided by the competitive access providers were exempt from state regulation, but the CAPs also provided services that were not a part of interstate access. Both the CAPs and the telephone companies provided local private line circuits that could be classified as jurisdictionally interstate or intrastate, depending only on the service to which they were connected. There was consequently no sharp dividing line between the services subject to the respective jurisdictions, and the companies were able to seek regulatory support in the jurisdiction that appeared most favorable to their interests.

Interconnection: CAP to CLEC

The first step in expanding the scope of CAP services beyond specialized high-speed private line service was to arrange interconnection with local telephone companies for private line circuits. Interconnection could be beneficial in providing an emergency back-up service and also in extending the reach of CAP services by using telephone company facilities to connect their fiber ring to buildings not located on the fiber path. Interconnection could be achieved by voluntary agreement, by federal action (because access to an interstate circuit was considered interstate service), or by state action (because some services were local private lines that were considered intrastate).

Teleport achieved the first interconnection agreement through voluntary negotiation with New Jersey Bell in 1986 when both companies perceived advantages in being able to use the other company's facilities to provide route diversity to customers between Newark and Princeton. When Teleport attempted to negotiate a similar agreement with New York Telephone, it encountered strong resistance and filed a complaint with the New York Public Service Commission (NYPSC). After extensive consideration of Teleport's complaint and broader issues of local competition, in 1989 the NYPSC ordered New York Telephone to interconnect its private line service with that of Teleport and other CAPs. The order allowed the interconnection to be either by physical collocation of competitive equipment in the telephone company central office or by "virtual collocation" (interconnection without actually terminating competitive equipment in the central office), sidestepping a controversial issue of the telephone company's control over central office space (Tomlinson, 2000, p. 155).

In 1989, Teleport began negotiations with Illinois Bell seeking a voluntary interconnection agreement similar to the earlier agreement with New Jersey Bell. Illinois Bell declined to follow New Jersey Bell's example, suggesting that it had adequate back-up facilities of its own and had no need for interconnection to provide diversity to its customers. Rather than filing a complaint, Teleport lobbied Terry Barnich, the chairman of the Illinois Commerce Commission, for support. Barnich told the president of Illinois Bell that he was favorably impressed with the arguments for interconnection and suggested that Illinois Bell negotiate a voluntary agreement in order to preclude the necessity for formal commission action (Tomlinson, 2000, p. 161). Illinois Bell accepted the hint and began serious negotiations with Teleport, leading to a 1991 agreement to interconnect nonswitched services. While Teleport focused on state issues, MFS had been seeking FCC action to require interconnection for the "special access" lines that were under the FCC's jurisdiction. The MFS efforts led to a 1992 FCC order requiring interconnection of nonswitched lines under federal jurisdiction.

Soon after the initial interconnection agreement was reached for nonswitched service in Illinois, Barnich proposed in a November 1, 1991, speech that the Chicago Loop, the city's dense downtown area, be classified as a special zone in which all telecommunication services could be offered competitively. MFS, Teleport, and Illinois Bell all responded favorably to the proposal. The new competitors perceived an opportunity to gain entry into the mainstream switched market while the incumbent perceived an opportunity to free itself of restrictive regulations. The Barnich speech and favorable industry reaction initiated an extensive series of proceedings in several different states to establish rules for switched local telephone competition.

Teleport was particularly active in arguing the case for competition. It issued a set of conditions that it considered necessary for competition in 1991, hired Gail Garfield Schwartz as Vice President of Government Affairs in 1992 soon after she left her position as deputy chairman of the New York Public Service Commission, and issued a series of White Papers on the benefits of competition and the regulatory changes necessary to make local competition feasible. By 1994, CAPs were beginning to win authorization from the state commissions to provide local switched telephone service and to interconnect with the incumbent carriers. States leading the development of local competition rules included New York, Illinois, Massachusetts, and Maryland, while many states continued to prohibit competition with the incumbent local telephone company.

Each state developed its own rules after conducting a formal hearing in which incumbents and potential entrants argued their cases with slightly revised versions of the earlier arguments over long distance competition. Incumbents generally argued that the regulated monopoly model worked well, that they provided efficient service with close attention to social concerns in developing their pricing structure, and that competitive opportunities only occurred because certain prices were high in order to keep other prices below cost. They argued that competition was unnecessary but that if it was allowed, the entrants should be required to pay substantial interconnection fees to the incumbents in order to compensate them for lost revenue and allow them to continue subsidizing favored classes of customers. The potential entrants argued that the internal subsidies among services within the local exchange had not been proved or required by regulatory authorities, that their new networks would provide socially beneficial and technologically progressive services at lower rates than those charged by the incumbents, and that they should be allowed to interconnect with incumbents on a "co-carrier" basis.

The co-carrier model was a critical part of the CAP proposals to the states and was adopted as federal policy in the Telecommunications Act of 1996. It assumed that each carrier was providing a service to the other and that symmetric payments would be made between carriers for terminating traffic received from the other. For example, when a CAP customer originated a call to a customer of the incumbent, the CAP would pay a fee to the incumbent for terminating service, but if the customer of the incumbent originated a call to a CAP customer, the incumbent would pay a fee to the CAP for terminating the call. The co-carrier model was consistent with the established interactions among monopoly telephone companies and was more favorable to the entrants than the customer model. In the customer model, the CAPs were treated as customers of the incumbent telephone companies and paid them for service, but received no payments from the incumbent when it sent calls to the CAP. Several states accepted the general concepts advocated by the potential competitors and established rules requiring interconnection on terms reasonably favorable toward competition, along with other necessary conditions to create the legal environment for potential competition.

As the CAPs installed switches and initiated switched service from 1994 forward, they were renamed competitive local exchange carriers (CLECs). Despite rapid growth and regulatory victories, they remained a tiny segment of the telecommunication industry. Their optical fiber networks provided alternative telephone service in the center of major cities, but were limited in scope with no economical way to offer service to all customers. By 1994, ten years after the divestiture, the CAPs/CLECs owned networks with a total of 400,000 fiber miles and were growing at 72 percent per year. In that year, local service telephone companies reported $83.9 billion in revenue while the CAPs and other local competitors reported $269 million, a revenue market share of 0.3 percent. While the market share was tiny, the new competitors already placed significant pricing constraints on portions of the local exchange market, and their growth rate and success at gaining interconnection rights from a small number of crucial state regulatory commissions suggested that competition could develop in the local exchange market (FCC, 1999b, chart 2.1 and table 2.1).

The Telecommunications Act of 1996

The political effort that eventually resulted in the Telecommunications Act of 1996 originated in the efforts of the Bell Operating Companies to free themselves from the restrictions imposed by the divestiture. The divestiture theory required that the BOCs be restricted to providing natural monopoly local exchange service and prohibited from providing potentially competitive services. The MFJ prohibited the BOCs from providing long distance service, from manufacturing telephone equipment, and from providing information services. The BOCs vigorously disagreed with the rationale for the restrictions and developed a sustained campaign to win freedom to participate in any market. Their first effort was to utilize the waiver process in the MFJ in which the restrictions could be modified by the judge overseeing the decree. The BOCs filed numerous requests before Judge Harold Greene of the U.S. District

Court for the District of Columbia, but did not gain his support for relaxing the restrictions. Judge Greene stated in a 1987 ruling:

> Almost before the ink was dry on the decree, the Regional Companies began to seek the removal of its restrictions. These efforts have had some success, in that they have tended to cause the public to forget that these companies, when still part of the Bell System, participated widely in anticompetitive activities, and that, were they to be freed of the restrictions, they could be expected to resume anticompetitive practices in short order, to the detriment of both competitors and consumers. (U.S. District Court (D.C.), 1987, pp. 2614–2620)

The BOCs also sought relief before the FCC where they received a more sympathetic hearing. The FCC's 1980 Computer II decision required that AT&T (and the BOCs after they were created) provide "enhanced services" only through a "fully separate subsidiary." The FCC's definition of "enhanced services" was similar to the MFJ's definition of "information services," and both terms were understood to apply to services that provided substantial computer processing along with communication. During the 1980s the telephone companies began moving from a network in which all the information and processing for a call were performed by the central office switch to one in which switches routinely queried distant databases for necessary information (the Advanced Intelligent Network). Strict application of the 1980 rules could have limited the options of the telephone company to create new services utilizing computer technology. Consequently, the FCC relaxed its rules in 1986 (the Computer III proceeding) by substituting nonstructural safeguards for the structural restrictions of Computer II. When the Department of Justice used the FCC's new rules as the basis for a change in position and argued that the BOCs should be relieved of the information services prohibition, Judge Greene still disagreed but was overruled by the D.C. Circuit Court of Appeals, which ordered him to give more deference to the views of the DOJ that had imposed the restriction initially. Following that court's order, Judge Greene reluctantly lifted the information services restriction in 1991.

Judge Greene's vigorous defense of the MFJ restrictions made it unlikely that the BOCs would succeed in their efforts to relax the rules through waivers. While the FCC was receptive to BOC arguments that the restrictions were counterproductive, it had no authority to overturn them. Consequently, the BOCs turned to Congress to seek legislation freeing them from the restrictions. They developed a strong lobbying effort that included procedural and substantive arguments for new legislation. Procedurally, they argued that telecommunication policy should be made by Congress, not by Judge Greene's rulings interpreting the MFJ. Substantively, they argued that technological progress and economies of scope were being sacrificed by limiting their activities. Congressional approval had neither been required nor sought prior to implementing the divestiture. Many members of Congress were skeptical of the divestiture theory and sympathetic to the BOC arguments that telecommunication policy should be made in Congress rather than by the DOJ and a federal judge.

Congressional efforts to modify the MFJ began soon after the divestiture was implemented when then-Senate Majority Leader Robert Dole introduced the Federal Telecommunications Policy Act of 1986. Dole argued that Judge Greene was micromanaging the telecommunication industry and that the FCC was the appropriate agency to administer telecommunication policy. The Reagan administration and the BOCs supported the Dole bill, while AT&T and the American Newspaper Publishers Association, among others, opposed it. The Dole bill did not pass, but it initiated a series of congressional attempts to modify or overturn the MFJ that continued for ten years. The BOCs were able to gain enough support to continue having bills introduced, but not enough to get them passed in the face of opposition from interexchange carriers, manufacturers, newspaper publishers, consumer groups, and others. In general, the bills were considered a benefit to the BOCs and a detriment to the various parties that offered products or services that the MFJ prohibited the BOCs from offering.

Congressional efforts to develop a federal policy for local telephone competition began in 1993 with the introduction of the Danforth-Inouye Telecommunications Infrastructure Act. The bill, sponsored by Senators John C. Danforth and Daniel Inouye, proposed the interconnection of competitive local carriers and the unbundling of the local exchange network, but did not change the MFJ. That bill alone would have been detrimental to the BOCs because it would have further reduced their monopoly power in the local exchange while not changing the restrictions on their other activities imposed by the MFJ. However, the developing state rules for local competition and the Danforth-Inouye bill created the possibility of establishing political support for a law that freed the BOCs from the MFJ restrictions and also imposed conditions to allow competition in the local market. The essential outline of the new law was negotiated in 1994 and then passed in separate bills by the Republican-controlled House and Senate during 1995. After extensive negotiations to resolve important differences between the House and Senate versions and to gain the support of President Clinton and Vice President Gore, the Telecommunications Act of 1996 was passed and signed into law in February 1996.

The 1996 Act was an amendment to the Communications Act of 1934 rather than an entirely new law. Consequently, it maintained the FCC and all the regulations issued by the FCC; however, the 1996 Act abolished the MFJ and replaced it with a set of provisions that provided conditions under which the FCC could authorize BOC entry into long distance, manufacturing, and electronic publishing services. The law also abolished state provisions that guaranteed a legal monopoly to incumbent telephone companies. The essential point of the new law was that the BOCs would have freedom to enter the competitive services prohibited to them by the MFJ in exchange for opening their local markets to competition. The statute provided specific conditions (known as the "competitive checklist") that must be met prior to allowing the BOCs to enter long distance service. Interpretation and administration of the conditions were assigned to the FCC with an advisory role given to both the Department of Justice and the state regulatory commissions.

The 1996 law abandoned the MFJ concept of rigid boundaries with separate companies operating in different markets and accepted much more fluid industry boundaries. It assumed that all parts of the industry were potentially competitive even though the incumbent local exchange carriers had an effective monopoly in most markets at that time. The economic conception underlying the 1996 Act was that the source of monopoly power in the local exchange was the network effect rather than the natural monopoly nature of the available technology. In the early twentieth-century competition, rival telephone companies were not interconnected. Consequently, any company that gained a majority of the subscribers in the area had an advantage over a smaller company because it could offer wider access to a new subscriber. The network effect makes size, as such, a substantial competitive advantage, even if there are not physical economies of scale. The 1996 Act eliminated the network effect as a major competitive weapon by requiring interconnection on favorable terms. Thus it was possible for a small company to sign up a limited number of subscribers and still offer access to all subscribers through interconnection with the incumbent company.

The law imposed a general duty on all telecommunication carriers "to interconnect directly or indirectly with the facilities and equipment of other telecommunication carriers." Incumbent local exchange carriers were required to negotiate the terms and conditions of interconnection agreements with potential competitors. If agreement could not be reached, the dispute could be submitted to the state regulatory commission for arbitration. Arbitrated agreements must "provide for the mutual and reciprocal recovery by each carrier of costs associated with the transport and termination on each carrier's network facilities of calls that originate on the network facilities of the other carrier." Incumbent local exchange carriers were also required to provide "non-discriminatory access to network elements on an unbundled basis at any technically feasible point on rates, terms, and conditions that are just, reasonable, and non-discriminatory." Incumbents were also required "to offer for resale at wholesale rates, any telecommunication service that the carrier provides at retail to subscribers who are not telecommunications carriers" (47 U.S.C. §§251, 252).

The requirements to interconnect with competitors and to make available unbundled services and services for resale to competitors were imposed on all incumbent local exchange companies regardless of their desire to enter long distance service. However, those requirements were also repeated in the competitive checklist for consideration of entry into long distance service. Thus one enforcement mechanism of the requirements was a prohibition of opportunities to enter long distance until the market-opening conditions were satisfied. The competitive checklist required additional measures to ease the entry of competitors into the local exchange, including number portability (the ability of a customer to switch service from an incumbent to a competitor without changing the telephone number) and access to telephone company databases and associated signaling necessary for call routing and completion.

The 1996 law completed the transition from a policy based on the assumption that service would be provided by a monopoly to a policy based on the assumption that service would be provided by interconnected competitive companies. Each of the intermediate steps assumed that some portion of the telephone network would remain a monopoly and that the problem was to define appropriate relationships between the monopoly and competitive portions of the industry. The 1996 law reversed the natural monopoly assumption that had been built into previous policy and replaced it with an assumption that all portions of the industry were potentially competitive. The 1996 Act was a particular contrast with the widely supported but not passed Packwood-Dingell-Wirth bill of 1983 (see Chapter 12) that would have prohibited bypass and guaranteed a strict legal monopoly to the incumbent local telephone companies. There was some empirical support for the changed assumption in the developing optical fiber systems and the rapidly expanding wireless systems. However, there was no attempt to rigorously show that a significant change had occurred in the conditions for local service. Rather, the assumption that local service could be competitive was plausible and politically convenient in order to break the political deadlock over previous MFJ-related bills.

The ordinary operation of a competitive market tends to push prices toward cost and eliminate either prices that are far above cost or prices that are below cost. The regulated monopoly pricing structure did not attempt to align individual prices with the cost of the various telephone services but instead created a politically determined price structure. Opposition to long distance competition was in part based on protecting the subsidies funded by high long distance prices. That argument was settled with a policy of long distance competition and high access charges imposed on long distance carriers that continued to provide funding for the subsidies. The ability to impose high access charges came from the market power retained by the local exchange companies. If local exchange competition was widespread, then access to long distance company POPs would become another competitive service. Consequently, it was necessary to either allow the remaining subsidies to be eroded away or to replace them with another funding source in the presence of local exchange competition.

The new law created arrangements to maintain and expand the subsidy structure while separating the funding of subsidies from the maintenance of monopoly prices. The law provided that "consumers in all regions of the nation, including low-income consumers and those in rural, insular, and high-cost areas, should have access to telecommunications and information services, including inter-exchange services and advanced telecommunications and information services, that are reasonably comparable to those services provided in urban areas and that are available at rates that are reasonably comparable to rates charged for similar services in urban areas" (47 U.S.C. §254). Earlier policies had assumed universal service was adequately provided if basic dial-tone service was available, even if that service was provided over older equipment with less functions available than were common in urban areas. The new law maintained previous subsidies for rural and high-cost areas but extended the subsidies to include support for advanced services and a more explicit requirement for equal pricing than had previously existed.

The new law substantially extended the previous universal support functions to include discounts for telecommunication services and Internet access to schools and libraries. The subsidies for schools and libraries were pursued by a coalition that included Vice President Gore, FCC chairman Reed Hundt, and education lobbyists. Senator Jay Rockefeller of West Virginia, a Democrat, sponsored the provision in order to promote distance education in his rural state of West Virginia. Republican Senator Olympia Snowe of Maine joined the Democrats in supporting the provision in order to expand distance education in her rural state, allowing the Senate Commerce Committee to add the provision to the bill against the opposition of the other Republican senators. The schools and libraries provisions were not included in the House bill, but were included in the final bill as part of the negotiations to secure President Clinton's support. Reed Hundt writes:

> Senator Rockefeller decided to champion the goal of the President and the Vice President to connect every classroom to the information highway. The necessary step was to amend the bill so that the FCC had the power not just to lower prices to schools, but to pay for building networks inside schools. This change was a matter of words. But its significance was to give the FCC the authority to command the spending of not just millions per year, but billions a year. My staff did not want to emphasize this cost . . . We were debating at relatively whisper-like levels, with virtually no media attention, one of the most important education bills of the century. The funding that might come from the proposed authority granted to the FCC would be, in time, greater than the G.I. Bill, which gave a college education to more than 15 million Americans. (2000, p. 109)

The statutory language authorizing subsidies to connect schools and libraries to the Internet was intentionally vague in order to blunt political opposition and avoid an examination of the cost, but the interpretation of the vague provisions was up to the FCC led by proponent Reed Hundt.

In order to provide revenue for the subsidies, the new law instituted the economic equivalent of a tax on telecommunication carriers. The law provided "every telecommunication carrier that provides interstate telecommunication services, shall contribute, on an equitable and non-discriminatory basis, to the specific, predictable, and sufficient mechanisms established by the Commission to preserve and advance universal service" (47 U.S.C. §254). Significantly, Internet service providers and Internet backbone providers were excluded from the definition of telecommunication carriers required to contribute to universal service. Thus a distinction continued to be made between the regulated sector subject to socially determined cross-subsidy structures and the unregulated market-oriented data communications sector.

Implementation of the Telecommunications Act of 1996

The 1996 Act modified the long-standing division of responsibility between the FCC and state regulatory commissions, but did not clearly specify the new jurisdictional structure. Prior to the Act, local competitive issues were subject to state authority and not to federal authority. The 1996 law adopted policies for local competition that were based in part on what state regulatory commissions had arranged, but incorporated the new policies into federal law while leaving the arbitration of disputed agreements to state commissions. Furthermore, the new law was an amendment to the old law and did not repeal its jurisdictional provisions, creating considerable confusion over exactly how jurisdictional boundaries were to be drawn under the new law.

The FCC assumed that it was authorized and obligated to develop regulations and to administer all provisions of the law not explicitly assigned to the state regulatory commissions in the ordinary operation of its long-standing responsibility to interpret and enforce the Communications Act of 1934. Many states assumed that because the law was dealing with matters previously reserved to the states, the FCC should have no role other than that mentioned explicitly in the language of the law.

The jurisdictional disputes between the FCC and state regulatory agencies reflected substantive industry disputes on how the law should be interpreted and applied. The FCC was generally sympathetic to the arguments of the long distance companies, CLECs, and other potential BOC competitors regarding the need to strictly control BOC power and give a regulatory helping hand to competition. The state regulatory agencies were generally sympathetic to the arguments of incumbent local exchange carriers (ILECs, including both BOCs and independent telephone companies) on the need to preserve stability and established rate structures against the disruption that could be created by extensive competition.

In proceedings before the FCC regarding the interpretation of the 1996 Act, the ILECs generally argued that the FCC should not prescribe detailed regulations. The ILECs contended that the statute provided the necessary general guidance and left implementation to private negotiations, with state arbitration as necessary, leaving no place for detailed federal regulations. The potential entrants generally argued that private negotiations would fail to reach good results because ILEC dominance gave them a much stronger bargaining position than potential entrants, and that consequently national rules were necessary in order to fully implement the statutory local competition provisions.

In August 1996, the FCC adopted a detailed 700-page order to implement the local competition provisions of the 1996 Act. The order largely adopted the positions of the potential entrants and generally rejected the proposals of the incumbents. The FCC order required that interconnection, unbundled network elements, and wholesale ILEC services be provided to the entrants on favorable terms. The FCC's interpretation of the local competition provisions in a way that favored entrants, together with strict FCC interpretation of the provisions for BOC entry into long distance, transformed the BOC congressional victory into a potential loss. Under the FCC interpretation, new companies could enter the local market previously monopolized by the BOCs while the BOCs remained unable to enter the long distance market.

The ILECs vigorously opposed the FCC's interpretation of the Act's local competition provisions, first by seeking relief from the FCC and then by seeking relief from the federal courts. The FCC refused to stay its rules, and many opponents (including all of the regional Bell Operating Companies, GTE, and numerous state public utility commissions) appealed the order to several different circuits of the federal appeals court. The appeals were consolidated in St. Louis before the Eighth Circuit Court of Appeals by random chance among the circuits in which the appeals were filed, in accordance with established procedure for cases filed in multiple circuits. The Eighth Circuit found that the FCC had exceeded its authority and vacated the FCC's pricing rules in 1997. The court held that the FCC's general rulemaking authority extended only to interstate matters and that the commission needed specific congressional authorization before implementing provisions of the 1996 Act addressing intrastate communications.

The various parties appealed the decision to the Supreme Court. In January 1999, the Supreme Court reversed the lower court's jurisdictional finding. The Supreme Court acknowledged that the 1996 Act was ambiguous. It stated:

> It would be a gross understatement to say that the Telecommunications Act of 1996 is not a model of clarity. It is in many important respects a model of ambiguity or indeed even self-contradiction. That is most unfortunate for a piece of legislation that profoundly affects a crucial segment of the economy worth tens of billions of dollars. The 1996 Act can be read to grant (borrowing a phrase from incumbent GTE) "most promiscuous rights" to the FCC vis-à-vis the state commissions and to competing carriers vis-à-vis the incumbents—and the Commission has chosen in some instances to read it that way. But Congress is well aware that the ambiguities it chooses to produce in a statute will be resolved by the implementing agency. (Supreme Court, 1999)

The majority opinion placed primary weight on the fact that the 1996 Act was constructed as an amendment to the 1934 law and that the 1934 law gave general authority to the FCC to make regulations implementing the law.

The problem that created confusion over the authority of the FCC to specify rules for local competition was the failure of Congress to either explicitly grant or deny the FCC the authority to interpret the pricing rules in the 1996 Act. If that failure were simply a drafting error, it would have been a straightforward matter to pass a minor amendment clarifying the intent of the law. However, the ambiguity in the law was intentional in order to gain agreement from those who disagreed on the substantive question. After the FCC issued its August 1996 decision, two groups of legislators who had been closely involved in the passage of the bill presented briefs to the appeals court in order to clarify "the intent of Congress" in the law. One group supported the ILECs and the state utility commissions in their assertions that Congress had not intended for the FCC to issue pricing rules. The second group supported the FCC in its assertion that Congress clearly intended the commission to issue the pricing rules.

Although the Supreme Court decision settled the jurisdictional issue, further litigation over the substance of the FCC's 1996 rules prevented their implementation. Consequently, the state regulatory commissions became the initial interpreters of the 1996 Act through their arbitration decisions on disputed CLEC-ILEC agreements. Incumbents and entrants continued to disagree over the appropriate prices to be paid for interconnection, transport and termination services, and unbundled elements but the statutory provisions narrowed the range of allowed disputes. State regulatory commissions no longer heard arguments on broad policy questions such as whether or not local competition was desirable, but instead focused attention on much narrower and detailed questions of exactly how the new competitors would interact with the incumbents. The statutory provision that any company could accept an interconnection agreement that had been negotiated or arbitrated made it feasible for small companies to enter the market without extremely high legal costs. A smaller company that did not wish to participate in arbitration could wait for one of the larger companies to work out an agreement and then adopt that as its guideline for interconnection and other interaction with the incumbent. Consequently, while the states continued to take the primary role in adjusting the relationships among companies as they would have in the absence of congressional action, the 1996 Act facilitated the entry of new competitors by establishing a general federal policy in favor of competition that limited the range of arguments before the state commissions.

The FCC's implementation of the universal service portion of the 1996 Act was complicated by Chairman Hundt's determination to adopt an expansive version of the vague statutory provisions for school Internet subsidies. In an unusual strategy, Hundt enlisted congressional and administration leaders to lobby recalcitrant commissioners, as well as encouraging the more normal route of a complex industry compromise.

Hundt described the efforts leading to the FCC's expansive interpretation of the subsidy legislation as follows:

> On May 20, 1997, the FCC commissioners were scheduled to vote . . . to pass a rule paying for the Internet in every classroom. The issue was part of a complicated proposal. For consumers, we would order lower long distance prices for low-volume users. For Internet users, we would make access cheap by prohibiting local phone companies from charging extra tolls for Internet communication across state lines in the way they did for long distance voice traffic—just as Steve Case's e-mails had urged. We proposed to order all communications companies to contribute about one percent of revenues every year to the fund for connecting classrooms. However, we would let local telephone companies reimburse themselves by charging long distance companies higher access charges in an amount equal to the contribution. At the same time, we ordered a reduction in those charges on the grounds that technology made telephone networks cheaper to operate.
>
> So we raised access charges by including in them the payments to the classroom funds, and we lowered them by ordering the local telephone companies to reflect their productivity gains . . . Under Senator Rockefeller's aegis, Bell Atlantic, Nynex, AT&T, and the education groups had worked out this complicated compromise on the Snowe-Rockefeller rule . . . In the days before the May 20 vote, the Vice President and Secretary of Education Dick Riley wrote to all the commissioners. Riley walked the eighth floor [location of commissioners' offices] to make his points. George Lucas encouraged the commissioners to vote for the rule: the power of the Force was with us. An army of lobbyists from education groups swarmed over the Commission. Senators Snowe and Rockefeller called and visited with the commissioners. (2000, pp. 214, 215)

After the commission voted to use universal service funds to connect classrooms to the Internet, Vice President Gore announced the decision at a news conference attended by Senators Rockefeller and Snowe.

Although political and legal controversies continued over the schools fund and other aspects of the universal service plan, the plan was implemented and continued to grow in scope. The assessment for supporting the schools and libraries fund rose from 0.8 percent of interstate end-user revenue in 1998 to 3 percent in 2002. The assessment for supporting the traditional universal services in high-cost areas and for low-income consumers rose more modestly from 3.2 percent of interstate end-user revenue in 1998 to 4.3 percent in 2001, for a total universal service assessment of 7.3 percent of interstate end-user revenue (FCC, 2002, table 20.5). The steady rise in the universal service fund "tax" rate created increasing discrimination between the cost of communicating by traditional long distance service and by the Internet that was exempt from universal service payments.

For the first three years after the 1996 Act was passed, it appeared to have little effect on either eliminating monopoly service in the local exchange or allowing the BOCs into long distance service, but it began to change the industry structure after 1999. The law helped create financial optimism with associated stock price increases, and it facilitated mergers among telecommunication companies, but litigation over its MFJ-substitute framework slowed its implementation. The FCC denied all BOC requests for permission to enter the long distance market until it approved the application for New York in September 1999 and the application for Texas in April 2000. The BOCs succeeded in their litigation to prevent the implementation of the FCC's local competition rules, but the FCC would not approve the BOC applications for long distance service until the BOCs provided more favorable opportunities for competitors than the state regulators required. By the end of 2000, BOCs in four states had received approval to initiate long distance service, and six more state applications were approved in 2001, providing clear precedents on the requirements for approval.

At the time the 1996 Act was passed, many companies announced optimistic plans for rapid entry into the local exchange market through resale of ILEC services, combining unbundled elements to create services, upgrading cable television systems to provide telephone service, expanding or creating optical fiber networks, and the deployment of fixed wireless systems. Most of those plans failed or were delayed. Controversies over the prices for resale and unbundled elements kept deployment at a minimal level for the first three years after the 1996 Act. Cable television systems required more expensive and time-consuming upgrades to provide telephone service than originally forecast and did not begin to serve significant numbers of telephone subscribers until 2002. Major fixed wireless companies Winstar and Teligent declared bankruptcy.

CLECs grew rapidly from a small base both before and after the 1996

Act. They increased total revenue from $174 million to $949 million between 1993 and 1996 (57 percent annual growth rate) and to $4.5 billion between 1996 and 1999 (52 percent annual growth rate) (FCC, 2002, table 9.7). After 1999, the CLECs began taking increasing advantage of the benefits conferred by the 1996 Act. In June 2001, CLECs reported 17.3 million end-user switched-access lines (9.9 percent of the ILECs' 174.5 million lines), of which 5.8 million were provided by CLEC-owned plant, 3.9 million were acquired from ILECs for resale, and 7.6 million were acquired from ILECs as unbundled network elements. The percentage of CLEC lines varied substantially by state, with the highest CLEC shares in New York (23 percent) and Texas (14 percent) (FCC, 2002, tables 9.3 and 9.5).

15

The Internet and the World Wide Web

By the mid-1990s a number of different elements were in place to facilitate a major transformation of the country's information infrastructure. These included:

1. Widespread use of personal computers, equipped with voice-grade telephone line modems and/or Ethernet capabilities.
2. Extensive development of local area networks (LANs) connected to information servers in organizations.
3. Widespread use of TCP/IP and Ethernet standards to create an interoperable system composed of elements from many different companies.
4. Continued rapid decline in the prices of transmission, routing, and end-user equipment.
5. Favorable regulatory treatment in both domestic and international forums for value-added or enhanced services (Internet-based services), allowing them to utilize the established infrastructure without being bound by the rules developed for an earlier technology.

While those elements provided the necessary foundation, growth in data communications was restrained by the absence of a standardized way of accessing information. That deficiency was solved with the development of the World Wide Web. The Web became a practical tool with the release of Netscape's browser and server software in December 1994, followed by Microsoft's browser a few months later and then a flood of additional products to facilitate the location and retrieval of information contained on Web servers through the public Internet.

Before the development of the Web, there were many variations in the methods by which one accessed data over the Internet. In some cases, it

266

was necessary to have an account at the remote computer, and in other cases, one could log onto the remote computer as "guest"; but some effort was required to access the computer and to find the relevant information even if the information owner desired to make it public. Finding information on the Internet was sometimes described as the equivalent of finding information in a library in which many people contributed books and dropped them haphazardly on the floor with no index or organization. Earlier tools to structure Internet information such as the University of Minnesota's Gopher system of the early 1990s helped but did not solve the problem of indexing and finding the desired information. This problem limited the incentive to provide commercial information. Consequently, prior to the Web, there was little electronic commerce over the Internet. There were important electronic commerce transactions over private networks (including electronic funds transfer for banking, electronic data interchange (EDI), and subscription-based provision of information), but most Internet usage was noncommercial in nature.

The Web was widely recognized as a significant development that had great potential. Rapid acceptance of Netscape products led to an initial public offering (IPO) in August 1995, less than a year after the company's first programs were released. Extensive positive publicity for Netscape prior to the offering suggested that it was becoming dominant in a rapidly growing segment without any significant competition and led to extraordinary demand for the company's stock. Netscape's IPO on August 9 valued the company at $2.2 billion, despite its short lifetime and total revenue of only $10 million in the preceding quarter (Cusumano and Yoffie, 1998, p. 330). The stock market success in turn garnered far more publicity, as the public became aware of the potential money in the net. Marc Andreessen's two-year rise from earning $6.85 per hour as a student programmer to a paper wealth of over $100 million in Netscape stock was widely publicized with a *Time* cover picture and accompanying article titled "The Golden Geeks" (February 19, 1996). The Netscape IPO served as a powerful attraction for venture capitalists and potential entrepreneurs, beginning a rush to establish net-related businesses.

Passage of the Telecommunications Act of 1996 also contributed to the acceleration of data communications. The 1996 Act was not specifically directed toward the Internet, the Web, or electronic commerce, but its general policy in favor of competition and its relaxation of earlier regulatory boundaries contributed to the belief that new approaches to telecommunication would not be restricted by regulation. At about the same time, wave division multiplexing (WDM) equipment for optical fiber systems became commercially available. WDM multiplied the capacity of optical fibers by transmitting simultaneous signals on different wavelengths. WDM equipment could be added to existing optical fibers or installed with new fibers and created a sharp drop in the cost of transmitting very high-speed bit streams.

The combination of a standardized addressing method to facilitate locating information, the 1996 Act to reduce regulatory barriers to the adoption of new technology, and WDM to allow great reductions in the cost of transmitting information created explosive growth of the Internet with the Web as the primary method of presenting information. The rapid growth increased stock market valuations and further attracted many entrants to Web, Internet, and telecommunication markets. Stock market valuation of Internet and telecommunication companies reached a peak in early 2000, followed, however, by substantial declines in stock prices and numerous bankruptcies.

While the stock market plunge for Web, Internet, and new telecommunication companies in 2000–2001 halted speculative projections on the extinction of traditional forms of commerce, it did not change the fundamental benefits of the new technology. Standardized access to information through Web addressing and standardized transmission of all kinds of information as TCP/IP packets provided a powerful new way of combining previously disparate kinds of information. The new approach added overhead in order to transmit and index information in a standardized way rather than the traditional separate media for data transmission, voice communication, audio broadcasting, and video broadcasting. However, as the cost of routers and bulk transmission capacity have continued to decline, the benefits of combining information types in a single standardized way are beginning to outweigh the additional overhead of structuring the information. Separate facilities optimized to the characteristics of particular media were desirable when transmission capacity was expensive, but standardized approaches that allow easy combining of media types are efficient when transmission costs are low. Supplying a variety of types of information through the Web and TCP/IP interface does not fit neatly into continuing legal distinctions among common carrier, enhanced, broadcasting, and cable television services and creates new pressure for further institutional evolution.

The Commercial Internet and Backbone Interconnection

During the 1980s the Internet remained an academic and military communications structure and had little effect on consumer and business communications. After the Defense Communications Agency (DCA) took control of the Arpanet in 1975, it attempted to impose more structured procedures and to prohibit unauthorized use as it tried to transform the research network into a reliable form of military communications. DCA used TCP/IP to connect the Arpanet to other military networks and required all Arpanet sites to convert to TCP/IP in place of the older ARPA protocol by 1983. Controversies between the goals of academic researchers and the security requirements of military communications led to splitting the Arpanet into two separate networks in 1983: a secure limited-access network called MILNET that would be connected to other military networks and a research-oriented open network still called Arpanet (Abbate, 1999, p. 143).

The Arpanet connected only a small set of universities that had large ARPA research contracts. Researchers from computer science departments not connected to the Arpanet secured a $5 million grant from the National Science Foundation (NSF) in 1981 to create the CSnet, a network designed to link computer science researchers around the country and provide limited e-mail gateways to other countries. The CSnet was linked to the Arpanet but was designed as a much more inclusive network (including dial-up connections for inexpensive limited use) without the $100,000 per node cost of the Arpanet. A number of other data communications networks designed to provide inexpensive access to particular information were established (USEnet, BITnet, Fidonet) but were not initially connected to other networks.

In the early 1980s the NSF also began designing its own network to connect university supercomputer sites. NSF planned an open network and encouraged universities to connect to regional networks that would then be connected to the NSF backbone network. The NSF backbone began operating in 1985 with a speed of 56 kilobits per second, the same speed as the Arpanet lines or a current high-speed dial-up modem. The backbone was upgraded to T-1 speed (1.544 megabits per second) in the later 1980s and eventually to T-3 speed (45 megabits per second). When completed in 1988, the NSF backbone connected thirteen sites across the country, and those sites served as connection points for regional networks. A college or university paid a fee to a regional network that provided connection to the NSFnet, but there was no charge for using the NSFnet. With NSF encouragement of networking and the rapid growth of university LANs in the late 1980s, the number of Internet-connected computers rose from 2,000 in 1985 to 30,000 in 1987 and to 159,000 in 1989 (Abbate, 1999, p. 143). The comparatively fast NSF backbone made the Arpanet obsolete and in 1990 it was decommissioned after the host sites were connected to the NSFnet.

Because the NSFnet was funded by the government, it was formally restricted to research and educational activities. The NSF's Acceptable Use Policy specifically prohibited commercial traffic on the NSFnet. However, the NSFnet functioned as the only set of interconnection points for the Internet. The increasing number of business LANs in the late 1980s either remained computer islands or were connected to other LANs through private networks. Many business users sought connection to the Internet. They could connect to the regional networks and could connect to the NSFnet as well because there was no way to distinguish academic from business packets routed to the backbone, but routine business operations required an alternative structure that did not depend on the NSF's inability to enforce its rules.

Regional networks could be either nonprofit or commercial and sometimes changed over time. For example, William Schrader led the development of the regional network NYSERNet. He then in 1989 founded Performance Systems International, which purchased NYSERNet and expanded its network into what became known as PSINet (Abbate, 1999, p. 198), an important commercial Internet backbone company until its bankruptcy. Descendants of the regional networks, established long distance telephone companies, and new entrants began building nationwide networks and seeking commercial customers.

In order to exchange traffic among the commercial networks without violating the NSF Authorized User Policy, three providers (PSINet, CERFNet, and Alternet) formed the Commercial Internet Exchange (CIX) in 1991. The companies connected to a gateway to exchange traffic and agreed to accept traffic from each other without charge. The "peering" arrangement recognized that interconnection increased the value of their networks and that each was performing a service for the other. As commercial traffic increased, the companies established additional interconnection points through private agreements. They generally maintained the practice of terminating traffic for each other at zero cost rather than adopting the access charge or settlements models from the telephone industry that split revenue between the originating and terminating carriers. The voluntary interconnection of competitive companies marked a sharp contrast to the extensive arguments over interconnection and payment that occurred in the telephone industry.

The simple interconnection arrangements among commercial Internet backbone providers were motivated by two distinct factors:

1. No single provider had a dominant position in the market, and each provider needed interconnection with the others in order to deliver complete service to its customers. If one provider had refused interconnection, it would have reduced the value of its own service and caused it to lose customers. In contrast, the telephone companies began with a dominant position and could maintain that position by refusing interconnection to potential competitors.

2. The simple structure of the TCP/IP protocol and the routers used to forward packets did not provide any straightforward way of measuring and recording traffic flows in order to construct a financial settlements system. The telephone company had built recording functions into its equipment in order to bill customers and could record traffic received from another company as well. The Internet's origin as a military and academic communications network had made accounting and billing unimportant.

With the growth of commercial traffic over the Internet in the early 1990s and the interconnection of commercial providers, the NSF backbone became unnecessary and was shut down in 1995. NSF helped develop network access points to facilitate the interconnection of commercial providers as part of the transition away from connecting networks through the NSF backbone. NSF also continued to fund academic experiments on networking and to support the development of specialized research networks, but after 1995 Internet growth and development were determined by market forces.

The Development of the Web

The World Wide Web is a specific implementation of hypertext approaches to linking information. Numerous implementations of hypertext occurred prior to the development of the Web, but they were local in nature, allowing, for example, a reader to quickly jump from one portion of an electronic document to another. Tim Berners-Lee, a computer specialist at the European particle research facility CERN, originated the Internet version of the Web while attempting to facilitate communication among the facility's diverse machines and documentation systems. He wrote of the late 1980s environment at CERN:

> Machines from IBM, Digital Equipment Corp. (DEC), Control Data—we had them all, as well as the new choice of PC or Mac in personal computers and different word processors.
>
> People brought their machines and customs with them, and everyone else just had to do their best to accommodate them. Then teams went back home and, scattered as they were across time zones and languages, still had to collaborate. In all this connected diversity, CERN was a microcosm of the rest of the world, though several years ahead in time. (Berners-Lee with Fischetti, 1999, p. 14)

The goal of the CERN project was an improved documentation system that was flexible enough to connect diverse types of files and organizational structures. Earlier, the TCP/IP protocol had allowed communication among diverse computer systems and networks without imposing the uniformity and structure required by typical telephone systems or the CCITT data communication protocols (see Chapter 8). Such flexibility and decentralization were purchased at the cost of some quality control; packets were transmitted on a "best efforts" basis across the various networks, and the user rather than the network was responsible for ensuring that adequate accuracy was achieved. Berners-Lee's insight was that a similar system could be developed for linking different kinds of data, regardless of the location or the specific type of computer that contained the data, by developing minimal common protocols. In attempting to develop a minimalist system, Berners-Lee concluded that the system "had to be completely decentralized" so that "a new person somewhere could start to use it without asking for access from anyone else." He noted that this approach "was good Internet-style engineering, but most systems still depended on some central node to which everything had to be connected—and whose capacity eventually limited the growth of the system as a whole" (Berners-Lee with Fischetti, 1999, p. 16).

At the time Berners-Lee developed his initial concept of the Web in 1988, he was not familiar with the Internet in any detail. However, assisted by others from CERN who were knowledgeable about the Internet, Berners-Lee soon recognized that the TCP/IP protocols and the Unix operating system furnished a way to provide access to his proposed hypertext method of referencing data. After finding little interest in supporting development of the system at CERN, Berners-Lee purchased a NeXT personal computer in 1990 and began programming portions of his hypertext concept. With the help of an intern, Berners-Lee programmed an initial crude browser and server and set up his NeXT personal computer as a server machine, with information about the Web project made freely available. In an attempt to show benefit to CERN, the internal telephone book was converted to hypertext and made available through the new structure as its first practical project.

According to Berners-Lee, the essential structure of the Web consisted of three basic protocols:

1. Universal resource identifiers (URIs, later known as URLs for uniform resource locators) in order to provide a unique label to the information referenced.
2. The Hypertext Transfer Protocol (HTTP) in order to define the communication session between server and browser.
3. The Hypertext Markup Language (HTML) in order to structure the documents and to provide links to other documents.

Berners-Lee writes: "What was often difficult for people to understand about the design was that there was nothing else beyond URIs, HTTP, and HTML. There was no central computer 'controlling' the Web, no single network on which these protocols worked, not even an organization anywhere that 'ran' the Web. The Web was not a physical 'thing' that existed in a certain 'place.' It was a 'space' in which information could exist" (Berners-Lee with Fischetti, 1999, p. 36).

Of course, the specification of the basic protocols for the Web did not create an effective Web of information anymore than the specification of TCP/IP in the 1970s created an effective Internet. In both cases, the protocols had to be implemented in widely used software and used as the basis for an extensive communications infrastructure. The concept of the Web and the specification of basic protocols for adding information on a decentralized basis were critical, but not sufficient, steps toward effective utilization.

Despite Berners-Lee's enthusiastic promotion, the early 1990s version of the Web failed to attract substantial usage either inside or outside CERN. The established hypertext research community was largely unrelated to the Internet research community, and the members of the hypertext research group were so unimpressed with the Berners-Lee approach that they rejected his request to present a paper at their 1991 conference (Berners-Lee with Fischetti, 1999, p. 50). The initial browser was written for the innovative but rarely used NeXT computer, greatly limiting the set of people who could experiment with it, and Berners-Lee lacked the personal time or the support staff to rewrite the browser for such mainstream systems as Unix workstations, IBM-compatible personal computers, and Macintosh computers.

Interest in the Web increased when several academic groups wrote Web browsers for the Unix operating system. The most important of these were the University of Kansas Lynx text-oriented system, released in March 1993, and the University of Illinois Mosaic graphics-oriented system, released in February 1993. Mosaic was developed at the National Center for Supercomputing Applications (NCSA) at the University of Illinois by student Marc Andreessen and staff member Eric Bina. It was the most sophisticated of the early browsers and attracted considerable interest. NCSA soon developed versions of the Mosaic browser for the Microsoft Windows and Macintosh operating systems to supplement the original Unix version. From the NCSA point of view, the essence of the Web was working software for browsers and servers, not the initial protocols, leading to some tension over credit for the new technology (Berners-Lee with Fischetti, 1999, p. 71).

At about the same time as the release of Mosaic, the University of Minnesota decided to request a license fee from commercial users of its popular Gopher system for accessing information over the Internet. The uncertainty created by the potential fee reduced corporate interest in Gopher and also raised questions about the intellectual property involved in the nascent Web. In order to end worries about CERN's control, Berners-Lee obtained a formal statement from CERN allowing free usage of its property in the Web without royalty or constraint (Berners-Lee with Fischetti, 1999, pp. 72–74).

The wide availability of free software from NCSA together with the disclaimer of property rights by CERN persuaded many people to set up servers. The Internet was growing rapidly and desktop computers linked by LANs were common, providing a base of networked users that could assimilate the new capabilities of the Web. The graphical capabilities of the Mosaic browser made it much more flexible than the text-only browsers, but also raised concerns about utilization of the limited Internet capacity. Images required far more bandwidth than text, and downloading of "frivolous" images (including personal pictures and risqué photographs scanned from magazines) potentially threatened to displace serious scientific communication on the limited capacity of the Internet at that time. A number of universities refused to support Mosaic and required the use of the Lynx text-only browser to avoid wasting data communications capacity. Marc Andreessen reported criticism from Tim Berners-Lee for adding graphical capability (Reid, 1997, p. 12).

Andreessen graduated in December 1993 and moved to Silicon Valley where he joined Jim Clark to establish the company that became Netscape Communications Corporation in early 1994. Clark was a former Stanford computer science professor with specialization in computer graphics who had earlier founded Silicon Graphics, Inc. Clark's own money and contacts, along with support from the venture capital firm of Kleiner Perkins Caufield & Byers, allowed a quick start to the company. Clark and Andreessen hired the original Mosaic development team and the author of the University of Kansas Lynx browser, as well as experienced senior managers.

Netscape began an intense period of development with the initial goal of developing a "Mozilla," a "Mosaic killer" browser and server combination that would be far superior to the original Mosaic. One Netscape executive recalled the early days: "a lot of times, people were there straight forty-eight hours, just coding. I've never seen anything like it, in terms of . . . human endurance, to sit in front of a monitor and program." Programmer Lou Montulli described the schedule: "sit at your cube, type a lot, basically continuous work until you hit a major roadblock . . . Then you'd quickly form a quick meeting at twelve midnight and figure it out in ten minutes, and then go back to work" (quoted in Reid, 1997, p. 27). Microsoft, Netscape, and numerous other software companies found that they could accomplish an extraordinary amount in a short time with a small group of unusually talented and dynamic young programmers who worked well together. Their stories are a striking contrast to the reports of IBM's effort to develop the complex operating system for the System/360 in which 2,000 people attempted to rush the delayed system to completion and complained of spending most of their time in meetings getting updated specifications on what related programming groups were changing.

The strenuous programming effort was matched by an expansive vision of the Web browser as a universal interface and a replacement for Microsoft's dominant Windows operating system:

> Clark and Andreessen . . . believed that the browser had the potential to become a universal interface that would tie the networks of the future together. The browser had two key strengths. First, it could simplify and integrate the management of data and resources, whether located locally on a hard drive or somewhere out on the Web. Consequently, as applications migrated to the network, the browser would replace the operating system (OS) as the primary user interface. Andreessen liked to say that when this happened, the OS would revert to its original role as a set of drivers for devices such as the computer's keyboard and mouse . . . Second, the emergence of a simple, universal interface would allow the network to grow in size and scope. New devices such as smart phones, televisions, and interactive games could all use the browser to communicate with computers of more traditional types . . . The browser would be a universal interface that would allow any user to walk up to and use any communications device. (Cusumano and Yoffie, 1998, p. 23)

It was only six months from the time Netscape was formed in April 1994 until the Beta release of its first browser, Navigator 1.0. The Beta release was posted to the company's file servers for free downloads. The Navigator brought the new company into conflict with the University of Illinois and its Mosaic licensee, Spyglass, Inc., over claims that the Netscape product infringed on the Mosaic property rights. The Netscape product was superior to the original Mosaic and threatened to eliminate any revenue stream that the university could have received from its Mosaic software. The conflict was settled out of court by Mosaic Communications Corporation changing its name to Netscape Communications Corporation and by a payment from Netscape.

In December 1994, Netscape shipped its browser and server software and began earning revenues. The company adopted a "free, but not free" pricing policy for the browser in an attempt to dominate the new market. That policy made the product free to students and educators and charged $39 to other users, but all users were allowed to download for free in order to test the software for a trial period with no efforts to disable it after the test period. Netscape's goal was to establish a dominant role in browsers and then be able to earn revenue from products related to browsers, consciously copying Microsoft's success at establishing dominance in operating systems and then earning high profits from applications software.

The popular Netscape software helped propel the Web from the eleventh-place source of traffic on the Internet backbone at the beginning of 1994 to the first-place source of traffic by early 1995 (Reid, 1997, p. 38), creating high expectations for the company. However, Netscape did not keep the market to itself for long. Two weeks after Netscape's successful IPO in August 1995, Microsoft released its first Web browser (Explorer 1.0) along with its new operating system, Windows 95. Explorer 1.0 only worked with Windows 95 and therefore was initially only available to a small segment of personal computer users, but it came bundled with Windows 95. Not only did Explorer provide competition to Navigator at a zero price; it required some effort for users of Windows 95 to obtain and install Navigator. While Netscape's liberal download and trial policy allowed users to obtain the browser for free, many corporations still paid the stated price in order to have clearly legal browsers on their machines, and browser sales comprised most of Netscape's early revenue.

Microsoft's Internet initiative created a period of intense competition between the two companies. Both companies offered their browsers at a price of zero and sought to improve the capabilities and expand usage of their product with an expectation that a dominant position in the browser market would allow them to gain benefits in related services. Both companies focused on rapid upgrades and a large set of complementary products. Both provided major upgrades to their initial browsers in less than a year and both released their third-generation browsers in August 1996 (less than two years after Netscape's first browser and only a year after Microsoft's first browser). The new versions were far more complex programs than the originals. Netscape prepared Navigator 1.0 (approximately 100,000 lines of code) with ten programmers,

Navigator 2.0 (approximately 700,000 lines of code) with thirty programmers, and Navigator 3.0 (approximately 1,000,000 lines of code) with fifty programmers (Cusamano and Yoffie, 1998, p. 162).

As programmers rushed to add new features to the browsers, they gained much broader capabilities as Andreessen had expected, but Netscape did not gain an advantage over Microsoft as he had hoped. As Microsoft overcame Netscape's early technical superiority and continued integrating the browser into its operating system, Internet Explorer became the dominant browser. Netscape abandoned its effort to establish a dominant independent position in Web-related software and accepted a merger offer from America Online. While Netscape eventually lost the competitive battle, its pioneering efforts in Web software and the short intense battle for dominance between Netscape and Microsoft facilitated the quick transformation of the Web from an experimental addressing scheme to a widely used mainstream tool.

Five years after the 1993 release of the Lynx and Mosaic browsers, the Web was a mainstream business and personal tool with full-featured free browsers available from both Netscape and Microsoft and extensive server and supporting programs and editing tools available. In contrast, the transition to standardized numbering systems and direct distance dialing in the telephone industry extended over thirty years. Direct distance dialing (DDD) and the Web were both innovations in automated addressing schemes that required a standardized address system and a control system to allow individual customers to reach the desired address without human intervention. DDD implementation was slowed by regulatory structures that gave customers the ability to complain about changes (longer dialing sequences, replacement of place names with digits) and by the need to install new hardware and implement new operating procedures. AT&T managed the DDD implementation with regulatory oversight. The Web addressing scheme was intrinsically far more complex, allowing access to many different kinds of documents and images. It occurred on a decentralized basis with no regulatory or administrative oversight. Companies made individual decisions about what content they would place on a web site, and customers made individual decisions about what browsers they would use to access that content. Much of the infrastructure (personal computers, local area networks, the Internet) was already available, and the new software allowed that infrastructure to be adapted to Web use without regulatory approval or new hardware.

The New Economy Financial Boom and Bust

The new opportunities created by widespread inexpensive Internet communication with information organized by Web standards were widely recognized and publicized, including thousands of references in the general media to the "new economy" or "information economy." Widely held expectations of an economic revolution in which "bricks and mortar" commerce would be replaced by online commerce created a surge of entrepreneurial companies. Expectations of "first mover" advantages (that is, the first major firm in a new market has an opportunity to dominate that market and earn long-term profits) induced venture capital firms and others to invest in companies with little revenue and no profits. Rapid stock market appreciation on early Web-based companies and the observation that changes could happen much faster in the electronic economy ("Internet time") than in the physical economy created a rush to finance additional companies and benefit from the surging stock market. In a *Wall Street Journal* story at the height of the boom, George Anders summed up the prevailing financial strategy as follows:

> Financiers in Silicon Valley and elsewhere are pouring $300 million a month into tiny new businesses built around the Internet . . . more than the combined total for biotechnology, electronics and microchips . . . Hundreds of Internet companies are being built atop nearly identical computing platforms, with no clear edge for any one of them . . . Yet venture capitalists dare not walk away. For all its goofiness, the Internet economy is producing enormous jackpots for early investors. Three companies founded within the past five years now have boggling stock-market values: online bookstore Amazon.com Inc., with $21.4 billion; auction-company eBay Inc., with $19 billion; and Web directory provider Yahoo! Inc., with nearly $35 billion. In each case, venture backers have seen their stakes jump more than 500-fold in value. (Anders, 1999, p. A1)

Competition among investment banks for lucrative IPO underwriting opportunities helped fuel the boom, supported by securities analysts who placed glowing recommendations on stocks underwritten by their companies. At the March 2000 peak, Internet stocks had a market capitalization of $1.4 trillion (Ip et al., 2000, p. A1). Internet stocks then declined sharply and many Web-based companies went out of business. According to a *Wall Street Journal* article soon after the end of the boom:

"The Great Internet Bubble . . . ranks among history's biggest bubbles. Investment bankers, venture capitalists, research analysts and investors big and small, through cynicism or suspension of disbelief, financed and took public countless companies that had barely a prayer of prospering. Rarely have so many people willingly put prudence on hold to enter a game most were sure couldn't last" (Ip et al., 2000, p. A1). An index of Internet stocks (scaled to 100 at the end of 1996) rose to 763 by the first quarter of 2000 and then dropped to 206 one year later (Eisenach, Lenard, and McGonegal, 2001, p. 57).

A similar boom-and-bust cycle occurred with telecommunication infrastructure but far more physical capital was used. While the Internet companies primarily invested in software and modest amounts of computer equipment to develop web sites, the infrastructure companies made massive investments in laying optical fiber cable. The two booms were closely related and based on similar optimistic forecasts. The transformation into a new economy required Internet companies to provide the information content and electronic commerce and also required a tremendous expansion in the infrastructure. It was obvious that the Internet capacity of the mid-1990s could not support extensive electronic commerce and other bandwidth-intensive applications.

Projections of capacity bottlenecks, together with the observation that technological advance allowed communication over new fiber networks at much lower cost than the average historical cost of existing networks, created expectations of high profits for new networks optimized to serve the booming Internet demand. The extraordinary growth rates of Internet usage during the 1995–1996 time frame when graphical Web browsers first came into widespread use was projected into the future with a frequently repeated claim that Internet traffic was doubling every hundred days (equivalent to an annual growth rate of over 1,000 percent). WorldCom's UUNET subsidiary (the largest Internet backbone carrier) continued to promote the high growth forecasts after actual growth slowed to near 100 percent per year, adding credibility to the growth forecasts because of its own knowledge of the market ("The Power of WorldCom's Puff," 2002, p. 60). While 100 percent annual growth in demand is extraordinarily high compared to most markets, it was far below the effective multiplication in capacity (increase in fiber miles times improvement in throughput because of wave division multiplexing).

When the Internet stock bubble broke in early 2000, the telecommunication company stock prices also collapsed. The NASDAC Telecommunication index (scaled to late 1996 = 100) rose to a peak of 510 in early 2000 and then dropped precipitously. Interdependent expectations (rapid transformation to electronic commerce implies profitable opportunities for Web-based companies as well as rapid growth in Internet traffic, which in turn implies profitable opportunities for network infrastructure companies and for suppliers of innovative equipment that can multiply their throughput of optical fiber lines) mutually collapsed. Major telecommunication network companies (including Global Crossing and WorldCom) filed for bankruptcy, while the stock of optical fiber equipment innovators Ciena and Corvis fell to 1 percent of its peak. The financial problem created by excess capacity and resulting low prices was accentuated by financial scandals. The WorldCom bankruptcy (the largest ever at the time of its filing) was preceded by the disclosure of multibillion-dollar accounting errors that have been described as the largest corporate fraud in history. WorldCom grew rapidly by merger (including the purchase of then larger company MCI for $87 billion in 1997) and was valued at $145 billion at its mid-1999 peak (Knight, 2002, p. E6). However, the common stock lost all value after the company's bankruptcy filing, and its bonds began selling at a deep discount.

Allegations of inappropriate insider enrichment complicated the financial restructuring of the troubled telecommunication companies. A *Wall Street Journal* analysis concluded that telecommunication insiders sold $14.2 billion in stock during the boom. Large individual sellers included Qwest Communications International founder Philip Anschutz ($2 billion) and Global Crossing founder Gary Winnick ($734 million). According to Dennis Berman:

> [The insider sales are] one of the largest transfers of wealth from investors—big and small—in American history. Hundreds of telecom executives, almost uniformly bullish, sold at least some portion of their stock and made hundreds of millions of dollars, while many investors took huge, unprecedented losses. It dwarfs the much more highly publicized Internet boom and bust . . . With over 60 bankruptcies to date, it's now clear that the sector sank under too much capacity and debt. Telecoms have now shed half a million jobs and about $2 trillion in market capitalization. (2002, p. A7)

New York's Attorney General filed suit against several of the executives who sold large amounts of stock and sought return of $1.5 billion in alleged improper profits (Gasparino, 2002, p. A1).

The major local exchange companies were more stable than the long distance, wireless, and equipment companies but still shared in some of the financial turmoil. While they made steady profits on their continuing local exchange service, they also diversified into other services and into foreign telecommunication with less profitable results. The broadly defined Dow Jones Telecommunications Index (including fixed line, wireless, and equipment companies) rose by 120 percent in the two years following September 1997 and then fell back to 40 percent below its 1997 starting point by September of 2002. Alternatively stated, the broad index of telecommunication stocks declined by 70 percent between September 1999 and September 2002 (data from *cbs.marketwatch .com*, downloaded September 12, 2002).

Real Growth in Telecommunication and Price Benefits

The bankruptcies and massive stock market losses in Internet and telecommunication companies during 2001 and 2002 created deep pessimism about the success of the information revolution. Many media stories emphasized the failures and problems. In one example, *Washington Post* writer Jerry Knight noted:

> [For bankrupt telecommunication companies] their shareholders are toast. The measure of what the company is worth changes from the price of its stock to how much the banks and bondholders get paid out of the bankruptcy. According to Bloomberg, those creditors have been getting an average of around 11 cents on the dollar in telecom bankruptcies and as much as 15 cents in more successful restructurings . . . Blowing away the stockholders' investment and the billions upon billions of debt that telecom companies have borrowed is the first thing that has to happen before anybody in the business can make money. But somebody also needs to blow up the thousands of miles of fiber-optic cables that were built with those borrowed billions; the nation has 10 times to 20 times as much fiber as it is using. After that, blow up the switches that connect the fiber to the Internet—there is a vast oversupply of them, too—and then blow up the servers because we have way more computers to run Internet Web sites than even the exploding Internet needs . . . The telecom era is over. (2002, p. E6)

While the financial turmoil and fraud investigations generated a negative image of the integrated telecommunication industry, the industry continued to grow and provide inexpensive sophisticated services to consumers and businesses.

The financial problems in the telecommunication industry (other than those created by fraud and self-dealing) developed because the competitive low prices were not high enough to support the expectations of the companies building the networks. Prices for bulk transmission capacity dropped dramatically primarily because the underlying cost of supplying that transmission capacity dropped dramatically. The previously stable telecommunication industry took on many of the characteristics of the computer industry, including both its rapid technological progress and its instability. Large price reductions required new models of usage.

In the early 1990s both IBM and DEC encountered severe financial difficulties as the industry's previously leading practices became outmoded with the continuing drop in the cost of computing. However, that was not an indication that demand for computers had disappeared. Rather, it was an indication that computing had become so cheap that traditional applications could be performed at practically no cost. Instead, vast quantities of computer power were purchased to sit on a desk or in a briefcase waiting for a user to request the machine to paint pixels on a screen. In traditional computer terms, there is vast excess computing capacity because most of the computer capacity sits idle much of the time and is not fully utilized even during periods of activity. However, the low price of computing makes that arrangement efficient because the prices are low enough to allow the computers to serve the user's convenience rather than scheduling work to fit the computer capacity. Similarly, the early 2000 price decline in bulk transmission cost and prices led to financial difficulties for incumbent companies but new opportunities for consumers and for companies that can devise new ways to take advantage of communications at practically zero cost.

By late 2002 bulk communications capacity between high-density points had become extremely cheap, but prices were much higher per unit for lower-density locations or smaller units of capacity. For example, according to offers posted on *BandwidthMarket.com* in September 2002, one could obtain an OC-48 circuit (2.49 billion bits per second) between Herndon, Virginia, and Santa Clara, California, for $80,000 per month on a one-year lease. Similarly, one could obtain an OC-48 circuit between New York and London for $68,000 per month. Those two routes are among the least expensive long distance domestic and international routes. Herndon and Santa Clara are major centers of East Coast and West Coast Internet activity while many cables link New York and London. The Herndon-Santa Clara price is equivalent to $2.06 per month per voice-grade circuit while the New York-London price is equivalent to $1.74 per month per voice-grade circuit.

Even lower unit rates could be obtained by committing to higher capacity or longer terms. An OC-192 circuit (10 billion bits per second) between New York and London was offered for $136,500 per month (four times the capacity for twice the price of the OC-48 circuit), while a twenty-year Indefeasible Right of Use (full usage rights without legal title) for the same capacity circuit was offered for $3.85 million. Offering twenty-year rights at a price of only twenty-eight times the monthly rental indicates an expectation that prices will continue to fall rapidly. Prices per unit rose sharply for deviations from the highest density routes and for lower units of capacity. For example, a DS-1 circuit (1.544 million bits per second) between Richmond, Virginia, and Sacramento, California, was offered for $3,073 per month, equivalent to $128 per month per voice-grade circuit (sixty-four times the unit rate for the bulk circuit between Herndon and Santa Clara).

The very low bulk transmission costs produced forecasts that the traditional voice long distance market was no longer viable. Wireless telephone plans changed to distance-insensitive pricing with no distinction between local and long distance minutes. The Internet retained its original distance-insensitive pricing. Nevertheless, domestic interstate toll revenue rose every year between 1984 and 1999 (from $26.5 billion in 1984 to $54.5 billion in 1999) before falling back slightly in 2000, while total toll revenue in 2000 (including intrastate and international) reached $109.6 billion (FCC, 2002, table 10.2). Total toll revenue grew at an annual rate of 5.2 percent between 1984 and 1997 and then slowed to a 2.8 percent annual growth rate between 1997 and 2000. The slow growth in toll revenue during the late 1990s contrasted sharply with the (false) assertions of 1,000 percent per year growth in Internet usage and the actual 100 percent per year growth.

During the period of booming stock prices based on growth prospects, analysts often treated the voice toll market as irrelevant but the $100 billion in annual revenue provided an important source of continuing income after the collapse of optimistic projections and stock prices. While very low toll rates were available through various special pricing plans, the complexity of the numerous plans and the transactions cost of finding the appropriate plan caused many subscribers to continue using the higher standard rates. The average revenue per minute for all interstate switched services dropped from $.15 in 1992 to $.09 in 2000 while the comparable average price for international switched service dropped from $1.01 to $.53 (FCC, 2002, table 14.3), leaving the average price far above the minimum available price or the real cost of service. Four minutes of average-priced switched international service cost more than the monthly rental of a voice-grade line between New York and London when computed as a fraction of a price of a high-speed circuit.

Despite the failure of many Internet companies and the decline in stock market prices, Internet commerce and other activities continued to grow. Consumer purchases over the Internet doubled between 1999 and 2000, with online purchases particularly important for travel ($13.2 billion), computers ($4.3 billion), apparel ($2.8 billion), and books ($2.5 billion) (Eisenach, Lenard, and McGonegal, 2001, p. 65). The end of the boom period reduced emphasis on growth alone and caused the remaining companies to move toward normal economic behavior with attention to revenue, cost, and profits.

The continuing development of electronic commerce and other Internet activities provided an incentive to consumers to seek higher-speed access to the Internet than could be provided over a voice-grade telephone line and modem. Cable television technology was designed for one-way video distribution and could not be directly used for either Internet access or telephone service. However, upgraded cable television systems could provide both. Predictions of rapid development of high-speed Internet access over cable during the late 1990s underestimated the difficulty of providing the new services over cable plant. After several years of cable plant reconstruction, broadband access over cable began expanding. Internet access at a speed of over 200 kilobits per second in at least one direction over coaxial cable or hybrid optical fiber and coaxial cable systems increased from 1.4 million lines at the end of 1999 to 3.6 million at the end of 2000 and 5.2 million in June 2001. The primary alternative high-speed access for home users was a digital subscriber line (DSL) provided over copper telephone wires. DSL lines also increased rapidly from a small base, rising from 0.4 million at the end of 1999 (29 percent of the cable lines at that time) to 2.7 million in June 2001 (52 percent of the cable lines at that time) (FCC, 2002, table 2.1).

16

Conclusion

During the First Information Revolution, telephone service developed into a stable regulated monopoly structure that continued until the beginning of fringe competition in the early 1970s. That structure provided political benefits for the regulators and market protection benefits for the regulated monopoly. It also provided a voice for dissatisfied consumers and steady prices for consumers so that they could make long-term investments, confident that the price of telecommunication service would not be raised drastically. The telephone companies generally provided high-quality and reliable basic service and incorporated technological improvements into the system in a conservative way that, from a customer perspective, did not require major changes. The telephone companies credibly described the system as a natural monopoly. Local service was provided over a pair of copper wires to each location. For residential customers, one pair of wires generally provided far more capacity than was needed, and therefore it appeared inefficient to consider a second provider of wires to the home. Long distance communications links appeared to have substantial economies of scale and therefore greater efficiency when provided by a single company. The Department of Defense also endorsed the single-supplier approach as the best structure for emergency and defense communications.

The regulated monopoly telephone system of the 1950s satisfied government, corporate, and residential consumers. It appeared to be a reasonable accommodation to the observed technology and opportunities. Widely advertised innovations from Bell Labs helped sustain political support for AT&T as a technologically progressive company. The Bell System's accomplishments during World War II and the early Cold War in providing critically needed communications services and equipment made it an indispensable component of the defense industrial capability. While individual customers complained of specific problems, there was no widespread displeasure with AT&T or political support for creating competition.

The telephone companies of the 1950s and the supporting institutional structure were based on electromechanical technology, supplemented with vacuum-tube electronics for telephone amplifiers and wireless transmission systems. AT&T was a leader in that technology and designed reliable equipment with very long service lives. The institutional structure encouraged the long service lives, with the associated slow depreciation schedules that reduced the rate burden. Technological progress was carefully controlled to remain compatible with older generations of equipment and to avoid the necessity to replace equipment before the end of its designed service life.

Technological Progress and Policy Evolution

This stable and satisfactory structure was challenged by the rapid progress in electronic components. For many years after the development of the transistor and the initiation of sustained electronics price reductions, the changing relative prices of electronics and electromechanical components had no significant effect on the industry structure. Transistors began as extremely high-cost devices that were used in high-value applications such as military products. As the price of transistors declined, they became mass-market components in radios and computers, replacing the earlier vacuum tubes. Similarly, AT&T replaced vacuum tubes with transistors without any requirement to modify its overall corporate strategy or any influence on regulatory policies. During the first period of the Second Information Revolution (1950–1968), computers and communications were largely separate worlds with little interaction. Computers and communications were sometimes used as complementary products, as in the SAGE air defense system and the SABRE airline reservation system, but the specialized early computer-communications systems were created without changing the regulatory structure. AT&T developed data sets (modems) to transmit computer data over its existing analog voice network and offered regulated data services as a straightforward expansion of its traditional regulated communications services.

However, the rapid progress in electronic components during the 1950s and 1960s together with the very different responses to that progress by the computer and communications industries created pressure to modify the regulated monopoly structure. The price of computing power fell drastically in accordance with the price reductions in electronic components, creating a massive increase in the range of economically feasible uses for computers. Computer companies introduced multiple generations of products, each with greater flexibility and lower prices per unit of computing power than the preceding generation.

Rapid obsolescence of computers increased the depreciation rate and the corresponding annual cost of computing service. For example, if a company purchased a computer with a physical lifetime of ten years but that was expected to become obsolete in five years, it needed to charge 20 percent of its capital cost to annual depreciation expenses rather than the 10 percent required for its physical lifetime. Rapid obsolescence also created instability in the computer industry, with many companies exiting the industry after finding they could not maintain the competitive pace of technological progress. Customers enjoyed rapid improvements in the price and performance level of new computer systems, but had no protection for their investment in training and software if their computer supplier went out of business or introduced an incompatible upgrade.

In contrast to the computer industry, the telephone industry under AT&T's leadership remained very stable. AT&T was more technologically sophisticated than IBM in the early 1950s, but AT&T continued to deploy standardized compatible products using the mature electromechanical technology while IBM transformed itself into a high-technology company. AT&T remained a closed world, protected from competition by regulation and prohibited by the 1956 consent decree from participating in services outside of the regulatory boundary. With the encouragement of regulators, AT&T held down the accounting cost of providing service by spreading depreciation over very long service lifetimes that were determined by physical capability rather than obsolescence. If IBM attempted to continue collecting rent for an obsolete machine, a competitor would eventually offer the customer a better deal, but there was no market check on the decisions of AT&T and the regulators.

Technological progress substantially reduced the cost of providing long distance service during the 1950s and 1960s as advances in electronic components reduced the cost of microwave radio and coaxial cable transmission systems and customer dialing replaced operator-assisted calling. However, those cost reductions were not translated directly into price reductions for long distance service but were used instead to avoid raising the price of local telephone service. Similarly, technological progress provided opportunities for greater flexibility and lower costs in modems, PBXs, and other terminal equipment, but those cost reductions were not consistently translated into price reductions for the corresponding services. The practice of maintaining stable prices in the presence of rapid changes in technological opportunities and costs created an increasing disparity between the cost of providing individual services and the price of those services.

As discussed in Chapter 1, technological progress and the associated change in price ratios generally create pressure to modify the institutional framework. That pressure comes from the efforts of entrepreneurs who perceive opportunities available from the new technology that cannot be fully exploited because of the institutional framework. Those entrepreneurs seek to modify the framework to accommodate the new technological opportunities but encounter resistance from those who benefit from the implicit property rights associated with the existing framework.

By the late 1960s the divergent responses of the computer and communications industries to electronics innovations had created incentives for institutional evolution. While early time-sharing computer systems could be accessed over the telephone network using AT&T-supplied teletype terminals and AT&T-supplied modems, computer users desired more flexibility and variety in their options for combining computer and communications functions. The increasing gap between the cost of supplying long distance service and AT&T's toll rates created interest in establishing alternative long distance transport systems. During the second period of the SIR (1969–1984), the regulated monopoly was transformed into a structure that allowed competition in CPE and long distance services while continuing the regulated monopoly in local exchange services. The CPE competition policy developed over twelve years from the initial liberalization of AT&T's strict control of terminal equipment in the 1968 Carterfone decision to the deregulation of terminal equipment in the 1980 Computer II decision. The policy of competition in long distance services developed over a similar time frame between the 1969 MCI decision and the implementation of the divestiture and access charges in 1984.

While entry could have been prevented through strong regulation, the incentives to enter the market required those who supported legal barriers to develop politically acceptable reasons for maintaining the monopoly. Most state regulators found those justifications (particularly the social benefits of revenue sharing and non-cost-based pricing) compelling, but the FCC and the DOJ did not. The FCC was able to allow initial competition in CPE and long distance without the approval of either the state regulators or Congress and could therefore implement its policy of limited competition even while there was little political support for major change in telephone policy.

Once the first competition was allowed, continued progress in electronics helped its success and expansion. The rapid proliferation of improved low-cost CPE after competition eliminated support for returning to the monopoly structure. Some of those improvements would have come about under continued monopoly because of the new opportunities from electronics progress, but the benefits were attributed to competition. Similarly, continued technological progress after long distance competition was authorized helped support the case for expanding competitive opportunities.

Initial competition also created incentives for further regulatory change because of the activities of the competitors. In the monopoly period, AT&T was the primary source of information for the regulators. While individual staff members might question some of AT&T's arguments, there was no organized support for an alternative point of view. The early competitors provided an alternative perspective on the industry and its opportunities from that provided by AT&T. They forced the regulators to evaluate arguments that had been easily accepted earlier with no objection. The initial competitors (especially MCI) were also aggressive in promoting their perspective and creatively using the different approaches of the FCC, the court of appeals, and the DOJ to advance their interests.

During the limited competition of the 1970s, the market model gradually gained support over the regulatory model. AT&T lost credibility with its vigorous arguments that harm to the network would result from the attachment of customer-owned terminal equipment. When that equipment was attached with no observable harm, AT&T's assertions about other benefits of the regulated monopoly system were examined more skeptically as possible self-serving statements designed to protect its market position. The FCC's policy of limited competition in long distance service in order to protect the revenue flows from long distance to local companies was upset by the court rebuke in the MCI Execunet litigation and overturned entirely with the DOJ-imposed divestiture. The DOJ accepted MCI's perspective that the revenue flow argument was simply rhetorical justification for the continuation of AT&T's monopoly.

The divestiture agreement and the FCC's plan to allow prices to adjust toward the cost of service in both the long distance and local markets produced a political backlash in support of the older structure. Fears of rising local telephone rates and loss of subsidies to favored companies overcame the economic arguments for the efficiency benefits of matching prices and cost. State regulators gained congressional support for their position in favor of continued sharing of long distance toll revenue with local telephone companies and forced the FCC to modify its access charge plan in order to avoid having it overturned by legislation. The post-divestiture policy toward long distance service was a political compromise that gave enough benefits to conflicting positions to survive. It combined the conflicting goals of encouraging competition in all services other than local exchange (the DOJ market-oriented perspective) and of maintaining the revenue flows from long distance to local service (the state-regulated monopoly perspective). In contrast, the CPE policy was clearly based on the competitive model, with 1970s concerns about revenue flows and harm to the network no longer discussed. The contradictory foundations of post-divestiture long distance policy produced a five-year period of managed competition in which regulatory control over the details of access charges and AT&T's long distance price structure affected competitive outcomes.

The political conflict over allowing competition in long distance and CPE resulted from disputes over how to distribute the benefits of technological progress. The regulatory perspective sought to favor the established widespread basic telephone service at the expense of new services. State regulators perceived their role as maintaining low basic prices and maintaining a variety of social policies such as geographical averaging. The method of accomplishing that was to limit implementation of new technologies that might increase costs and to increase the contribution from CPE and long distance service in order to transfer the benefits of technological progress in those areas to basic local service. That method worked so long as the entire industry was under complete regulatory control, but it created incentives for entry into the services being discriminated against. The regulatory approach required strict boundaries around the regulated services, with limits on potential competitors in order to maintain the politically determined price structure. AT&T and the state regulators were strong proponents of the regulated monopoly approach.

An alternative perspective sought to maximize the ability of consumers to enjoy technological progress. In that view, new products and services should not be taxed to support old products. New products should either develop according to market-driven principles, or be given specific advantages in order to encourage progress. That perspective skeptically evaluated arguments for the benefits of maintaining a monopoly, especially when those benefits required the exclusion of competitors and limitations on consumer choice. The Department of Justice and potential competitors were proponents of the market-oriented approach. The FCC initially supported the regulated monopoly but gradually moved toward a market orientation.

The revised institutional structure established by 1984 rearranged the property rights of the monopoly era. AT&T lost the ability to control new services created by innovative CPE, and state regulators lost part of their power to arrange the rate structure to meet political goals. Prior to CPE liberalization, for example, an improvement in modem speed could be used to define a new class of data communications service with a price determined by the customer valuation of obtaining the higher speed and by political goals. After CPE deregulation, any customer was entitled to use an innovative modem to increase throughput while paying the telephone company the same basic rate for a voice-grade line as if it were used only for voice or with a low-speed modem.

While CPE deregulation simply transferred the rights to control CPE from AT&T and the regulators to consumers, the long distance liberalization created a more complex mixture of old and new property rights. The high initial access charges protected the established rights of local telephone companies to receive a portion of the long distance toll revenue, with continuing large subsidies for rural and high-cost telephone companies. The access structure established the right of long distance users to enjoy continuing technological progress, while paying a tribute to the past arrangements. The new structure included the right for enhanced service providers to use the local network freely for access to data communications services without paying the high access fees imposed on voice long distance providers.

The long distance and CPE liberalizations were primarily based on the technological progress of the previous era and managed to set up by 1984 a satisfactory structure for the problems of 1969: computer-communications interaction and overpriced long distance service. While that structure was being developed, progress continued in ways that created pressure for further evolution. Optical fiber transmission systems developed rapidly, slashing the cost of transmitting high-speed streams of data. Mobile phones were introduced without monopoly telephone company control, providing an alternative to copper wires. Personal computers and LANs proliferated. The early Internet developed with the connection of disparate networks using TCP/IP. While most of those matters were of little economic importance for the computer or telephone industry during the pre-divestiture period, they provided incentives for further institutional evolution in the post-divestiture period.

The immediate post-divestiture world provided monopoly power to the local exchange companies, but also imposed tight restrictions on the freedom of the BOCs to pursue business opportunities outside of the local exchange market. Innovations in wireless and optical fiber systems created incentives for new companies to offer novel types of local exchange service and created dissatisfaction with the monopoly policy for local exchange. The BOCs' goal of eliminating the restrictions on their business together with the desire of other industry participants to provide local exchange service allowed the political compromise incorporated into the Telecommunications Act of 1996. That legislation eliminated the strict boundary lines among various pieces of the telephone market and established a general policy in favor of competition in all parts of the market.

The 1996 Act moved telecommunication policy closer to that of the unregulated computer industry and reduced the distinctions between common carrier telephone service and unregulated data communications. However, it did not entirely eliminate those distinctions, and the dividing line between regulated and unregulated services remained significant. Regulated services continued to be subject to numerous requirements (including interconnection obligations and universal service taxes and subsidies) that were not imposed on unregulated data communications services.

Implementation of the 1996 Act was slow and controversial, with extensive litigation over the revised set of property rights imposed by the new law. The BOCs vehemently opposed the FCC's interpretation of the rights of competitive companies to create new services by utilizing portions of the BOC network, while potential competitors complained that the BOCs were refusing to follow the market-opening provisions of the law. Dissatisfaction with the 1996 Act, financial instability and bankruptcies among telecommunication companies, and continued technological progress created the likelihood of further institutional change.

The Process of Institutional Change

While technological progress and the interaction of the computer industry with the regulated communications industry created pressure for institutional change, the initial inclination of the policymakers was to make minimal adjustments in order to solve immediate problems. Moreover, there was great uncertainty regarding the future technological developments and the best way to respond to them. That uncertainty, coupled with the active opposition to change from the industry people who provided most of the information to the regulators, generated conservatively minimal responses to the observed problems. However, over time substantial evolution occurred. Three types of policy tools were used to implement institutional change amid political controversy and industry opposition.

The first type was the intellectual development of the case for modifying the regulatory structure, including economic and engineering analyses at many different levels of generality and detail. The intellectual development began with academic economic studies that emphasized the problems created by regulation and that proposed market-oriented reforms. Academic studies were supplemented by detailed intellectual support for politically feasible changes, often by staff members or consultants who were familiar with the current constraints and controversies. For example, Ronald Coase's 1959 FCC testimony and writings regarding market processes for spectrum were largely ignored by the FCC until staff studies in the 1980s provided a guide for modest changes. The combination of academic articles, think tank studies, and government studies provided an intellectual foundation for examining the need for monopoly and for regulation. The intellectual foundation for reforming the regulated monopoly system helped build public and political support for changes and provided an alternative view to that supplied by the regulated companies for policy discussions within the regulatory agencies.

The second type of policy tool used to facilitate institutional change consisted of methods of dealing with limited information. The early U.S. telephone liberalization occurred when there was little information about alternatives to the centralized control of the telephone network that AT&T and all the other telephone companies of the world claimed was necessary. Rational policy approaches would compare the expected results of various policy alternatives and choose the best one according to specified criteria. That approach is open to extensive political criticism by those who wish to maintain the status quo. While all actions (including no change from the present) are uncertain scenarios, the unchanged policy has a privileged position because it is the default if no other policy is adopted. Thus promoting change in the U.S. structure required finding ways around the information trap that we cannot change because we do not know enough.

The primary solution to the information problem was to structure policy changes as small incremental steps. Many major initiatives began gradually: price caps for AT&T, a small subscriber line charge (SLC), limited flexibility for spectrum users. That approach allowed backtracking on things that did not work and further development of those that did. In the midst of great uncertainty and political differences, starting small is both a way of overcoming the inertia created by inadequate information and a way of generating new information on what works and what does not. Once new players are in the market, they will make arguments that support their interests and provide an alternative to the information provided by the incumbent. The policy of gradualism makes the regulatory agencies seem sluggish because they may be working on similar things for many years, but it allows substantial cumulative change when there is inadequate information and political support for one major policy change.

An important part of the policy of gradualism was narrowly limiting the scope of information that would be considered in evaluating a policy decision. Important decisions were formally developed on narrow grounds: the Above 890 private microwave liberalization was concerned only with spectrum availability, not with long distance competition; the MCI decision was an experiment for a small-scale system; the divestiture was antitrust enforcement and not concerned with broader telecommunication policy questions. Such justifications often make government decisionmakers appear to be unaware of the significance of their action, but this narrowing avoids the impossible task of projecting the implications of the decisions and defending those implications against parties that prefer no action at all.

Incremental changes based on limited information also had disadvantages. It meant that regulatory policy was continually changing, and companies could not make long-term plans with confidence about the policies that would be in place for the duration. Incrementalism worked better for policies that were easily divisible into meaningful increments than for those that were not. For example, the SLC could be adjusted in small increments (easily divisible) while the policy of limited long distance competition (not easily divisible) had no stability. The practice of making many different policy changes on narrow grounds did not provide any guarantee that the decisions would be consistent or add up to any kind of coherent overall policy.

Another method of dealing with uncertainty and limited information was attempting to develop policies that are generally satisfactory over a wide range of environments rather than ones that are closely tailored to the expected conditions. Robust rules that are not closely tied to the expected "state of the world" have a greater chance of being useful as the world changes. Seeking rules that are useful without an accurate prediction of the future environment often means putting greater emphasis on market forces and opportunities for choice than on detailed regulations.

The third category of policy tools aimed to limit the political opposition of those whose benefits from the regulated monopoly system were endangered by institutional changes. The essential action was to protect the benefits and implicit property rights that were already in place while limiting the expansion of those benefits to new technologies and services. That included putting boundaries on the monopoly, so that the core monopoly could not be stretched to encompass new technologies and products. It also included clever use of legal definitions to create a space for alternatives to the dominant firm without challenging it directly. The introduction of private carriers and of enhanced service providers allowed for alternatives without direct competition. Insofar as the providers in those protected spaces developed, they could become competitors to the dominant firm at a later time.

The institutional framework for telecommunication has not adjusted smoothly or rapidly to changes in technology. The incremental approach to deal with uncertainty and the protection of existing interests to blunt political opposition to change have made the process slow and inconsistent. Contradictory policies have been adopted to avoid resolving political conflicts and to avoid having the political conflicts block change. Protecting the established interests has determined the overall shape of feasible reform and has slowed many potentially useful kinds of changes.

As common carrier communication policy has gradually evolved from a regulated monopoly to regulated interconnected competition, there has been continual dispute over two types of policy controversies: the distribution of income among the many different participants in the production and consumption of communications, and the distribution of power among the many different policy-influencing organizations. Income distribution activities occupy a great deal of regulatory time and attention and receive even more time and attention from companies as they attempt to influence regulations in a way favorable to themselves. The distribution activities of regulation generally create substantial efficiency losses. Those losses occur through direct rent dissipation (efforts spent to support changes that would direct distribution toward oneself and to oppose changes that would direct distribution away from oneself) and through changes in investment incentives and other managerial actions created by the regulatory action.

One form of income distribution is the distribution between the regulated carriers and the consumers, controlled by regulatory limits on profits or prices. Profit-limiting regulation is designed for situations of high capital intensity and relatively stable technology with natural monopoly characteristics. It is a method of reducing risk for both firms and consumers by guaranteeing a stable though limited profit rate to the firms and a stable set of prices for consumers. However, it also encourages risk-averse behavior on the part of the firm. Regulators disapprove of risky investments because if they fail, the firm will seek price increases with resulting political pain for the regulators. Firms will not find risky investments with potentially high payoffs attractive because they will bear some costs if the investments fail and will not be able to enjoy the full advantages if the investments succeed.

A second form of income distribution regulation is the control of the price structure. During the regulated monopoly, rates for all services provided by the firm were designed to generate total revenue equal to the total cost as computed by the regulated accounting system. Many different rate structures (changes in the relative prices of business, residential, extension, and private lines) could generate the desired revenue. The general practice was to seek a "contribution" from local services other than basic residential (as well as from interstate long distance service) in order to provide basic residential service at a rate below the accounting cost of supplying the service. That policy supported inexpensive basic telephone service but also imposed a tax on many other services. Control of the rate structure provided political benefits to the regulators because it gave them the power to redistribute the burden of paying for the telephone network among various classes of users. Political control of the rate structure also provided benefits to the regulated companies because their continuing monopoly power was necessary in order to protect the politically determined rate structure.

The politically determined price structure slowed the development of new services. In many markets, new services are introduced with promotional below-cost prices in order to gain consumer acceptance. In telephone service, new services generally had to show evidence that they would be profitable from the beginning in order to avoid burdening the basic rate payer. Enhanced services were able to develop because they were free of the constraints of rate regulation and its politically determined price structure, while the structure encouraged telephone companies to provide mass-market services with little attention to niche services that might eventually grow into major markets. Thus the rate structure control accentuated the risk aversion that was built into the management of the overall price and profit levels.

A third form of income distribution regulation is the political control of revenue flows across companies to meet specific goals of subsidizing rural companies and other "universal service" goals. The universal service program was expanded in the Telecommunications Act of 1996 to support services to schools, libraries, and rural health-care providers and to incorporate services beyond basic dial tone. The universal service payments were reformed and improved after the 1996 Act by converting to a "tax" on telecommunication revenue rather than the price structure controls of an earlier time. The expanded universal service payment scheme creates discrimination between services subject to the tax (including wireline and wireless telephone service) and services not subject to the tax (including Internet services). As more communication moves over the exempt services and less over the subject services, the tax discrimination will become a more substantial policy issue. As the cost of long distance transmission approaches zero and telephone service rate plans include bundled long distance and local minutes, interstate toll revenue is likely to decline and may not be able to support the current universal service obligations regardless of the tax rate imposed.

As noted earlier, a second major class of policy controversies has concerned the distribution of power among the many different organizations that influence telecommunication policy, including government agencies, advocacy groups, and regulated firms. Many different government organizations contribute to telecommunication policy, including Congress, the FCC, state Public Utility Commissions (PUCs), the Department of Justice, the Commerce Department, the State Department, and the U.S. Trade Representative. While the lines of authority are specified, they are not clear in practice, and many conflicts and overlapping responsibilities occur. For example, it is clearly specified that Congress makes federal legislation and that the FCC carries out duties assigned to it by Congress for interstate telecommunication while the state PUCs carry out duties assigned to them by state legislation for intrastate telecommunication services. However, Congress can also provide detailed intervention through the oversight and authorization process, often at the request of a single member. The same equipment is used for intrastate and interstate service with continual disputes over the boundaries of state and federal authority. The same issues can be examined from either a "public interest" regulatory standard administered by the FCC or an antitrust standard administered by the DOJ.

Conflicts among agencies for power often represent conflicts over policies supported by various industry interests. In the late 1970s, the potential competitors to AT&T found the DOJ more sympathetic than the FCC and sought antitrust intervention on issues that were before the FCC. The DOJ accepted the perspective of the potential competitors and sought to reduce the FCC's authority because the DOJ believed that the FCC was supporting continued monopoly for AT&T. In the early 1980s, the FCC sought to reduce state authority because it objected to state rate structure policies that created high per-minute rates for long distance service. The bitter political conflict over the subscriber line charge was accentuated by the underlying theme of removing power from the states. The intense controversy over state versus federal authority to interpret provisions of the Telecommunications Act of 1996 developed in significant part because the state interpretation was more favorable to incumbents and the federal interpretation was more favorable to potential entrants.

Final Comment

The technological transformation that created pressure for the previous institutional changes is continuing. The sustained extraordinary progress in basic electronic components is likely to continue. Further reduction in the price of electronic components will make it economically feasible to incorporate very complex electronic devices in low-cost items for routine occasional use. Continued technological progress is likely to induce further institutional evolution, especially in spectrum management and in the continuing regulatory distinctions among common carrier, enhanced, cable television, and broadcasting services.

While the story is not yet complete, we are moving toward an era of distance-insensitive information transmission at near zero price. Many individuals already enjoy zero marginal cost for transmitting e-mail and accessing Web information regardless of distance or national boundaries. When zero marginal cost transmission was observed in the early Internet, many commentators asserted that it only occurred because of the noncommercial nature of the Internet and that it would disappear as the Internet moved into mainstream operation. Yet as the Internet was transformed into commercial operation, the pricing model of a fixed access fee independent of usage volume or distance was retained because it is a reasonable approximation to the actual cost structure that saves the transaction costs of measuring and billing for actual usage.

Before the First Information Revolution, rapid communication over long distance was impossible and slow communication was expensive. Consequently, local arrangements were critical. During the First Information Revolution, slow communication became much cheaper and rapid communication became possible though at a higher price. While that change greatly influenced the pattern of business development (allowing the rise of large nationwide businesses), communication costs still remained an important concern. Telegraph rates were relatively high, especially for detailed information. During the Second Information Revolution, long distance communication costs have fallen and have become less distance-sensitive. While there is still some identifiable greater cost of transmitting information long distances than short distances, that cost is very low. The cost of supplying bulk long distance transport capacity is so low as to be insignificant for any communication with low to moderate bandwidth. As of 2002, it is still expensive to transmit high-bandwidth items such as full motion video for large numbers of subscribers.

The Second Information Revolution is a revolution in both price and products. Just as the First Information Revolution reduced the price of early products (mail) and made available new products (telephone and telegraph), so the Second Information Revolution has reduced the price of earlier products (telephone) and created new products (immediate access from one's desk to distant stored information). Just as the First Information Revolution induced major changes in business organization and the overall economy, the Second Information Revolution has already induced major changes in business and consumer behavior and can be expected to facilitate a more thorough transformation in the future as the full implications of immediate access to distant information at near zero cost are developed.

References

Index

REFERENCES

Abbate, Janet. 1999. *Inventing the Internet.* Cambridge, Mass.: MIT Press.

Anders, George. 1999. "You Expect Big Losses and Want $10 Million? Sure, We'll Consider It." *Wall Street Journal,* March 17, p. A1.

AT&T. 1980. "Defendants' Pretrial Brief," reprinted in C. H. Sterling, J. F. Kasle, and K. T. Glakas, eds., *Decision to Divest: Major Documents in U.S. v. AT&T, 1974–1984,* vol. 1, pp. 560–664. Washington, D.C.: Communications Press, 1986.

Beelar, Donald C. 1967. "Cables in the Sky and the Struggle for Their Control." *Federal Communications Bar Journal,* 21: 27–37.

Bekkers, Rudi, and Jan Smits. 1999. *Mobile Telecommunications: Standards, Regulation, and Applications.* Boston, Mass.: Artech House.

Bell Laboratories. 1977. *Engineering and Operations in the Bell System.* Murray Hill, N.J.: Bell Telephone Laboratories, Inc.

———. 1978. *A History of Engineering and Science in the Bell System: National Service in War and Peace (1925–1975).* Murray Hill, N.J.: Bell Telephone Laboratories, Inc.

———. 1982. *A History of Engineering and Science in the Bell System: Switching Technology (1925–1975).* Murray Hill, N.J.: Bell Telephone Laboratories, Inc.

———. 1985. *A History of Engineering and Science in the Bell System: Transmission Technology (1925–1975).* Murray Hill, N.J.: Bell Telephone Laboratories, Inc.

Beniger, James R. 1986. *The Control Revolution: Technological and Economic Origins of the Information Society.* Cambridge, Mass.: Harvard University Press.

Benjamin, Stuart M., Douglas G. Lichtman, and Howard A. Shelanski. 2001. *Telecommunications Law and Policy.* Durham, N.C.: Carolina Academic Press.

Berman, Dennis. 2002. "Before Telecom Industry Sank, Insiders Sold Billions in Stock." *Wall Street Journal,* August 12, p. A1.

Berners-Lee, Tim, with Mark Fischetti. 1999. *Weaving the Web: The Original Design and Ultimate Destiny of the World Wide Web by Its Inventor.* New York: HarperCollins.

Brand, Stewart. 2001. "Founding Father" (interview of Paul Baran). *Wired,* March, pp. 145–153.

Bresnahan, Timothy F., and Shane Greenstein. 1999. "Technological Competition and the Structure of the Computer Industry." *Journal of Industrial Economics,* 47: 1–40.

Brock, Gerald W. 1975. *The U.S. Computer Industry: A Study of Market Power.* Cambridge, Mass.: Ballinger.

———. 1981. *The Telecommunications Industry: The Dynamics of Market Structure.* Cambridge, Mass.: Harvard University Press.

———. 1989. "Dominant Firm Response to Competitive Challenge: Peripheral Equipment Manufacturers' Suits against IBM (1979–1983)," in John Kwoka, Jr., and Lawrence White, eds., *The Antitrust Revolution.* Glenview, Ill.: Scott, Foresman.

———. 1994. *Telecommunication Policy for the Information Age: From Monopoly to Competition.* Cambridge, Mass.: Harvard University Press.

Buderi, Robert. 1996. *The Invention That Changed the World: How a Small Group of Radar Pioneers Won the Second World War and Launched a Technological Revolution.* New York: Touchstone.

Calhoun, George. 1988. *Digital Cellular Radio.* Norwood, Mass.: Artech House.

Cantelon, Philip. 1993. *The History of MCI: 1968–1988, The Early Years.* Dallas, Tex.: Heritage Press.

Ceruzzi, Paul E. 1998. *A History of Modern Computing.* Cambridge, Mass.: MIT Press.

Chandler, Alfred D. 1977. *The Visible Hand: The Managerial Revolution in American Business.* Cambridge, Mass.: Harvard University Press.

———. 1990. *Scale and Scope: The Dynamics of Industrial Capitalism.* Cambridge, Mass.: Harvard University Press.

Christensen, Clayton M. 1997. *The Innovator's Dilemma.* Boston, Mass.: Harvard Business School Press (reprinted in paperback by HarperCollins, 2000).

Coase, Ronald. 1937. "The Nature of the Firm." *Economica,* n.s., 4.

———. 1988. *The Firm, the Market, and the Law.* Chicago, Ill.: University of Chicago Press.

Comer, Douglas E. 1997. *Computer Networks and Internets.* Upper Saddle River, N.J.: Prentice Hall.

Communications Act. 1934. Communications Act of 1934, as amended, 47 U.S.C. §151.

Computer Industry Census. 1971. Very detailed information on 2,700 companies originally collected in confidence for the *U.S. v. IBM* litigation and introduced into the public record in *California Computer Products v. IBM,* 613 F.2d 727 (1979).

Court of Appeals, D.C. Cir. 1977. *MCI Telecommunications v. FCC,* 561 F.2d 365.

Court of Appeals, 4th Cir. 1976. *North Carolina Utilities Commission v. FCC,* 537 F.2d 787.

Court of Appeals, 9th Cir. 1979. *California Computer Products v. International Business Machines Corp.,* 613 F.2d 727.

Cusumano, Michael A., and David B. Yoffie. 1998. *Competing on Internet Time: Lessons from Netscape and Its Battle with Microsoft.* New York: The Free Press.

Eisenach, Jeffrey, Thomas Lenard, and Stephen McGonegal. 2001. *The Digital Economy Fact Book.* 3rd ed. Washington, D.C.: Progress and Freedom Foundation.

Electronic Industries Association. 1979. *Electronic Market Data Book.* Washington, D.C.: Electronic Industries Association.

FCC. 1939. *Investigation of the Telephone Industry in the United States.* Washington, D.C.: U.S. Government Printing Office (reprinted Arno Press, 1974).

———. 1949. *Federal Communications Commission Reports,* 42: 1–23.

———. 1971. *Federal Communications Commission Reports, 2nd Series,* 29: 870–920.

———. 1974. *Statistics of Communications Common Carriers: Year Ended December 31, 1971.* Washington, D.C.: U.S. Government Printing Office.

———. 1980. *Federal Communications Commission Reports, 2nd Series,* 77: 384–495.

———. 1984. *Statistics of Communications Common Carriers: Year Ended December 21, 1984.* Washington, D.C.: U.S. Government Printing Office.

———. 1989. *Statistics of Communications Common Carriers: 1988/89 Edition.* Washington, D.C.: U.S. Government Printing Office.

———. 1998. "Fiber Deployment Update, End of Year 1998." Industry Analysis Division, Common Carrier Bureau *(www.fcc.gov/wcb/iatd/stats).*

———. 1999a. *Reference Book of Rates, Price Indices, and Expenditures for Telephone Service.* Industry Analysis Division, Common Carrier Bureau *(www.fcc.gov/wcb/iatd/stats).*

———. 1999b. "Local Competition Report, August 1999." Industry Analysis Division, Common Carrier Bureau *(www.fcc.gov/wcb/iatd/stats).*

———. 2001. "Trends in Telephone Service." Industry Analysis Division, Common Carrier Bureau *(www.fcc.gov/wcb/iatd/stats).*

———. 2002. "Trends in Telephone Service." Industry Analysis Division, Common Carrier Bureau *(www.fcc.gov/wcb/iatd/stats).*

Felker, Alex, and Kenneth Gordon. 1983. "A Framework for a Decentralized Radio Service." Staff Report, Office of Plans and Policy, Federal Communications Commission, Washington, D.C.

Flamm, Kenneth. 1988. *Creating the Computer: Government, Industry, and High Technology.* Washington, D.C.: Brookings Institution.

———. 1996. *Mismanaged Trade?: Strategic Policy and the Semiconductor Industry.* Washington, D.C.: Brookings Institution.

Freeman, Roger. 1999. *Fundamentals of Telecommunications.* New York: John Wiley & Sons.

Gasparino, Charles. 2002. "New York Sues Telecom Executives over Stock Profits." *Wall Street Journal,* October 1, p. A1.

Gleick, James. 1992. *Genius: The Life and Science of Richard Feynman.* New York: Pantheon Books.

Hafner, Katie, and Matthew Lyon. 1996. *Where Wizards Stay Up Late: The Origins of the Internet.* New York: Touchstone.

Hazlett, Thomas W. 1990. "The Rationality of U.S. Regulation of the Broadcast Spectrum." *Journal of Law and Economics,* 33: 133–170.

———. 2001. "The Wireless Craze, the Unlimited Bandwidth Myth, the Spectrum Auction Faux Pas, and the Punchline to Ronald Coase's 'Big Joke': An Essay on Airwave Allocation Policy." *Harvard Journal of Law and Technology,* 14: 335–567.

Henck, Fred, and Bernard Strassburg. 1988. *A Slippery Slope: The Long Road to the Breakup of AT&T.* New York: Greenwood Press.

Holcombe, A. N. 1911. *Public Ownership of Telephones on the Continent of Europe.* Cambridge, Mass.: Harvard University Press.

Horwitz, Robert. 1989. *The Irony of Regulatory Reform: The Deregulation of American Telecommunications.* New York: Oxford University Press.

Hughes, Thomas. 1998. *Rescuing Prometheus.* New York: Random House.

Hundt, Reed E. 2000. *You Say You Want a Revolution: A Story of Information Age Politics.* New Haven, Conn.: Yale University Press.

Ip, Greg, Susan Pulliam, Scott Thurm, and Ruth Simon. 2000. "The Internet Bubble Broke Records, Rules and Bank Accounts." *Wall Street Journal,* July 14, p. A1.

Jackson, Tim. 1997. *Inside Intel: Andy Grove and the Rise of the World's Most Powerful Chip Company.* New York: Penguin Putnam.

John, Richard R. 1995. *Spreading the News: The American Postal System from Franklin to Morse.* Cambridge, Mass.: Harvard University Press.

Kaplan, Fred. 1983. *The Wizards of Armageddon.* New York: Simon & Schuster.

Knight, Jerry. 2002. "WorldCom Woes Pop the Region's Telecom Bubble." *Washington Post,* July 1, p. E1.

Kwerel, Evan, and Alex D. Felker. 1985. "Using Auctions to Select FCC Licensees." Working Paper 16, Office of Plans and Policy, Federal Communications Commission, Washington, D.C.

McCraw, Thomas K. 1984. *Prophets of Regulation.* Cambridge, Mass.: Harvard University Press.

McMillan, John. 2002. *Reinventing the Bazaar: A Natural History of Markets.* New York: W. W. Norton.

Miller, Michael J. 1997. "Looking Back." *PC Magazine,* March 25, pp. 108–136.

Mountjoy, Richard. 1995. *100 Years of Bell Telephones.* Atglen, Pa.: Schiffer Publishing.

Mueller, Milton. 1996. *Universal Service: Competition, Interconnection, and Monopoly in the Making of the American Telephone System.* Cambridge, Mass.: MIT Press.

Murray, James B. 2001. *Wireless Nation: The Frenzied Launch of the Cellular Revolution in America.* Cambridge, Mass.: Perseus Publishing.

Noam, Eli. 1992. *Telecommunications in Europe.* New York: Oxford University Press.

Noll, Roger, and Bruce Owen, 1989. "The Anticompetitive Uses of Regulation: *United States v. AT&T,*" in John Kwoka and Lawrence White, eds., *The Antitrust Revolution.* Glenview, Ill.: Scott, Foresman.

North, Douglass C. 1981. *Structure and Change in Economic History.* New York: W. W. Norton.

———. 1990. *Institutions, Institutional Change, and Economic Performance.* Cambridge: Cambridge University Press.

"The Power of WorldCom's Puff." 2002. *The Economist,* July 20–26.

Redmond, Kent C., and Thomas M. Smith. 1980. *Project Whirlwind: The History of a Pioneer Computer.* Bedford, Mass.: Digital Press.

Reich, Leonard. 1977. "Research, Patents, and the Struggle to Control Radio: A Study of Big Business and the Uses of Industrial Research." *Business History Review,* 51: 208–235.

Reid, Robert H. 1997. *Architects of the Web: 1,000 Days That Built the Future of Business.* New York: John Wiley & Sons.

Rhodes, Richard. 1995. *Dark Sun: The Making of the Hydrogen Bomb.* New York: Simon & Schuster.

Riordan, Michael, and Lillian Hoddeson. 1997. *Crystal Fire: The Invention of the Transistor and the Birth of the Information Age.* New York: W. W. Norton.

Scherer, F. M. 1960. "The Development of the TD-X and TD-2 Microwave Radio Relay Systems in Bell Telephone Laboratories." Weapons Acquisition Research Project, Harvard Graduate School of Business Administration, Cambridge, Mass.

———. 1999. *New Perspectives on Economic Growth and Technological Innovation.* Washington, D.C.: Brookings Institution.

Stehman, J. Warren. 1925. *The Financial History of the American Telephone and Telegraph Company.* Boston: Houghton Mifflin.

Sterling, Christopher, and Michael Kittross. 2002. *Stay Tuned: A History of American Broadcasting.* 3rd ed. Mahwah, N.J.: Lawrence Erlbaum Associates.

Supreme Court. 1999. *AT&T Corp. v. Iowa Utilities Board,* 525 U.S. 366.

Temin, Peter, with Louis Galambos. 1987. *The Fall of the Bell System.* Cambridge: Cambridge University Press.

Thompson, Robert L. 1947. *Wiring a Continent.* Princeton, N.J.: Princeton University Press.

Tilton, John. 1971. *International Diffusion of Technology: The Case of Semiconductors.* Washington, D.C.: Brookings Institution.

Tomlinson, Richard G. 2000. *Tele-Revolution: Telephone Competition at the Speed of Light.* Glastonbury, Conn.: Connecticut Research, Inc.

U.S. Census (U.S. Bureau of the Census). 1975. *Historical Statistics of the United States, Colonial Times to 1970, Bicentennial Edition, Part 1.* Washington, D.C.: U.S. Government Printing Office.

U.S. Congress. 1958. House Committee on the Judiciary, *Hearings before the Antitrust Subcommittee,* 85th Cong., 2nd Sess., pt. 2, vol. 1 (March 25–May 22, 1958).

U.S. District Court (District of Columbia). 1982. Modification of Final Judgment, *United States v. AT&T,* 552 F. Supp. 131.

———. 1987. *United States v. Western Electric,* reprinted in C. H. Sterling and J. F. Kasle, eds., *Decision to Divest IV: The First Review, 1985–1987,* pp. 2402–2624. Washington, D.C.: Communications Press, 1988.

U.S. District Court (Eastern District, Pennsylvania). 1948. *Philco Corp. v. American Telephone and Telegraph Co.,* 80 F. Supp. 397.

Vail, T. 1915. "Some Truths and Some Conclusions." Speech to the Vermont State Grange, December 14. Bedminster, N.J.: AT&T Historical File.

Wallace, James, and Jim Erickson. 1992. *Hard Drive: Bill Gates and the Making of the Microsoft Empire.* New York: HarperCollins.

Walter-Carlson, Marilyn. 1974. "Prepared Statement of Mrs. Walter-Carlson," in U.S. Senate Committee on the Judiciary, *Hearings before the Subcommittee on Antitrust and Monopoly on S. 1167: The Computer Industry,* 93rd Cong., 2nd Sess. 1974, pp. 5412–5436.

Watson, Thomas J. Jr., and Peter Petre. 1990. *Father, Son & Co.: My Life at IBM and Beyond.* New York: Bantam Books.

Webbink, Douglas W. 1980. "Frequency Spectrum Deregulation Alternatives," Working Paper 2, Office of Plans and Policy, Federal Communications Commission, Washington, D.C.

Weiman, David, and Richard Levin. 1994. "Preying for Monopoly? The Case of Southern Bell Telephone Company, 1894–1912." *Journal of Political Economy,* 102: 103–126.

Williamson, Oliver E. 1975. *Markets and Hierarchies: Analysis and Antitrust Implications.* New York: The Free Press.

———. 1996. *The Mechanisms of Governance.* New York: Oxford University Press.

———. 2000. "The New Institutional Economics: Taking Stock, Looking Ahead." *Journal of Economic Literature,* 38: 595–613.

INDEX

Defense Advanced Research Projects Agency
(DARPA), 146
Defense Calculator (IBM 701), 65, 98
Defense Communications Agency (DCA),
143, 146, 269
Defense industry, 47–48, 56–57, 71, 83, 287–
288; code-breaking and, 3, 47, 56, 58–61;
nuclear weapons research and, 3, 47, 56,
60–63, 65, 71; air defense systems and, 4,
49–50, 56–57, 65, 68, 70–80, 99–101,
139, 170, 288; transistor technology and,
4, 55–56, 84; telegraph usage and, 25; radar development and, 48–53; Arpanet and,
142–144
DeForest, Lee, 33, 36
DeForest Radio Telephone Company, 36
Department of Commerce, 38–39, 203–204,
300
Department of Defense (DOD), 4, 55, 70,
117–118, 203–204, 205. *See also* Defense
industry
Department of Justice (DOJ): antitrust and,
32, 85, 116–120, 155–157; market orientation of, 126, 292–293; AT&T divestiture
and, 141, 200–202, 292; monopoly as
viewed by, 189–190, 291; policy authority
of, 200, 300
Desktop computers, 74, 140
Digital Equipment Corporation (DEC), 66,
105, 107–111, 148, 152, 160, 283
Digital subscriber line (DSL) service, 285
Digital time division multiple access
(TDMA) technology, 240
Dingell, John, 211, 257
Direct customer dialing, 83, 114, 129, 186,
278, 290
Distance education, 258, 262–263
Dole, Robert, 254
Doriot, Georges, 108
DOS operating system, 167

EasyWriter (software), 167
Eckert, J. Presper, 64, 97
Eckert, Wallace, 58
Eckert-Mauchly Computer Corporation, 97
Economies of scale/scope, 2, 24, 27, 32, 76,
102, 113, 201, 255
Edelstein, David, 157

Edison, Thomas, 28
Educational discounts, 100, 156
EDVAC computer, 64
Electrical relay computers, 57–58, 113
Electronic commerce, 267, 279–282, 285
Electronic Industries Association, 124
Electronic switches, 130–131
E-mail, 7, 145–146, 172–173, 182
ENFIA (Exchange Network Facilities for In-
terstate Access), 195–197, 209
Engineering Research Associates (ERA), 59–
60, 97, 100
England. *See* Great Britain
Enhanced service providers (ESPs), 266,
297–298; deregulation of, 182–184; rates
and pricing of, 197, 200; access charges
and, 212–214, 294; definition of, 219, 253
ENIAC computer, 61, 63–65, 67, 98
ERA 1103 computer, 59, 97
Erie Railroad, 24–25
Error handling, 146–147, 149, 151
Ethernet, 151–153, 168–169, 266
Europe, 8, 10, 31, 105–106, 227
Execunet service, 194–197, 208, 212, 292
Explorer (Internet browser), 277
Exxon Enterprises, 166

Faggin, Federico, 163–164, 166
Fairchild Camera and Instruments (firm), 88
Fairchild Semiconductor (firm), 88, 91–92
Federal Communications Commission
(FCC), 42–43; monopoly and, 15, 121,
140–141; telephone service/equipment
supply separation and, 116; rates/pricing
tariffs and, 125–126, 157, 187, 261–262;
limited competition and, 135, 141, 181,
291–292; data communications networks
and, 140; customer premises equipment
and, 175–179; policy authority of, 178,
200, 259–261, 300–301; specialized services and, 192–193; switched services and,
194–196; access charge rules and, 196,
207–212, 292; bypass issues and, 211,
247; cellular telephone licensing and,
228–233; antitrafficking rules of, 229, 232,
235; market orientation and, 293. *See also*
Computer Inquiry I, II, III; Spectrum allocation